Continuous *Color*

A MONTH-BY-MONTH GUIDE TO

SHRUBS AND SMALL TREES FOR

THE CONTINUOUS BLOOM GARDEN

Continuous Color

Pam Duthie

 Ball Publishing

Batavia, Illinois

Ball Publishing
P.O. Box 9
335 N. River St.
Batavia, IL 60510 U.S.A.
www.ballpublishing.com

Library of Congress Cataloging-in-Publication Data

Duthie, Pam, 1942-
  Continuous color : a month-by-month guide to shrubs and
small trees for the continuous bloom garden / Pam Duthie.
      p. cm.
Includes bibliographical references and index.
  ISBN 1-883052-38-6 (alk. paper)
  1. Flowering shrubs. 2. Flowering trees. 3. Color in gardening. I.
Title.

  SB435.D93 2004
  635.9'76—dc22

                    2003025553

Printed and bound in China by Imago.
10 09 08 07 06 05 04 1 2 3 4 5 6 7 8 9

Contents

"To every thing there is a season, and a time to every purpose under heaven."

—Ecclesiastes 3:1

With Heartfelt Thanks!

Without the supportive encouragement and patience of my family I could never have finished this book in four years! They cook for me, water and tend gardens, and have taken many side trips with me to visit gardens and nurseries. Many thanks to husband Angus Duthie, and children Ann Duthie, Todd and Michelle Duthie, and Laurie and Mark Martinelli. But more important is that they enjoy being in a garden, too!

I am ever grateful to the many people I have met over the years who were happy to share their garden experiences and love of *all* plants! Every place I have lectured or taught I have had great opportunities to learn about new plants and ideas that really work in the garden.

For this book I had a super assistant! Good friend Lorrie Burrows sorted and filed slides, slaved over endless lists, and kept me going when things got overwhelming. Everyone should have an assistant like Lorrie!

I have a whole list of experts who were very generous with their time and knowledge. Kris Bachtell, John Beaudry, Tim Boland, Peter Bristol, Dale Deppe, Mike Dirr, John Elsley, Jeff Epping, Rich and Susan Eyre, Ed Hasselkus, Richard Hawke, Dan Hinckley, Kris Jarantoski, Roy Klehm, Ed Lyon, Angie Palmer, Charles Price, Lee Rhandhava, Mark Rudy, Steve VanderWoude, Tim Wood, and Glenn Withey. And thanks also to the many friends across the country who shared their "favorite shrubs lists" with me.

A very special thanks goes to Rich's Foxwillow Pines (Rich and Susan Eyre, Vanessa Mueller), Song Sparrow Nursery (Roy Klehm, John Elsley, Renee Jaeger), Spring Meadow Nursery (Dale Deppe, Steve VanderWoude, Tim Wood) and Stonewall Nursery (Peter Moersch, Ed Lyon) who allowed me to photograph as often as I liked and helped me fill my garden with the *best companions* to perennials. I was also very blessed to always have ready access to the incredible plant collections at Chicago Botanic Garden, The Morton Arboretum, and Olbrich Botanical Garden.

In order to help others "see" the structure of the shrubs and small trees, I used the expertise of artist Nance Klehm in creating line drawings for each plant. Nance and I had a great time getting that visual aid down on paper, and it became a true learning experience for both of us.

And last but never least — thanks to all the people at Ball Publishing who were so easy to work with and very supportive in a difficult time. My editor, Rick Blanchette, helped me play with new ideas and jollied me along when I had a puzzle to work out.

Thank you all for helping to make *Continuous Color* blossom and grow!

Pam Duthie

Introduction

Like any good garden, this book has grown and matured, as has this gardener. The concept began in an effort to determine which shrubs and small trees would best fit in the mixed border and would complement the perennials I so love! To fit into this garden, the plants would need to have limited size—to begin with, I set the height limit at 15 feet. But then it was necessary to consider how much space width-wise these woodies would take up and whether they would shade out the perennials.

As a landscape designer, I do always start with structure (shrubs and trees) in the garden. The English call this the "bones," a term that aptly describes the backbone that ultimately highlights the colorful floral display of perennials and annuals. But the shrubs and small trees also provide myriad colors and extend the season right through winter—the dreariest season here in the Chicagoland area.

Loving the progression of change in the garden, I was amazed at how colorful shrubs and trees might be, even though their bloom times were more limited. Burgundy, blue, yellow-to-golden-yellow, silvery, or variegated foliage abounds with new plant introductions. Then there is the change to fall color and fruit and, finally, the winter interest of stems and bark, which were not just brown and gray.

Then I started paying attention to evergreens and had to learn as much as possible about dwarf conifers. These have different colors, too. And they are not static all season long either. New growth is different from that of mature growth. At varying times of the year, dependent on the species, needles brown and drop. And conifers get cones, also in various colors and textures.

Of course, I became totally hooked! And because I like to have firsthand knowledge, I started collecting every woody that excited me. It will be interesting to see if I chose correctly and my new additions won't outgrow their spaces. Or maybe I will just have to become "Pamela Scissorhands"?

The very first thing I learned about my new shrubs and small trees was that they did not demand a lot of attention.

I wasn't out there deadheading and staking, as I would be with my perennials. My heavy clay soils were already improved over many years with organic materials (compost), and the only major concern was allowing enough room and light. The "lamb's ear from hell" kept spreading its fuzzy leaves toward a tiny 'Little Bun' pine—the lamb's ear is now cut in half.

About the Book

The layout of *Continuous Color* is similar to the layout of *Continuous Bloom* (my perennials book). Remember that I like to plan for a progression of change in the garden. I have arranged many of the plants by month of bloom, but others are to be found grouped as all-summer color, fall color, fall fruit, winter interest, and evergreen.

Again I have used my "plant portrait" format, with easy-to-find information:

SCIENTIFIC NAME: Although standardized throughout the world, some names may change due to the latest studies of plants and interpretations of their origins. I still find that it is easiest to locate a source for plant material by using the Latin, or scientific, name. And I was surprised to find that it is easier than ever to find sources through the Internet—just "google" the name! Can you believe that Google.com will even correct the spelling?

COMMON NAME: Common names can be confusing since many are different depending on the region. A good example of this is *Thuja occidentalis*. Depending on where you grew up, you may call it a white cedar or an arborvitae, and may even confuse it with *Juniperus virginiana*, which is also called a red cedar. If you are trying to find the plant at a local garden center, you will have better luck by using the scientific name.

PLANT TYPE: For this book, the classification may be either shrub or tree. These plants are sometimes called woodies because the woody stems are evident in every season (unlike perennials, which dieback to their own roots each year). The trees and shrubs may also be evergreen or native and will be so noted.

ZONE: The USDA Hardiness Zone Map is printed in appendix A at the back of the book so you can better understand which plants will do well in your garden location. I did not include this map in the perennial book, thinking that everyone already had this information. I was *wrong!* Thank you for letting me know it is needed. I am a Zone 5 gardener in northern Illinois, but I like to push the zone parameters in protected microclimates in my own garden. I've noted these pushed zones in parentheses. Additional zone information is added, where necessary, in "Insiders Tips."

FLOWER/FRUIT: A brief description of color, appearance, and fragrance is given in this category. In some cases you may find that I have noted this category as "not ornamental," meaning that it is hidden by foliage or so small as to not be noticed.

HABIT/FOLIAGE: This section provides information about the form, or shape, of the plant and bark, stem, and leaf color, including the changes through the seasons. Understanding the seasonal "color" changes is key to planning color throughout the entire year! To aid in the understanding of how the shape of the plant works in the garden, I had artist/gardener Nance Klehm do line drawings.

HEIGHT: The projected mature height of a shrub or small tree is important because it can affect the scale and proportion of your garden—hence, the overall design and appropriateness of chosen plants. There is a plant to fit every garden size. I did arbitrarily choose plants that would mature at less than 15 feet *or* could be *easily* managed under this height with pruning.

WIDTH/SPACING: The mature width of a plant is an even more important consideration. If working to create a mixed border garden including perennials and annuals, the gardener must know how much space a shrub or small tree will need and how fast that plant may grow. Planning ahead to allow all plants the space they need to grow will ultimately save you from plant loss due to shading and/or competition. And, of course, this will likely save endless hours in pruning to keep plant material in bounds.

LIGHT: Correctly evaluating the light conditions for your garden site is an important part of planning a garden. If you don't get it right, too much sun can burn or retard growth, and too much shade will cause plants to become "leggy" and to show less bloom and have poor fall color.

SOIL: Soil type impacts plant performance. Brief descriptions of different soils are given, and like light conditions, the gardener will soon know if the plant has the best growing medium.

CARE: Special care requirements for each plant—particularly pruning and mulching—are noted here. Further discussions of care will be found in chapter 13.

USES: I have found that the uses I liked best were tied to highlighting the other plants in the garden. Very few of the shrubs were long blooming, but the foliage color, fall color and fruit, winter stem color and persistent fruit, and size and shape determine their usefulness in the garden.

PROBLEMS: Noted here are problems with disease, pests, invasiveness, and occasionally lack of performance due to light and soil conditions.

INSIDER'S TIPS: This is always my favorite catchall for additional information that may help in decision-making for your garden. Also included here are some other species or cultivars that might be worth trying.

COMBINES WITH: Because I look at shrubs and small trees as "companions" to my perennials, it was fun to imagine the perennials that might go well with the predominant season of the plant portrait. The choices are endless; I just wanted to get you started and know that you will have just as much fun thinking of your own combinations.

Garden Tips

Just as I "discovered" many new-to-me shrubs and small trees as I researched and wrote this book, I would encourage you to try new plants. My philosophy is: If I can afford to loose a plant, it is worth trying in my own garden. I also don't listen too much when someone says I cannot grow a plant because of zone or site limitations! I learned early on that it is worth trying in a protected site in good, well-drained soil. And if a plant is rated as short-lived, as are many cherry trees in my region that live only ten years,

I can rationalize spending $130 for that plant, as it will have cost me $13 per year.

And finally, be a constant observer of how plants look in every season. Each day in the garden brings changes and new colors. Progression-of-color thinking is a new way of looking at the shrubs and small trees. Look particularly at what has color in winter—persistent fruit, colored stems, and evergreens. But each season progressively adds new colors the gardener can use to create a garden of "continuous color."

CHAPTER 1

Color FOR THE NEW YEAR

LATE WINTER–SPRING

Hamamelis × *intermedia* 'Diana'

'DIANA' WITCH HAZEL

© Jim Ault

PLANT TYPE:	Deciduous tree
ZONE:	(5) 5b–8
FLOWER/FRUIT:	Copper-red clusters of crinkled straps are only lightly fragrant
HABIT/FOLIAGE:	Wider vase shape, can be rounded or flat-topped; oval green leaves are crinkled and turn yellow-orange to red in fall
HEIGHT:	6–10 feet
WIDTH/SPREAD:	10–12 feet
LIGHT:	Sun to part shade
SOIL:	Average to rich, moist but not wet
CARE:	Prune after blooming to shape
USES:	Winter flower, fragrant, fall color, background
PROBLEMS:	During the colorful summer season, the witch hazels look pretty plain
INSIDER'S TIPS:	The intermedias are crosses between *Hamamelis japonica* and *Hamamelis mollis* and provide winter-blooming flowers ranging from clear yellow to red. The selection among the intermedia hybrids is unbelievable and will probably be determined by the availability in local nurseries.
COMBINES WITH:	*Amsonia hubrectii, Perovskia atriplicifolia, Solidago rugosa* 'Fireworks', *Sedum* × 'Autumn Joy'

Corylus avellana 'Contorta'

HARRY LAUDER'S WALKING STICK, CONTORTED FILBERT

PLANT TYPE:	Deciduous shrub
ZONE:	4–8
FLOWER/FRUIT:	Dull yellow catkins are showy on bare stems
HABIT/FOLIAGE:	Very twisted and curling stems cascade to form a rounded shrub; dark green leaves are twisted, too; may have yellow-green fall color
HEIGHT:	6–8 feet
WIDTH/SPREAD:	4–6 feet
LIGHT:	Sun to part shade
SOIL:	Rich, moist, well-drained
CARE:	The plant will benefit from an occasional thinning of its branches to better emphasize the structure.
USES:	Winter interest, architectural accent, early bloom
PROBLEMS:	Suckers from rootstock when not grown on its own roots
INSIDER'S TIPS:	Gardeners choosing the contorted filbert want a plant that is a little different but not too big. While the structure of the branches in winter is very interesting, the overall feeling of the plant is a little "lumpy." even when leafed-out. This can be improved with pruning or by being very choosey when purchasing.
COMBINES WITH:	*Galanthus nivalis* (bulb), *Hosta* 'Loyalist' or 'Lemon Lime', *Lamium maculatum* 'Beedham's White'

3

Cornus mas

CORNELIAN CHERRY

PLANT TYPE:	Deciduous tree
ZONE:	4–7 (8)
FLOWER/FRUIT:	Clusters of fuzzy yellow flowers on leafless stems; fruit is a bright red cherry
HABIT/FOLIAGE:	Oval to almost pyramidal form usually with multi-stemmed trunks; leafs out after blooming; tinged bronze-purple in fall
HEIGHT:	20 feet
WIDTH/SPREAD:	15 feet
LIGHT:	Sun, part shade, shade
SOIL:	Rich, moist, well-drained
CARE:	Easy; may be kept pruned as a hedge or even "limbed up" as a single-trunk small tree
USES:	Screen, hedge, early bloom, fall fruit, attracts birds, shade garden
PROBLEMS:	Pest free
INSIDER'S TIPS:	'Golden Glory' is a preferred cultivar in the north for its profuse bloom and more upright form. It is said to have more profuse bloom than the species. I personally cannot tell the difference and am happy to grow either particularly in a shady spot where it "glows" in early spring.
COMBINES WITH:	*Hosta fortunei* 'Gold Standard', *Stylophorum diphyllum, Teucrium chamaedys* 'Summer Sunshine', *Polemonium reptans*

Cornus mas 'Golden Glory'

CORNELIAN CHERRY

PLANT TYPE:	Deciduous tree
ZONE:	4–7 (8)
FLOWER/FRUIT:	Profuse clusters of fuzzy yellow clusters, along bare stems; bright red cherries
HABIT/FOLIAGE:	Densely oval, upright form usually with multi-stemmed trunks; leafs-out after blooming; tinged bronze-purple in fall
HEIGHT:	20 feet
WIDTH/SPREAD:	15 feet
LIGHT:	Sun, part shade, shade
SOIL:	Rich, moist, well-drained, slightly acidic
CARE:	May be kept pruned as a hedge
USES:	Screen, hedge, early bloom, fall fruit, attracts birds, shade garden
PROBLEMS:	None
INSIDER'S TIPS:	'Golden Glory' is a preferred cultivar in the North for its profuse bloom and more upright form.
COMBINES WITH:	*Pulmonaria longifolia* 'Bertram Anderson', *Astilbe* x *arendsii* 'Bressingham Beauty', *Brunnera macrophylla* 'Dawson's White'

Forsythia x 'Courtasol', 'Gold Tide'

'GOLD TIDE' FORSYTHIA

© Steve VanderWoude

PLANT TYPE:	Deciduous shrub
ZONE:	(4) 5–8
FLOWER/FRUIT:	Bright yellow flowers engulf the stems
HABIT/FOLIAGE:	Dwarf, arching branches are low spreading; light green leaves become purple-tinged in fall
HEIGHT:	18–24 inches
WIDTH/SPREAD:	3–4 feet
LIGHT:	Sun to part shade
SOIL:	Adaptable to most soils
CARE:	If necessary, prune right after blooming to curb spread of the plant
USES:	Adaptable, groundcover, floriferous, early bloom
PROBLEMS:	While taller forsythias are nipped by late frosts in the North, this one may not be.
INSIDER'S TIPS:	Because I had an extra plant, I have tried it in a site with only late afternoon sunlight. So far, it is thriving.
COMBINES WITH:	*Hemerocallis* 'Barbara Mitchell', *Hosta* 'Whirlwind', *Alchemilla mollis*

Forsythia x 'Northern Gold'

'NORTHERN GOLD' FORSYTHIA

PLANT TYPE:	Deciduous shrub
ZONE:	3–8
FLOWER/FRUIT:	Profuse yellow flowers along the stems
HABIT/FOLIAGE:	Upright, vase shape with dense tan stems; medium green leaves turn yellow in the fall
HEIGHT:	6–8 feet
WIDTH/SPREAD:	5–7 feet
LIGHT:	Sun to part shade
SOIL:	Average, well-drained
CARE:	Easily maintained with pruning or even shearing right after bloom
USES:	Profuse early bloom, hedge, screening, background
PROBLEMS:	None
INSIDER'S TIPS:	An old-time favorite here shown as a hedge around the backyard of a property on an exposed corner. Because of the dense, upright habit, the owner can easily maintain it with shearing. This is one of the first shrubs to bloom in the Midwest.
COMBINES WITH:	*Scilla sibirica, Aruncus dioicus, Phlox paniculata* 'David', *Gaura lindheimeri*

Mahonia aquifolium

OREGON GRAPE HOLLY

PLANT TYPE:	Broadleaf evergreen
ZONE:	(4) 5–8
FLOWER/FRUIT:	Fragrant, bright yellow clusters; blue-black berries in August
HABIT/FOLIAGE:	Upright growing with an irregular form (shape of the one in photograph); dark, blue-green, glossy leaves similar to holly turn bronze purple in fall; evergreen
HEIGHT:	3–6 feet
WIDTH/SPREAD:	3–5 feet
LIGHT:	Shade, part shade
SOIL:	Rich, moist, well-drained
CARE:	Prune out any winterkill in early spring. Control any suckering. Protect from winter wind and sun.
USES:	Winter color, fragrant, foundation
PROBLEMS:	Suckers; becomes chlorotic in alkaline clay soils
INSIDER'S TIPS:	*Mahonia repens* is a lower-growing species often used as an evergreen groundcover.
COMBINES WITH:	*Hosta montana* 'Aureomarginata', *Aruncus dioicus*, *Brunnera macrophylla* 'Dawson's White'

CHAPTER 2

April

WHY WAIT FOR APRIL SHOWERS
TO BRING MAY FLOWERS?

Corylopsis glabrescens

FRAGRANT WINTER HAZEL

PLANT TYPE:	Deciduous shrub
ZONE:	5–8
FLOWER/FRUIT:	Fragrant soft yellow "chains" of drooping bells on bare stems
HABIT/FOLIAGE:	Densely branched rounded form often flat-topped; dark green leaves become yellow-green to gold in fall if not killed by early frosts
HEIGHT:	8–15 feet
WIDTH/SPREAD:	8–15 feet
LIGHT:	Part shade
SOIL:	Rich, moist, well-drained, acidic
CARE:	Grow in a sheltered spot to protect from late winter frosts.
USES:	Winter shape, fragrant, early spring bloom, background
PROBLEMS:	None
INSIDER'S TIPS:	Michael Dirr calls this the hardiest of the winter hazels and is a great choice for northern gardeners.
COMBINES WITH:	*Mertensia virginica, Narcissus cyclamineus, Helleborus orientalis, Kirengeshoma palmata*

Lindera benzoin

SPICEBUSH

PLANT TYPE:	Native, deciduous shrub
ZONE:	4–8
FLOWER/FRUIT:	Small, yellow wispy flowers have a nice spicy fragrance, scarlet fruit in fall
HABIT/FOLIAGE:	Loose, open, rounded form; light green leaves become yellow to golden yellow in fall
HEIGHT:	8–12 feet
WIDTH/SPREAD:	6–8 feet
LIGHT:	Sun, part shade, shade
SOIL:	Average to rich, moist to wet
CARE:	Can be pruned into a small tree
USES:	Fragrant, shade tolerant, naturalistic, early bloom, fall color
PROBLEMS:	Little noticed in the shady landscape; flowers very early, and fall colors are not as vibrant as other shrubs
INSIDER'S TIPS:	This plant has the showiest flowers and fall color in full sun but still an important shrub to use in shade.
COMBINES WITH:	*Hosta fortunei* 'Gold Standard', *Anemone sylvestris, Arisaema triphullum, Aquilegia candadensis*

Acer truncatum

PURPLEBLOW MAPLE

PLANT TYPE:	Deciduous shrub
ZONE:	4–8
FLOWER/FRUIT:	Showy chartreuse or yellow-green flowers in clusters; fruit is purple-tinged winged samara
HABIT/FOLIAGE:	Slow-growing upright oval shape on a single trunk; bark resembles that of Japanese maples; glossy, dark green typical maple leaves begin lightly tinged with purple; fall color is yellow, but orange and red in colder zones (yellow-orange in the South)
HEIGHT:	15–20 feet
WIDTH/SPREAD:	8–10 feet
LIGHT:	Sun to part shade
SOIL:	Average to rich, evenly moist
CARE:	Easy care-if it fits your garden space, you will need minimal pruning.
USES:	Specimen, anchor, four-season interest
PROBLEMS:	Hard to find in nurseries!
INSIDER'S TIPS:	Here is a tree that could be a substitute for Japanese maple in colder zones.
COMBINES WITH:	*Tradescantia* 'Sweet Kate' (aka 'Blue and Gold'), *Veronica spicata* 'Royal Candles', *Echinacea purpurea* 'White Swan'

Amelanchier x *grandiflora*

APPLE SERVICEBERRY

PLANT TYPE:	Deciduous tree
ZONE:	4–9
FLOWER/FRUIT:	White clusters from pink buds before leaves; edible red fruit in June turning blue-black
HABIT/FOLIAGE:	Upright rounded; new leaves purple tinted, red-orange fall color
HEIGHT:	20 feet
WIDTH/SPREAD:	15–20 feet
LIGHT:	Sun, part shade
SOIL:	Rich, moist, well-drained
CARE:	Because of a moderate growth rate, it is easily pruned to control height.
USES:	Specimen, anchor for mixed border, long season of interest, attracts birds
PROBLEMS:	Some powdery mildew
INSIDER'S TIPS:	Some cultivars: 'Princess Diana' has red-orange fall color. 'Autumn Brilliance' holds this same fall color longer. Newer, hard-to-find 'Prince William' has a shrubbier habit for the smaller garden—only 6 feet tall.
COMBINES WITH:	*Hemerocallis* 'Rosy Returns', *Salvia* x *superba* 'May Night', *Rosa* 'Flower Carpet White', *Iris pallida* 'Variegata'

Amelanchier × *grandiflora* 'Spring Glory', 'Sprizam'

'SPRING GLORY' SERVICEBERRY

PLANT TYPE:	Deciduous shrub
ZONE:	4–8
FLOWER/FRUIT:	Large white, fragrant flowers become purple-black fruit in June
HABIT/FOLIAGE:	Broadly columnar, upright form; medium green ovals turn bright yellow and red-orange in fall
HEIGHT:	10–12 feet
WIDTH/SPREAD:	7–9 feet
LIGHT:	Sun to part shade
SOIL:	Rich, moist, somewhat acidic
CARE:	Rarely needs pruning
USES:	Multiseason interest, fragrant, early flowering, attracts birds, fall color
PROBLEMS:	None
INSIDER'S TIPS:	'Spring Glory' serviceberry can fit into a narrower space than the species, which increases its usefulness in the mixed border.
COMBINES WITH:	*Narcissus* 'Jack Snipe', *Muscari armeniacum, Aster novae-angliae* 'Purple Dome', *Weigela florida* 'Midnight Wine'

Aronia melanocarpa 'Morton', 'Iroquois Beauty'

'IROQUOIS BEAUTY' BLACK CHOKEBERRY

© Don Brennan

PLANT TYPE:	Deciduous shrub, native
ZONE:	4–8
FLOWER/FRUIT:	Fragrant white flower with purple-black berries
HABIT/FOLIAGE:	Compact, horizontal oval shape—not as leggy as the species; glossy green leaves with bright, red-orange fall color
HEIGHT:	2–3 feet
WIDTH/SPREAD:	4–5 feet
LIGHT:	Sun to part shade
SOIL:	Tolerant of most soil types either wet or dry
CARE:	Easy
USES:	Attracts birds, hedge, fall color
PROBLEMS:	None
INSIDER'S TIPS:	This is a much more compact selection from the Morton Arboretum and Chicagoland Grows Inc. program.
COMBINES WITH:	*Hemerocallis* 'Happy Returns', *Campanula carpatica* 'Samantha', *Alchemilla mollis*

Cercis canadensis 'Alba'

WHITEBUD

PLANT TYPE:	Native, deciduous tree
ZONE:	5–9
FLOWER/FRUIT:	White pea-shaped flowers—almost buds—flowering in bunches along branches
HABIT/FOLIAGE:	Rounded crown with "graceful ascending branches" (Dirr); makes an effective winter architecture; heart-shaped leaves turn yellow in fall
HEIGHT:	20–30 feet
WIDTH/SPREAD:	30 feet
LIGHT:	Part shade to sun- okay with afternoon sun
SOIL:	Rich, moist, well-drained
CARE:	Prune to open canopy for interior light
USES:	Specimen, architectural anchor, focal point, open woodland, winter architecture
PROBLEMS:	Canker is possible, also check for scale, verticillium wilt
INSIDER'S TIPS:	The ultimate size of any whitebud can be kept smaller if pruning begins at an early age of development, and the ones available at nurseries generally are small to begin with.
COMBINES WITH:	*Tulipa* 'Esther', *Narcissus* 'Ice Wings', *Pulmonaria longifolia* 'Majeste', *Anemonella thalictroides*

Cercis canadensis 'Lavender Twist', 'Covey'

'COVEY' WEEPING REDBUD

PLANT TYPE:	Deciduous tree
ZONE:	5b*–9
FLOWER/FRUIT:	Small, budlike, lavender-rose flowers along the stems
HABIT/FOLIAGE:	Upright main stem, then weeping tip; twisting lateral branches also cascade; large heart-shaped leaves are medium green, turning yellow in fall
HEIGHT:	5–6 feet
WIDTH/SPREAD:	6–8 feet
LIGHT:	Part shade to sun—OK with afternoon sun
SOIL:	Rich, moist, well-drained
CARE:	Stake the leader shoot to achieve desired height
USES:	Specimen, architectural accent, fall into winter interest, small space
PROBLEMS:	None
INSIDER'S TIPS:	Introduced by the Brotzman Nursery in Madison, Ohio.
COMBINES WITH:	*Arabis caucasica* 'Snowcap', *Heuchera villosa* 'Autumn Bride', *Lilium* 'Casa Blanca', *Geranium pratense* 'Mrs. Kendall Clark'

*Growing at the Chicago Botanic Garden in the Circle Garden

Daphne genkwa

LILAC DAPHNE

PLANT TYPE:	Deciduous shrub
ZONE:	5–7
FLOWER/FRUIT:	Rosy lilac clusters all along the stems before plant has leafed out
HABIT/FOLIAGE:	Somewhat open, mounded form; branches arch upward; emerald green leaves appear after flowers and may have yellow fall color
HEIGHT:	3–4 feet
WIDTH/SPREAD:	3–5 feet
LIGHT:	Sun to part shade
SOIL:	Average to poor, well-drained
CARE:	May need to prune for tip dieback.
USES:	Textural background, profuse early bloom, small space
PROBLEMS:	Not tolerant of heavy clay soil and unfortunately is not fragrant
INSIDER'S TIPS:	Lilac daphne has been evaluated at the Chicago Botanic Garden and must be grown in well-drained, not-too-rich soils to avoid chlorotic leaves (yellowing). If you are looking for fragrance, consider *Daphne caucasica* or *Daphne* x 'Carol Mackie', also included in this book. *Daphne mezereum* is also fragrant (Zones 4–7).
COMBINES WITH:	*Arabis caucasica* 'Snowcap', *Baptisia minor*, *Centranthus ruber* 'Coccineus'

Fothergilla gardenii 'Beaver Creek'

'BEAVER CREEK' DWARF FOTHERGILLA

PLANT TYPE:	Deciduous shrub
ZONE:	4–9
FLOWER/FRUIT:	Fragrant white bottlebrush spike; fruit is a non-showy capsule
HABIT/FOLIAGE:	Low, densely mounded form; leaves blue-green to dark green, turn orange and red in fall; will be more yellow in shadier sites
HEIGHT:	2–3 feet
WIDTH/SPREAD:	3–4 feet
LIGHT:	Part shade to sun
SOIL:	Rich, moist, well-drained, slightly acidic
CARE:	Easy
USES:	Fragrant, small space, fall color, disease free
PROBLEMS:	No pests or diseases
INSIDER'S TIPS:	The "native" alkaline, clay soil in my garden has been amended over a twenty-year period with compost and "leaf mold" so that it drains better and has a lower pH (more neutral than alkaline).
COMBINES WITH:	*Tulipa* 'Pink Diamond', *Uvularia grandiflora*, *Phlox stolonifera* 'Sherwood Purple'

Fothergilla major

LARGE FOTHERGILLA, LARGE BOTTLEBRUSH BUSH

PLANT TYPE:	Native, deciduous shrub (mountains of southeastern United States)
ZONE:	4–8
FLOWER/FRUIT:	Fragrant bottlebrush flowers are larger than those of other fothergillas
HABIT/FOLIAGE:	Upright, rounded oval form; dark green leaves turn yellow-orange to red in fall
HEIGHT:	5–6 feet
WIDTH/SPREAD:	5–6 feet
LIGHT:	Sun, part shade, shade
SOIL:	Acid, moist, well-drained but adaptable
CARE:	Requires only minimal pruning.
USES:	Fragrant, early blooming, fall color, background
PROBLEMS:	No pests or diseases but looks leggy until it leafs out
INSIDER'S TIPS:	*Fothergilla* 'Mt. Airy' is a Mike Dirr selection for best fall color. The best color is in full sun, but color is also affected by water stress and nutrients.
COMBINES WITH:	*Doronicum caucasium, Polemonium reptans, Dennstaedtia punctilobula*

Halesia tetraptera 'UConn Wedding Bells'

'WEDDING BELLS' CAROLINA SILVERBELL

PLANT TYPE:	Native, deciduous tree
ZONE:	4–8 (9)
FLOWER/FRUIT:	Flowers are cluster of white, dangling bells; the flowers on this selection are larger than the species
HABIT/FOLIAGE:	A low-branched, rounded form that is taller than it is wide spreading; light green oval leaves turn yellow in fall but drop early
HEIGHT:	15–20 feet
WIDTH/SPREAD:	12–15 feet
LIGHT:	Sun, part shade, shade
SOIL:	Rich, moist, well-drained, acidic
CARE:	Prepare soil as you would for rhododendrons; these will also be good garden companions
USES:	Shade tolerant, naturalistic, early blooming
PROBLEMS:	Becomes chlorotic in heavy clay soil
INSIDER'S TIPS:	Silverbells seen in the wild are often understory trees growing on the slopes of ridges or mountains. 'Wedding Bells' is a smaller-sized silverbell introduced by Mark Brand of the University of Connecticut.
COMBINES WITH:	*Mertensia virginica, Tiarella wherryi, Dryopteris marginalis, Stylophorum diphyllum*

Kerria japonica 'Golden Guinea'

'GOLDEN GUINEA' JAPANESE KERRIA

PLANT TYPE:	Deciduous shrub
ZONE:	4–9
FLOWER/FRUIT:	Golden-yellow, single roselike blooms are larger than the species
HABIT/FOLIAGE:	Rounded habit with arching stems; bright green stems showy in winter; sharply pointed bright green leaves with only occasional yellow fall color
HEIGHT:	3–5 feet
WIDTH/SPREAD:	3–5 feet
LIGHT:	Part shade, shade
SOIL:	Average, well-drained
CARE:	Blooms on old wood, so pruning should be done right after bloom. Prune at least a third of older stems to improve appearance. Stems may be cut back to a few inches from the ground.
USES:	Profuse bloom, winter color, light texture, shade tolerant
PROBLEMS:	No pests or diseases; spreads by runners; soil that is too rich promotes rampant growth
INSIDER'S TIPS:	'Pleniflora' has double flowers, 'Picta' has creamy white variegation, and 'Albiflora' has creamy white flowers.
COMBINES WITH:	*Narcissus* 'Ice Follies', *Tulipa* 'Temple's Favorite', *Hosta fortunei* 'Gold Standard'

Magnolia stellata 'Royal Star'

'ROYAL STAR' MAGNOLIA

PLANT TYPE:	Deciduous tree
ZONE:	5–8
FLOWER/FRUIT:	Pink buds open to pure white, fragrant flowers with up to 18 petals
HABIT/FOLIAGE:	Densely rounded shape with smooth, gray bark; medium to deep green large, oval leaves turn golden yellow in fall; star magnolias have the best fall color compared to other magnolias
HEIGHT:	15–20 feet
WIDTH/SPREAD:	15–20 feet
LIGHT:	Sun to part shade
SOIL:	Rich, moist, well-drained
CARE:	Clay soils should be supplemented with well-composted 'leaf mold'. Prune right after flowering to assure flowers for the next year.
USES:	Specimen, mixed border, foundation, anchor
PROBLEMS:	Trouble free
INSIDER'S TIPS:	Mike Dirr calls star magnolias the most cold- and heat-tolerant species. In northern climates, plant this in a protected location to avoid frost damage, but not a southern exposure, which will bring on early bloom.
COMBINES WITH:	Annual pansies, *Heuchera* 'Midnight Claret', *Veronica spicata* 'Royal Candles'

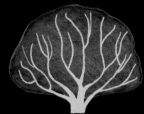

Magnolia x 'Betty'

'BETTY' MAGNOLIA, LITTLE GIRL HYBRID MAGNOLIA

PLANT TYPE:	Deciduous tree
ZONE:	(4) 5–9
FLOWER/FRUIT:	Large red-purple blooms before tree leafs-out, sporadic blooms later in the season, which are lighter in color
HABIT/FOLIAGE:	Broadly rounded, multi-stemmed form with smooth gray bark; medium-green leaves begin bronze-tinged and are typical of most magnolias, including the golden brown fall color
HEIGHT:	10–15 feet
WIDTH/SPREAD:	10–15 feet
LIGHT:	Full sun
SOIL:	Rich, moist, well-drained, slightly acidic
CARE:	Clay soils should be supplemented with 'leaf mold' compost or peat. Prune right after flowering.
USES:	Specimen, anchor, background, winter architecture
PROBLEMS:	Watch for powdery mildew, water sprouts
INSIDER'S TIPS:	The "little girl" hybrids are often confused in the trade, so be sure you are really getting 'Betty'.
COMBINES WITH:	*Paeonia officinalis* 'Krinkled White', *Rosa* 'Flower Carpet White', *Salvia* x *superba* 'May Night', *Hydrangea paniculata* 'Little Lamb'

Magnolia x 'Elizabeth'

'ELIZABETH' MAGNOLIA

PLANT TYPE:	Deciduous tree
ZONE:	4–8
FLOWER/FRUIT:	Fragrant, creamy-yellow, tulip-shaped flowers
HABIT/FOLIAGE:	Upright, pyramidal shape with smooth gray bark; large, oval, medium-green leaves may turn golden brown in fall
HEIGHT:	10–12 feet in 10 years; 30 feet or more at maturity
WIDTH/SPREAD:	8–10 feet
LIGHT:	Sun to light shade
SOIL:	Rich, moist, well-drained
CARE:	Prune right after blooming so you don't risk losing next year's flower buds. Keeping this one smaller than its projected mature height will require a lot of pruning management after the first 10 years!
USES:	Fragrant, specimen, foundation, background
PROBLEMS:	Occasional scale
INSIDER'S TIPS:	This magnolia is the first yellow-flowered variety, and since it blooms later in spring, the flowers a less likely to be nipped by late frosts in the North. A Brooklyn Botanic Garden introduction, it is a cross between *Magnolia acuminata* and *Magnolia denudata*. Other "newer" yellow-flowered varieties are worthwhile choices, too: 'Butterflies', 'Goldfinch', and 'Yellow Bird'.
COMBINES WITH:	*Tulipa* 'Sweetheart', *Lamium maculatum* 'Beedham's White', *Paeonia lactiflora* 'Flame', *Anemone sylvestris*

25

Malus 'Donald Wyman'

'DONALD WYMAN' CRABAPPLE

PLANT TYPE:	Deciduous tree
ZONE:	4–7(8)
FLOWER/FRUIT:	Light pink buds open to white flowers; glossy, bright-red fruit persists into spring
HABIT/FOLIAGE:	Oval (somewhat upright) shape with multi-stemmed trunk; glossy, medium-green leaves with bronzed yellow fall color
HEIGHT:	20 feet
WIDTH/SPREAD:	20 feet
LIGHT:	Full sun
SOIL:	Rich, moist, well-drained
CARE:	Judicious pruning starting at an early age will control the size of this plant.
USES:	Persistent fruit, specimen, anchor, disease resistant
PROBLEMS:	Not as small as some crabapples; less bloom appears in alternate years, but it is still very showy
INSIDER'S TIPS:	I like the multi-stemmed trunk habit of this crabapple, as well as its multi-seasonal interest! It continues to be well-used in the landscape, particularly in commercial settings. Each year this crab can be underplanted with a carpet of pansies—you pick a color!
COMBINES WITH:	*Myosotis sylvatica, Polemonium reptans, Tulipa* 'Christmas Dream', *Hosta* 'Kabitan'

Malus 'Louisa'

'LOUISA' CRABAPPLE

PLANT TYPE:	Deciduous tree
ZONE:	4–7 (8)
FLOWER/FRUIT:	Rose-colored buds open to true pink flowers; small yellow to amber persistent fruit
HABIT/FOLIAGE:	Broadly weeping form, stems weep to the ground; glossy, light green leaves with little fall color
HEIGHT:	15 feet
WIDTH/SPREAD:	15 feet
LIGHT:	Full sun
SOIL:	Rich, moist, well-drained
CARE:	If any pruning is needed, it should be done by early June.
USES:	Weeping form, persistent fruit, winter interest
PROBLEMS:	None; resistant to apple scab
INSIDER'S TIPS:	There is a crabapple for every garden! Choose by the features you want—flowers, fruit, form. (See Easy "You Can Plan" Crabapple Chart at back of this book.) Companion planting should be done outside the area where stems come to the ground. 'Louisa' was selected at Polly Hill Arboretum in 1962.
COMBINES WITH:	*Scilla sibirica*, *Stachys byzantina* 'Silver Carpet', *Veronica spicata* 'Red Fox'

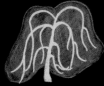

Malus 'Sugar Tyme', 'Sutyzam'

'SUGAR TYME' CRABAPPLE

PLANT TYPE:	Deciduous tree
ZONE:	4–8
FLOWER/FRUIT:	Pale pink buds open to fragrant white flowers; half-inch red fruit persists into midwinter
HABIT/FOLIAGE:	Upright oval shape with dark branches arching outward at the tips; dark green leaves with only slight yellow fall color
HEIGHT:	15–18 feet
WIDTH/SPREAD:	10–15 feet
LIGHT:	Full sun
SOIL:	Rich, moist, well-drained
CARE:	Prune right after blooming if you need to manage the ultimate size of this crabapple.
USES:	Persistent fruit, fragrant, attracts birds
PROBLEMS:	Touted for its resistance to Japanese beetle
INSIDER'S TIPS:	I love 'Sugar Tyme' for its fragrance! I know you will think I have gone "crab crazy," as there are 12 represented in the book. But think of it as an opportunity to choose by shape, size, color, and, most important, disease resistance.
COMBINES WITH:	*Iris sibirica* 'Caesar's Brother', *Paeonia lactiflora* 'Flame', *Caryopteris* x *clandonensis* 'First Choice'

Malus 'Tina'

'TINA' CRABAPPLE

PLANT TYPE:	Deciduous shrub
ZONE:	4–8
FLOWER/FRUIT:	Rosy buds open to white fragrant flowers; small red fruit persists until frost
HABIT/FOLIAGE:	Dwarf, wide-spreading mound; although it is often single-trunked, branches tend to start close to the ground; dark green with some yellow fall color
HEIGHT:	5 feet
WIDTH/SPREAD:	8–10 feet
LIGHT:	Full sun
SOIL:	Rich, moist, well-drained
CARE:	Easily maintained at this small size.
USES:	Small stature, disease resistance, fragrance, background
PROBLEMS:	Highly resistant to disease
INSIDER'S TIPS:	Although relatively short, remember that it is more widely spreading and will eventually shade out plants underneath. It provides a good location to plant smaller hostas and wildflowers.
COMBINES WITH:	*Tulipa* 'Peachblossom' or 'Arabian Nights', *Hosta* 'Kabitan', *Anemone nemerosa, Corydalis lutea*

Pieris japonica

JAPANESE PIERIS, LILY-OF-THE-VALLEY SHRUB

PLANT TYPE:	Broadleaf evergreen
ZONE:	4b–7, needs protection in Zone 4b
FLOWER/FRUIT:	White, scented flowers hang in drooping clusters
HABIT/FOLIAGE:	Arching mound of young green stems to older gray-brown stems; evergreen leaves begin bronze or red-tinged and become glossy dark green
HEIGHT:	6–8 feet, but often only 3–4 feet
WIDTH/SPREAD:	6 feet
LIGHT:	Sun, part shade, shade
SOIL:	Rich, moist, well-drained, acidic
CARE:	Prune after blooming to maintain height and spread.
USES:	Evergreen, shade tolerant, deer resistant, fragrant
PROBLEMS:	Not as dependent on acid soils as other "ericaceous" plants, short lived if grown in wet soils
INSIDER'S TIPS:	For my clay soils, I add layers of leaf mold every fall to increase drainage as well as to lower alkalinity.
COMBINES WITH:	*Lamium maculatum* 'White Nancy', *Hosta* 'Lime Krinkles' or 'Kabitan', *Heucherella* x 'Burnished Bronze', *Persicaria microcephala* 'Red Dragon'

Prunus tomentosa

NANKING CHERRY

PLANT TYPE:	Deciduous shrub
ZONE:	3–7
FLOWER/FRUIT:	From pink buds come fragrant white flowers in April, followed by edible red fruit in June and July
HABIT/FOLIAGE:	Broadly spreading habit becomes more open with age; stems are reddish-brown; dark green foliage turns yellow in fall with tomentose undersides
HEIGHT:	6–8 feet
WIDTH/SPREAD:	10–12 feet
LIGHT:	Full sun
SOIL:	Average to rich, moist but not wet
CARE:	Easily pruned right after blooming
USES:	Early blooming, fragrant, background, winter interest
PROBLEMS:	No pests are serious
INSIDER'S TIPS:	Cherries tend to be short-lived (10–15 years), but I have been watching the Nanking cherry and think it may be one with greater longevity.
COMBINES WITH:	*Polemonium reptans, Phlox paniculata* 'Laura' and 'Katherine', *Aster novi-belgii* 'Bonningdale White'

Prunus × *cistena*

PURPLELEAF SAND CHERRY

© Jim Ault

PLANT TYPE:	Deciduous tree
ZONE:	3–7
FLOWER/FRUIT:	Light pink clusters are lightly fragrant; black fruit
HABIT/FOLIAGE:	Upright vase shape with black stems; red-purple leaves
HEIGHT:	8–10 feet
WIDTH/SPREAD:	6–8 feet
LIGHT:	Full sun
SOIL:	Rich, moist, well-drained
CARE:	Hard prune some of the stems to the ground to cause lower growth, which keeps the plant from becoming leggy.
USES:	Early blooming, fragrant, color accent, background, hedge
PROBLEMS:	Short lived plant (10–15 years)
INSIDER'S TIPS:	This seems to be the most trouble-free and widely available purpleleaf cherry in the Midwest, so is not too costly to replace. A similar species is used for taller hedging in England and the eastern United States—the purpleleaf pissard plum (*Prunus cerasifera*).
COMBINES WITH:	*Crambe cordifolia, Dictamnus albus, Gaura lindheimeri* 'So White', *Sanguisorba canadensis*

Prunus 'Snofozam', 'Snow Fountains'
'SNOW FOUNTAINS' WEEPING CHERRY

© Lake County Nursery, Perry, Ohio

PLANT TYPE:	Deciduous tree
ZONE:	5–8
FLOWER/FRUIT:	Single white profusion of flowers; few black fruits
HABIT/FOLIAGE:	Narrowly weeping; dark green leaves turn gold in fall
HEIGHT:	10–15 feet
WIDTH/SPREAD:	6–12 feet
LIGHT:	Sun to light shade
SOIL:	Average to rich, moist but not wet
CARE:	If you prune branches that are touching the ground, remember to prune closer to the top crown—the stems branch outward from where you have pruned.
USES:	Early blooming, unusual shape, fall color
PROBLEMS:	Reported to be "short-lived" in Zone 5
INSIDER'S TIPS:	'Snow Fountains', even if it lives only 10 years in my garden, will be well worth replacing! *Prunus subhirtella* 'Pendula' is another weeping form but gets too big (40 feet by 40 feet). My perennial monkshood stems intertwined in the weeping stems of 'Snow Fountains' and gave the appearance of having blue blossoms in September and October.
COMBINES WITH:	*Aconitum napellus, Pulmonaria longifolia* ssp. *cevennensis, Heuchera* 'Plum Pudding', *Astilbe* x *arendsii* 'Glow' (has red new growth in spring)

Prunus x *yedoensis* 'Shidare Yoshino'

WEEPING YOSHINO CHERRY

PLANT TYPE:	Deciduous tree
ZONE:	5–8
FLOWER/FRUIT:	Profuse white with a hint of pink flowers all along the stems; black fruit is not very showy
HABIT/FOLIAGE:	Weeping, rounded form from a main trunk; dark green leaves emerge after bloom and become yellow in fall
HEIGHT:	Grows slowly to 15 feet in 10 years
WIDTH/SPREAD:	20–25 feet
LIGHT:	Sun to light shade
SOIL:	Rich, moist, well-drained
CARE:	Since I have not seen mature forms of this cherry, I can only imagine that pruning while the tree is young might be the method to curb growth, particularly the width.
USES:	Specimen, architectural accent, early blooming
PROBLEMS:	May be short-lived
INSIDER'S TIPS:	This weeping cherry deserves a special place in the landscape and looks fantastic growing alongside a large water feature, such as a pond. It would be wasted in the mixed border and should only be underplanted with low plants.
COMBINES WITH:	*Scilla sibirica, Muscari armeniacum, Lamium maculatum* 'Beedham's White'

Rhododendron 'Aglo'

'AGLO' RHODODENDRON

PLANT TYPE:	Broadleaf evergreen
ZONE:	4–7
FLOWER/FRUIT:	Clear pink blooms with a darker center
HABIT/FOLIAGE:	Compact mound; small, evergreen leaves turn red in fall through winter; lepidote
HEIGHT:	2–4 feet
WIDTH/SPREAD:	2–4 feet
LIGHT:	Sun to light shade
SOIL:	Rich, moist, well-drained
CARE:	I only prune out any winterkill. You may choose to remove browned, spent flowers. With too much shade, 'Aglo' first gets very leggy then finally declines. Rhodie experts recommend "high shade."
USES:	Evergreen, early blooming, fall color
PROBLEMS:	None; this is the easiest of the PJM hybrids to grow in the Midwest
INSIDER'S TIPS:	The sister to 'Aglo' (also from Weston Nursery and Wayne Mezitt breeding program) is 'Olga Mezitt', with light pink blossoms and a little more open habit. Did you guess that 'Aglo' is 'Olga' spelled backwards?
COMBINES WITH:	*Dicentra spectabilis, Leucojum aestivum* 'Gravetye Giant', *Myosotis sylvatica* 'Victoria Dark Blue'

Rhododendron 'PJM'

'PJM' RHODODENDRON

PLANT TYPE:	Broadleaf evergreen
ZONE:	4–7
FLOWER/FRUIT:	Purple-pink flowers vary in intensity
HABIT/FOLIAGE:	Rounded and dense; small, glossy leaves turn purple or mahogany in fall; lepidote
HEIGHT:	3–6 feet
WIDTH/SPREAD:	3–6 feet
LIGHT:	Sun to light shade
SOIL:	Rich, moist, well-drained, is not so acid-specific
CARE:	Care is identical to that of *Rhododendron* 'Aglo'.
USES:	Evergreen, early blooming, fall color
PROBLEMS:	Now found to be prone to virus
INSIDER'S TIPS:	The smaller leaf rhododendrons do best in sun. This plant does particularly well in Midwest gardens, although it is very overused for this reason. Introduced by Weston Nurseries in Hopkinton, Massachusetts, in 1943.
COMBINES WITH:	*Hosta montana* 'Aureomarginata', *Narcissus* 'King Alfred', *Muscari armeniacum, Mertensia virginica*

Spiraea × *cinerea* 'Grefsheim'

'GREFSHEIM' SPIREA

PLANT TYPE:	Deciduous shrub
ZONE:	4–7 (8)
FLOWER/FRUIT:	Tiny white flower bloom all along the stems before leaves appear; a more delicate bridalwreath spirea
HABIT/FOLIAGE:	A dense mound of dark brown, arching stems; medium green, narrow leaves create a fine texture that turns yellow-gold in fall
HEIGHT:	4–5 feet
WIDTH/SPREAD:	4–5 feet
LIGHT:	Sun to part shade
SOIL:	Average, well-drained
CARE:	When older plants become too twiggy, renovate prune by cutting a third of the stems to the ground.
USES:	Early blooming, profuse bloomer, textural contrast, fall color
PROBLEMS:	Becomes leggy in too much shade
INSIDER'S TIPS:	This spirea is the first to bloom and explodes in spring in a profusion of white flowers. It is a more manageable size than bridalwreath spirea and has the added bonus of even finer texture.
COMBINES WITH:	*Iris sibirica* 'Caesar's Brother', *Geranium* 'Brookside', *Aquilegia chrysantha, Aster novi-belgii* 'Alert'

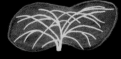

Viburnum carlesii 'Compactum'

COMPACT KOREAN SPICE VIBURNUM

PLANT TYPE:	Deciduous shrub
ZONE:	(4) 5–7
FLOWER/FRUIT:	Spicy fragrant pink buds become white snowballs; red to black fruit is not showy
HABIT/FOLIAGE:	Densely rounded shrub; dark green leaves have burgundy fall color
HEIGHT:	30–40 inches
WIDTH/SPREAD:	30–40 inches
LIGHT:	Sun to part shade
SOIL:	Average to rich, evenly moist
CARE:	Pruning by "heading back" is best done right after flowering.
USES:	Fragrant, small space, fall color, screening
PROBLEMS:	Korean spicebushes are more resistant to leaf spot
INSIDER'S TIPS:	"True" *Viburnum carlesii* 'Compactum' should be under 4 feet tall. A warning: I have seen some that grow to be 6 feet because they were not labeled correctly at the nursery.
COMBINES WITH:	*Phlox subulata, Lysimachia nummularia* 'Aurea', *Hemerocallis* 'Happy Returns', *Kirengeshoma palmata*

Viburnumx x *juddii*

JUDD'S VIBURNUM

PLANT TYPE:	Deciduous shrub
ZONE:	4–8
FLOWER/FRUIT:	Pink buds open to white semi-snowballs; fruit sparse
HABIT/FOLIAGE:	Upright and nicely rounded; stems are a little more coarse than those of *Viburnum carlesii;* dark green oval leaves become red-purple in fall, particularly if it gets cold early
HEIGHT:	6–8 feet
WIDTH/SPREAD:	6–8 feet
LIGHT:	Sun to part shade
SOIL:	Average to rich, evenly moist
CARE:	Any pruning should be done right after blooming.
USES:	Fragrant, early blooming, background, foundation
PROBLEMS:	Resistant to bacterial leaf spot
INSIDER'S TIPS:	Judd's viburnum has overtaken the Korean spice viburnum for popularity in the Midwest. Both are fragrant and have similar rounded forms.
COMBINES WITH:	*Tulipa* 'Angelique', *Phlox divaricata, Hemerocallis* 'Cherry Cheeks', *Hakonechloa macra* 'Aureola', *Spiraea japonica* 'Dakota Goldcharm'

Spiraea japonica 'Neon Flash'

'NEON FLASH' SPIREA

PLANT TYPE:	Deciduous shrub
ZONE:	3–8
FLOWER/FRUIT:	Deep reddish-rose clusters that continually repeat bloom into October
HABIT/FOLIAGE:	Roundy-moundy with red-brown stems; very twiggy, like most spireas; leaves emerge red-tipped then become dark green; late fall color is green suffused with burgundy
HEIGHT:	3–4 feet
WIDTH/SPREAD:	3–4 feet
LIGHT:	Sun to light shade
SOIL:	Average to rich, moist but not wet
CARE:	Shearing spent blossoms gives a neater appearance—brown seedheads detract from the constantly repeat-blooming flowers.
USES:	Long blooming, easy care, foundation
PROBLEMS:	None
INSIDER'S TIPS:	The species *Spiraea japonica* has been put on the invasives list at the Chicago Botanic Garden. The cultivars will be evaluated as to which *japonica* types have the potential to seed about in natural landscapes.
COMBINES WITH:	*Hemerocallis* 'Summer Wine', *Gaura lindheimeri, Geranium pratense* 'Midnight Reiter', *Euphorbia myrsinites*

CHAPTER 3

May

NOW LET THOSE MAY
FLOWERS COME!

Aesculus pavia
RED BUCKEYE

PLANT TYPE:	Deciduous tree
ZONE:	5–9
FLOWER/FRUIT:	Bright red tubular flowers become brown buckeyes in fall
HABIT/FOLIAGE:	Round-top small, shrubby tree; shiny, dark green leaves typical of buckeyes with no fall color
HEIGHT:	10–20 feet
WIDTH/SPREAD:	10–20 feet
LIGHT:	Sun to light shade
SOIL:	Rich, moist, well-drained
CARE:	Allow enough space for ultimate growth
USES:	Specimen, winter structure, landscape tree
PROBLEMS:	May be too big for most gardens
INSIDER'S TIPS:	It is worth having a red buckeye as a specimen if you can give it space, perhaps outside the garden border. Although a real standout when in flower, there is no fall color.
COMBINES WITH:	*Brunnera macrophylla, Campanula poscharskyana, Phlox stolonifera*

Chionanthus virginicus

FRINGE TREE

PLANT TYPE:	Native, deciduous tree
ZONE:	4–9
FLOWER/FRUIT:	Long white, drooping and thready-looking panicles; fruit is a dark blue drupe in August and September
HABIT/FOLIAGE:	Rounded open pyramid similar to magnolia, multi-stemmed with smooth bark; leaves are shiny green and elliptical, turning yellow in fall
HEIGHT:	20 feet, in the landscape is usually 10–15 feet
WIDTH/SPREAD:	6–10 feet
LIGHT:	Sun to part shade
SOIL:	Rich, moist, slightly acid
CARE:	Easy. I have only pruned mine when the spruce next to it caused it to grow out toward the sunlight.
USES:	Specimen, early flowering, fall color
PROBLEMS:	Occasional leaf spot and powdery mildew
INSIDER'S TIPS:	I have had no foliar problems with my fifteen-year-old plant. It is planted in highly organic soil with only morning sun. Because the plant is dioecious (flowers being only one sex), plants produce fruit only if there are other clones nearby. Mine has never set fruit!
COMBINES WITH:	*Iris sibirica* 'Orville Fay', *Salvia* x *superba* 'May Night', *Chrysanthemum parthenium* 'Aureum', *Aster divaricatus*

Cornus kousa var. *chinensis*

CHINESE KOUSA DOGWOOD

PLANT TYPE:	Deciduous tree
ZONE:	5–8
FLOWER/FRUIT:	Creamy-white four-pointed bracts; strawberry-like fruit September–October
HABIT/FOLIAGE:	Stiffly upright when young, becoming more horizontally spreading with age; dark green sometimes glossy leaves, becoming reddish purple to scarlet in fall
HEIGHT:	15–20 feet, possibly to 30 feet
WIDTH/SPREAD:	15–20 feet
LIGHT:	Sun to part shade
SOIL:	Rich, consistently moist, slightly acidic
CARE:	This can become a good-sized tree. Pruning decisions need to be made at a young age. Mulch to maintain soil moisture and to improve heavy clay soils.
USES:	Specimen, showy flowers, fall fruit, fall color
PROBLEMS:	This variety does not show the disease problems that have recently affected *Cornus florida*.
INSIDER'S TIPS:	Kousa dogwoods have become the cold-climate substitute for *Cornus florida*. This tree tends to be smaller in colder climates.
COMBINES WITH:	*Alchemilla mollis, Rosa* 'Knockout', *Heuchera* 'Plum Pudding', *Digitalis purpurea*

Deutzia x *kalmiiflora* 'Magician'

'MAGICIAN' DEUTZIA

PLANT TYPE:	Deciduous shrub
ZONE:	5–8
FLOWER/FRUIT:	Large pink flowers edged in white and purple-veined appear in clusters along the stems
HABIT/FOLIAGE:	Mounded form with thin, twiggy arching stems producing an open look; light green lance-like leaves become yellow in fall
HEIGHT:	5–7 feet
WIDTH/SPREAD:	5–7 feet
LIGHT:	Sun to light shade
SOIL:	Average to rich, moist but not wet
CARE:	Prune for a neater appearance right after bloom.
USES:	Profuse bloom, specimen, background, fall color
PROBLEMS:	Twiggy, open habit needs judicious pruning
INSIDER'S TIPS:	Newer pink-flowered, more compact forms are slowly becoming available. Look for cultivars 'Pink Minor' or 'Perle Pink'.
COMBINES WITH:	*Iris sibirica* 'Steve', *Rosa* 'Iceberg', *Hydrangea paniculata* 'Little Lamb'

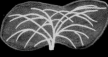

Enkianthus campanulatus

REDVEIN ENKIANTHUS

PLANT TYPE:	Deciduous shrub
ZONE:	(4) 5–7
FLOWER/FRUIT:	Creamy yellow clusters of bells with red veins
HABIT/FOLIAGE:	Narrow upright habit with tiered branching pattern; glossy, blue-green leaves with yellow to orange-red fall color
HEIGHT:	6–8 feet, 12–15 feet in the Northeast
WIDTH/SPREAD:	6–8 feet
LIGHT:	Sun to partial shade
SOIL:	Rich, moist, well-drained, acidic
CARE:	Does best in acidic soils with similar needs to the rhododendrons.
USES:	Interesting flower display, fall color, shade tolerant
PROBLEMS:	Not tolerant of wet clay soil!
INSIDER'S TIPS:	Check *Enkianthus perulatus* as a more "elegant" shrub, which also grows to 6 feet tall. Those growing this plant with clay soils in the Chicagoland region have worked hard to create the soil needed for enkianthus.
COMBINES WITH:	*Alchemilla mollis*, *Lilium* 'Stargazer', *Astilbe chinensis* 'Purple Candles'

Kalmia latifolia
MOUNTAIN LAUREL

PLANT TYPE:	Broadleaf evergreen, native
ZONE:	4–8
FLOWER/FRUIT:	Brightly colored clusters of pink and dark pink cup-shaped, starry flowers
HABIT/FOLIAGE:	Compact, roundy-moundy; glossy foliage reminiscent of rhododendron, new leaves are lighter green, becoming dark green
HEIGHT:	4–8 feet
WIDTH/SPREAD:	4–8 feet
LIGHT:	Sun, part shade, shade
SOIL:	Rich, moist, well-drained, acidic
CARE:	Needs protection from drying winds in winter and well-mulched soil to conserve soil moisture. Prepare soil as you would for rhododendrons.
USES:	Evergreen, small space, showy flowers
PROBLEMS:	More open habit in shade
INSIDER'S TIPS:	Unfortunately, with the heavy clay soils in the Midwest, few mountain laurels are being grown, and then only by gardeners who are willing to work at changing their soils. There are numerous kalmias available by mail order, with flower colors ranging from white, pink, and red.
COMBINES WITH:	*Rodgersia aesculifolia, Digitalis purpurea* 'Alba', *Hosta* 'Blue Angel'

Philadelphus x *virginalis* 'Belle Etoile'

'BELLE ETOILE' MOCK ORANGE

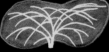

PLANT TYPE:	Deciduous shrub
ZONE:	5–8
FLOWER/FRUIT:	Masses of fragrant white 2-inch flowers with light maroon center
HABIT/FOLIAGE:	Broadly arching branches form a wide mound; medium green leaves do not have fall color
HEIGHT:	6–8 feet
WIDTH/SPREAD:	6–8 feet
LIGHT:	Sun to light shade
SOIL:	Average to rich, moist but not wet
CARE:	In England I have seen Belle Etoile espaliered on walls.
USES:	Background, fragrance, floriferous, Victorian garden
PROBLEMS:	Only one season of interest
INSIDER'S TIPS:	Most gardeners do not have garden space to grow a plant that only has one season of interest, but if you have the room, it's a great shrub.
COMBINES WITH:	*Geranium* x *cantabrigiense* 'Karmina', *Hemerocallis* 'Joan Senior', *Spiraea japonica* 'Dakota Goldcharm'

Rhododendron 'Album Novum'

'ALBUM NOVUM' RHODODENDRON

PLANT TYPE:	Broadleaf evergreen
ZONE:	4–7
FLOWER/FRUIT:	Lilac-tinged buds open to large clusters of white flowers with a yellow-green spot near the centers
HABIT/FOLIAGE:	Dense, bushy, rounded outline; large, dark green and glossy leaves are evergreen; elepidote
HEIGHT:	4–6 feet
WIDTH/SPREAD:	3–4 feet
LIGHT:	Open shade, part shade—needs more shade in the South
SOIL:	Rich, moist, well-drained, acidic
CARE:	Root balls need to be drastically cut apart before planting. I know that can be particularly scary to do, but this encourages new horizontal root growth and is recommended by rhododendron aficianados. I've done it, and it works!
USES:	Specimen, evergreen, woodland edge
PROBLEMS:	Needs soil improvement to ensure good drainage
INSIDER'S TIPS:	A *Rhododendron catawbiense* hybrid, it shows greater cold hardiness, as well as some tolerance for hot summer sun. Another 'ironclad' hybrid is *Rhododendron* 'Roseum Elegans'.
COMBINES WITH:	*Alchemilla mollis, Allium* 'Purple Sensation', *Tulipa humilis* 'Persian Pearl', *Hosta fortunei* 'Gold Standard'

Rhododendron calendulaceum

FLAME AZALEA

PLANT TYPE:	Native, deciduous shrub
ZONE:	5–7
FLOWER/FRUIT:	Yellow to orange or coral; not fragrant
HABIT/FOLIAGE:	Large open, naturalistic rounded shrub; medium green leaves become yellow to red in fall
HEIGHT:	4–8 feet
WIDTH/SPREAD:	4–8 feet
LIGHT:	Open shade, part shade—needs more shade in the South
SOIL:	Rich, moist, well-drained, acidic
CARE:	Must meet the soil requirements to grow—acid soil that is well drained! See page 293.
USES:	Bold color, shade tolerant, fall color, specimen
PROBLEMS:	Clay soils lead to iron deficiencies
INSIDER'S TIPS:	While there has been hybridization done for more cold hardiness, the issue is still the need for acidic soil. You want a soil that is high in iron but lower in other nutrients.
COMBINES WITH:	*Mertensia virginica, Tiarella wherryi, Dryopteris goldiana*

Rhododendron 'Northern Lights'

'NORTHERN LIGHTS' AZALEA

PLANT TYPE:	Deciduous shrub
ZONE:	4–7
FLOWER/FRUIT:	A profusion of very pale pink, fragrant flowers
HABIT/FOLIAGE:	Upright, rounded, somewhat more open in more shade; rich green ovals turn bronzed-orange in fall
HEIGHT:	5–7 feet
WIDTH/SPREAD:	4–5 feet
LIGHT:	Part shade
SOIL:	Rich, moist, well-drained, slightly acidic
CARE:	Prepare soil as you would for other azaleas—plant high and mulch with pine needles or pine bark.
USES:	Fragrant, profuse bloom, fall color
PROBLEMS:	Not as mildew resistant as some of the later introductions
INSIDER'S TIPS:	There is a whole series of the very cold-hardy 'Lights' azaleas developed in Minnesota by Albert Johnson and Harold Pellet. *Rhododendron prinophyllum*, one of the parent plants, is more tolerant to higher pH and also gives the clove scent to the flowers. Two other hardy (to –20°F) azaleas I hope to try are *Rhododendron schlippenbachii* and *Rhododendron vaseyi*.
COMBINES WITH:	*Pulmonaria* 'Majeste', *Tradescantia* x *andersoniana* 'Concord Grape', *Geranium pratense* 'Mrs. Kendall Clark'

Rhododendron catawbiense 'Nova Zembla'

'NOVA ZEMBLA' CATAWBA RHODODENDRON

PLANT TYPE:	Broadleaf evergreen
ZONE:	4–8
FLOWER/FRUIT:	Showy clusters of crimson red bells
HABIT/FOLIAGE:	Dense, upright rounded form; large, glossy, dark green leaves are evergreen; elepidote
HEIGHT:	6–10 feet
WIDTH/SPREAD:	6–10 feet
LIGHT:	Part shade, shade
SOIL:	Rich, moist, well-drained, acidic
CARE:	If this sits in a saucer of clay soil, it will definitely develop *Phytophthora* root rot. Good tips on any care issues can be found at: www.rhododendron.org. Click on plant care to find articles that will be helpful.
USES:	Color accent, evergreen
PROBLEMS:	Rhododendrons with red flowers are more susceptible than other rhododenrdons to *Phytophthora*
INSIDER'S TIPS:	The Briggs Nursery has introduced *Rhododendron* 'Super Nova', a polyploid of 'Nova Zembla'. Rare Find Nursery's catalog calls this a Franken Child!
COMBINES WITH:	*Pulmonaria longifolia* ssp. *cevennensis, Anemonella thalictroides, Athyrium nipponicum* 'Pictum'

Rhododendron x 'Scintillation'

'SCINTILLATION' RHODODENDRON

PLANT TYPE:	Evergreen shrub
ZONE:	5–8
FLOWER/FRUIT:	Heavy trusses (clusters may have as many as 15 flowers) of clear pink, golden spots in the centers; mid-season bloomtime
HABIT/FOLIAGE:	Round with strong branching habit; glossy, medium evergreen leaves that are a little more elliptical than other elepidotes
HEIGHT:	4–6 feet
WIDTH/SPREAD:	4–6 feet
LIGHT:	Part shade, shade
SOIL:	Rich, moist, well-drained, acidic
CARE:	Good tips on any care issues can be found at: www.rhododendron.org. Click on plant care to find articles that will be helpful.
USES:	Specimen, strong grower, evergreen, foundation
PROBLEMS:	You must acidify clay soil
INSIDER'S TIPS:	This grows at the Chicago Botanic Garden in a very protected site, and the soils have probably been amended for acidity.
COMBINES WITH:	*Phlox divaricata* 'Montrose Tricolor', *Brunnera macrophylla* 'Dawson's White', *Hosta plantaginea* 'Aphrodite'

Rhodotypos scandens

BLACK JETBEAD

PLANT TYPE:	Deciduous shrub
ZONE:	4–8
FLOWER/FRUIT:	White, four-petaled flowers followed by glossy black fruit that persists thru winter
HABIT/FOLIAGE:	Medium sized, open mound; light green leaves emerge early in the season and have some yellow fall color
HEIGHT:	3–6 feet
WIDTH/SPREAD:	3–6 feet
LIGHT:	Sun, part shade, shade
SOIL:	Widely adaptable
CARE:	Easy
USES:	For difficult sites, background, shade tolerant, naturalistic garden
PROBLEMS:	No pests or diseases
INSIDER'S TIPS:	Although not a mover and shaker in the mixed border, jetbead performs well in shade and in other difficult sites with little or no care.
COMBINES WITH:	*Stylophorum diphyllum, Athyrium nipponicum* 'Pictum', *Hosta fluctuans* 'Variegata' ('Sagae'), *Lysimachia nummularia* 'Aurea'

Spiraea fritschiana 'Pink Parasols'

'PINK PARASOLS' SPIREA

© ColorChoicePlants.com

PLANT TYPE:	Deciduous shrub
ZONE:	(3) 4–7
FLOWER/FRUIT:	Big, pale pink spirea flower that resembles a parasol
HABIT/FOLIAGE:	Rounded form with dense reddish brown stems; dark green leaves turn yellow-orange in fall; leaves are larger than most spireas
HEIGHT:	2–3 feet
WIDTH/SPREAD:	3–4 feet
LIGHT:	Sun to light shade
SOIL:	Average to rich, moist but not wet
CARE:	'Pink Parasols' benefits from thinning out the oldest stems every other year before spring growth.
USES:	Bold accent, large flowers, fall color, foundation
PROBLEMS:	None
INSIDER'S TIPS:	Because I get so carried away with the yellow-leafed spireas, I like to suggest others that have a bold dark green presence. 'Pink Parasols' also has showier, large blooms.
COMBINES WITH:	*Hemerocallis* 'Ice Carnival', *Iris pallida* 'Variegata', *Perovskia atriplicifolia* 'Little Spire'

Spiraea japonica 'Goldmound'

'GOLDMOUND' JAPANESE SPIREA

PLANT TYPE:	Deciduous shrub
ZONE:	4–8
FLOWER/FRUIT:	Light pink clusters of tiny flowers with some repeat into September
HABIT/FOLIAGE:	Rounded, low mounding; yellow-gold foliage fades to yellow green and turns orange-red in fall
HEIGHT:	2–3 feet
WIDTH/SPREAD:	3–4 feet
LIGHT:	Sun to light shade
SOIL:	Average to rich, moist but not wet
CARE:	Prune to shape in early spring before growth has started. Removing faded flowers will promote new growth and repeat flowering.
USES:	Bright foliage, roundy-moundy shape, fall color
PROBLEMS:	Seems to be resistant to powdery mildew
INSIDER'S TIPS:	Newer cultivars that may hold yellow foliage color better throughout the summer are 'Candle Light' and 'Lemon Princess'.
COMBINES WITH:	*Campanula poscharskyana, Paeonia officinalis* 'Paula Fay', *Hemerocallis* 'Cherry Cheeks', *Lilium* 'La Reve'

Syringa meyeri 'Palibin'

DWARF KOREAN LILAC

PLANT TYPE:	Deciduous shrub
ZONE:	3–7
FLOWER/FRUIT:	Pale lilac-pink in smaller panicles; very lightly fragrant
HABIT/FOLIAGE:	Broadly rounded form on a standard; form showy in winter; small, dark green leaves show good mildew resistance but no fall color
HEIGHT:	4–5 feet
WIDTH/SPREAD:	5–6 feet
LIGHT:	Full sun
SOIL:	Rich, moist, well-drained
CARE:	Keep formally pruned, pruning right after blooming
USES:	Foundation, hedge, specimen, formal garden, winter outline
PROBLEMS:	None
INSIDER'S TIPS:	Flowers show best against an evergreen backdrop. As compared to 'Miss Kim' lilac, this one has a more profuse bloom but smaller flower panicles.
COMBINES WITH:	*Iris sibirica* 'Caesar's Brother', *Paeonia* x 'Petticoat Flounce', *Agastache* x 'Blue Fortune'

Viburnum plicatum var. *tomentosum* 'Mariesii'

'MARIESII' DOUBLEFILE VIBURNUM

PLANT TYPE:	Deciduous tree
ZONE:	5–8
FLOWER/FRUIT:	White lacecap-like flowers are not fragrant; red and black fruit only appear where there is another clone
HABIT/FOLIAGE:	Rounded form with horizontally branched and tiered branches; light green leaves have a tendency to drop, complimenting the tiered habit; red purple in fall
HEIGHT:	8–10 feet
WIDTH/SPREAD:	9–12 feet
LIGHT:	Sun to part shade—needs more shade in southern regions
SOIL:	Rich, moist, well-drained
CARE:	Pruning should only be done to improve the lateral structure—take time and do it artfully. It is best to allow this plant space to grow as a specimen.
USES:	Specimen, profuse flower, architecture, fall color
PROBLEMS:	Does not do well in heavy clay soils, especially with poor drainage
INSIDER'S TIPS:	Soil improvement to amend compacted clay is an absolute necessity if you want to successfully grow doublefile viburnum. The time and expense will be well worth it.
COMBINES WITH:	*Carex elata* 'Bowles Golden', *Hosta fluctuans* 'Variegata' ('Sagae'), *Tiarella wherryi* 'Oakleaf'

Viburnum rufidulum 'Morton', 'Emerald Charm'

'EMERALD CHARM' SOUTHERN BLACKHAW

© Chicagoland Grows Inc.

PLANT TYPE:	Deciduous shrub
ZONE:	5–9
FLOWER/FRUIT:	Profuse, creamy-white domed clusters; fruit is dark blue
HABIT/FOLIAGE:	Rounded, multi-stemmed habit is more open in shaded sites; oval leaves are glossy, dark green with rich burgundy fall color
HEIGHT:	10–12 feet
WIDTH/SPREAD:	8–10 feet
LIGHT:	Sun to part shade
SOIL:	Rich, moist, well-drained
CARE:	Gets really big! Prune as needed after blooming.
USES:	Screen, profuse bloom, fall color
PROBLEMS:	None
INSIDER'S TIPS:	Viburnums are very popular in the Midwest. The Chicagoland Grows Inc. program—through the Morton Arboretum, Chicago Botanic Garden, and the Ornamental Growers Association—has worked hard to introduce plants through selection and trialing. This "southern" blackhaw was selected for winter hardiness.
COMBINES WITH:	*Aquilegia candadensis, Iris sibirica* 'Caesar's Brother', *Miscanthus sinensis* 'Variegatus'

Weigela florida 'Alexandra', 'Wine & Roses'

'WINE & ROSES' WEIGELA

© Steve VanderWoude

PLANT TYPE:	Deciduous shrub
ZONE:	4–8
FLOWER/FRUIT:	Profuse trumpet-shaped rosy-red flowers
HABIT/FOLIAGE:	Upright rounded shrub with somewhat arching stems; dark, shiny burgundy-purple foliage
HEIGHT:	4–5 feet
WIDTH/SPREAD:	4 feet
LIGHT:	Sun to light shade
SOIL:	Average, well-drained
CARE:	Prune immediately after blooming.
USES:	Profuse bloom, foliage color, specimen
PROBLEMS:	None, disease resistant
INSIDER'S TIPS:	The foliage of 'Wine & Roses' weigela with more shade is only bronzed green. This recent introduction comes from Herman Geers of Holland and is a great improvement over 'Foliis Purpureis', which always looked brownish to me.
COMBINES WITH:	*Phlox paniculata* 'Fairest One', *Sedum* x 'Autumn Joy', *Hydrangea paniculata* 'Limelight'

Weigela florida 'Briant's Rubidor'

'BRIANT'S RUBIDOR' WEIGELA

PLANT TYPE:	Deciduous shrub
ZONE:	4–8
FLOWER/FRUIT:	Ruby-red funnel-shaped flowers
HABIT/FOLIAGE:	Upright rounded form; very bright yellow leaves are almost shocking
HEIGHT:	5–7 feet
WIDTH/SPREAD:	4–5 feet
LIGHT:	Part shade
SOIL:	Average, well-drained
CARE:	Pruning is not necessary if the plant height fits your garden.
USES:	Bold color accent, profuse bloom, easy care
PROBLEMS:	Color is shocking!
INSIDER'S TIPS:	Because the foliage gets a bit "crisped" in hot summer sun, I would put it in a site that is shaded at noontime. This picture was taken at Crathes Castle, Scotland, in a "yellow garden." The plant will stand out even more in gardens of green foliage. In the picture shown above, 'Briant's Rubidor' has been pruned to present different levels of bloom and colored foliage.
COMBINES WITH:	*Primula florindae, Coreopsis verticillata* 'Golden Showers', annual *Helichrysum* 'Limelight'

Potentilla fruticosa 'Primrose Beauty'
BUSH CINQUEFOIL

PLANT TYPE:	Deciduous shrub
ZONE:	2–6
FLOWER/FRUIT:	Pale yellow buttercups with darker yellow centers
HABIT/FOLIAGE:	Mounded, very shrubby with brown stems; tiny grayish green leaves; fall color not particularly ornamental
HEIGHT:	2–3 feet
WIDTH/SPREAD:	3–4 feet
LIGHT:	Sun to light shade
SOIL:	Rich, moist, well-drained, tolerates drier soils
CARE:	If plant becomes too woody, renovate leafless stems by cutting them to the ground.
USES:	Long blooming, foundation, facer plant, massing
PROBLEMS:	Needs pruning to rejuvenate
INSIDER'S TIPS:	I am partial to this cultivar because the flowers do not seem so brassy.
COMBINES WITH:	*Hemerocallis* 'Ice Carnival', *Euphorbia polychroma*, *Phlox paniculata* 'Blue Paradise', *Berberis thunbergii* 'Bonanza Gold', *Euonymus fortunei* 'Gold Splash'

Syringa x *tribida* 'Josee'

'JOSEE' LILAC

PLANT TYPE:	Deciduous shrub
ZONE:	3–6
FLOWER/FRUIT:	Fragrant, lavender-pink panicles that repeat intermittently through summer and fall
HABIT/FOLIAGE:	Semi-dwarf rounded form; small, dark green heart-shaped leaves
HEIGHT:	4–6 feet
WIDTH/SPREAD:	4–6 feet
LIGHT:	Full sun
SOIL:	Rich, moist, well-drained
CARE:	Needs very little pruning, if any at all
USES:	Long blooming, smaller space, fragrant
PROBLEMS:	Disease resistant
INSIDER'S TIPS:	When choosing which lilacs to grow in your garden, first consider the size and spacing. The next decision will be the bloom color, ranging from lilac to pink to purple and white or yellow! And since most do not have fall color, look for ones that have another season of interest, as this long-bloomer or others with an interesting winter outline, such as the standard form of 'Paliban'.
COMBINES WITH:	*Iris sibirica* 'Caesar's Brother', *Leucanthemum* x 'Ryan's White', *Miscanthus sinensis* 'Little Zebra'

Daphne caucasica

CAUCASIAN DAPHNE

© Richard Hawke

PLANT TYPE:	Deciduous shrub
ZONE:	(4) 5–7
FLOWER/FRUIT:	Clusters of white fragrant flowers on the end of plant stems, with repeat into early fall
HABIT/FOLIAGE:	Tightly rounded shape; light green to blue green fine-textured ovals
HEIGHT:	4–5 feet
WIDTH/SPREAD:	4–5 feet
LIGHT:	Light shade to part shade
SOIL:	Rich, moist, well-drained (neutral pH)
CARE:	Prune out winterkill as necessary. Plant in a protected location.
USES:	Fragrance, repeat bloom, foundation, small space
PROBLEMS:	Needs winter protection, especially if there is no snow cover in the North
INSIDER'S TIPS:	There are varying reports as to the difficulty keeping this plant alive. All daphnes resent transplanting or any disturbance of soil around their roots.
COMBINES WITH:	*Ligularia dentata* 'Desdemona', *Ajuga reptans* 'Gaiety', *Phlox* x 'Chattahoochie'

Weigela florida 'White Knight'

'WHITE KNIGHT' WEIGELA

PLANT TYPE:	Deciduous shrub
ZONE:	5–8
FLOWER/FRUIT:	Large white trumpets with a hint of pink; flowers all along the stems with lesser repeat bloom
HABIT/FOLIAGE:	Upright open form with black stems arching outward; medium green foliage has no fall color
HEIGHT:	5–6 feet
WIDTH/SPREAD:	5–6 feet
LIGHT:	Sun to light shade
SOIL:	Average, well-drained
CARE:	Easy—prune occasionally if needed.
USES:	Long blooming, easy care, background
PROBLEMS:	No pests
INSIDER'S TIPS:	An Iowa State University introduction that has repeat bloom into September.
COMBINES WITH:	*Myosotis sylvatica* 'Victoria Dark Blue', *Geranium wallichianum* 'Buxton's Blue', *Amsonia hubrectii*

Abelia x *grandiflora*
GLOSSY ABELIA

PLANT TYPE:	Semi-evergreen
ZONE:	6–9
FLOWER/FRUIT:	Lightly fragrant, white-tinged pink tubular bells that repeat intermittently until frost; fruit not ornamental
HABIT/FOLIAGE:	Mounds of arching stems; new growth bronzed; oval, dark glossy green leaves turn purple in fall
HEIGHT:	3–6 feet
WIDTH/SPREAD:	5–6 feet, spreading
LIGHT:	Sun to part shade
SOIL:	Rich, moist, well-drained, acidic
CARE:	Prune in winter or early spring to maintain mounded form
USES:	Hedge, foundation, long blooming
PROBLEMS:	Mildew and root rot
INSIDER'S TIPS:	The hardiest and most prolific of the abelias, glossy abelia typically dies back to its own roots in the North and does not put out sufficient height to use it as a dieback shrub in Zone 5. *Abelia mosanensis* is the best species for northern gardens. Just remember that it will not have the repeat bloom or be semi-evergreen.
COMBINES WITH:	*Hosta* 'Sum and Substance' (or other sun-tolerant hostas), *Hemerocallis* 'Strawberry Candy', *Phlox paniculata* 'Red Riding Hood'

Viburnum plicatum var. *tomentosum* 'Watanabei' ('Summer Snowflake')

'SUMMER SNOWFLAKE' DOUBLEFILE VIBURNUM

PLANT TYPE:	Deciduous shrub
ZONE:	5–8
FLOWER/FRUIT:	Repeat-blooming, small white pinwheels become red then black fruit, although sparsely produced
HABIT/FOLIAGE:	Rounded form with horizontally branched and tiered branches; small, light green leaves turn red-purple in fall
HEIGHT:	5–6 feet
WIDTH/SPREAD:	5–6 feet
LIGHT:	Sun, part shade, shade
SOIL:	Rich, moist, well-drained
CARE:	Be sure to prune out "water sprouts" to maintain tiered shape.
USES:	Long blooming, accent, background, fall color, tiered winter branches, attracts birds
PROBLEMS:	Because this plant is so busy blooming, it does not have much fruit.
INSIDER'S TIPS:	I have seen it growing well in full shade and am evaluating it in my own shady garden site. 'Pink Beauty', 'Mariesii', 'Shasta', and 'Shoshoni' are other popular cultivars with the horizontal branching pattern, but these only bloom in May and June.
COMBINES WITH:	*Hosta* 'Patriot' or 'Pilgrim', *Polygonatum odoratum* 'Variegatum', *Lamium maculatum* 'White Nancy'

CHAPTER 4

June

TAKE TIME TO SMELL
THE FLOWERS!

Sambucus nigra 'Laciniata'

CUTLEAF ELDERBERRY

PLANT TYPE:	Deciduous shrub
ZONE:	3–7
FLOWER/FRUIT:	Creamy white flat clusters in June becomes purple edible fruit in August and September
HABIT/FOLIAGE:	Very upright vase shape; finely cut, medium green foliage—"looks like a giant fern!"
HEIGHT:	6–8 feet
WIDTH/SPREAD:	4–6 feet
LIGHT:	Sun to part shade
SOIL:	Rich, moist
CARE:	This shrub is often cut to the ground in spring to keep in bounds, but doing so decreases the amount of bloom and fruit.
USES:	Texture, specimen, wet garden, background
PROBLEMS:	None
INSIDER'S TIPS:	The cutleaf elderberry is a somewhat weaker grower than the species and is not as spreading. Use as a textural contrast that will be showy all season long.
COMBINES WITH:	*Nepeta subsessilis*, *Anemone vitifolia* 'Robustissima', *Hemerocallis* 'Rocket City' or 'Pink Lavender Appeal'

Aesculus parviflora

BOTTLEBRUSH BUCKEYE

PLANT TYPE:	Native, deciduous shrub
ZONE:	4–8
FLOWER/FRUIT:	8–12 inch long white, pointed bottlebrush or pyramidal spike
HABIT/FOLIAGE:	Rounded and spreading outline; dark green, boldly lobed leaves turn yellow in fall
HEIGHT:	8–12 feet
WIDTH/SPREAD:	10–15 feet, spreading
LIGHT:	Sun, part shade, shade—prefers afternoon shade
SOIL:	Average to rich, evenly moist, slightly acidic
CARE:	Pruning is seldom necessary, but it can be rejuvenated by cutting it to the ground right after flowering.
USES:	Massing, space filler, specimen, fall color, shade tolerant
PROBLEMS:	Although there a no problems with pest or disease, remember that it is a spreader.
INSIDER'S TIPS:	Please note that I have called the bottlebrush buckeye a "space filler." Beware: It will take over other plants! Look for the larger-flowered *Aesculus parviflora* 'Rogers'. Also, it is best planted with other shrubs that can compete with this shrub.
COMBINES WITH:	*Taxus* x *media* 'Tauntonii', *Spiraea* x *cinerea* 'Grefsheim', *Astilbe* x *arendsii* 'Bridal Veil'

Genista tinctoria 'Royal Gold'

DYER'S GREENWOOD, 'ROYAL GOLD' SUMMER BROOM

PLANT TYPE:	Deciduous shrub
ZONE:	4–7
FLOWER/FRUIT:	Rich yellow, pea-like terminal clusters
HABIT/FOLIAGE:	Mounds of twiggy bright green stems give winter interest; bright green, thin leaves have no fall color
HEIGHT:	2–3 feet
WIDTH/SPREAD:	3 feet
LIGHT:	Full sun
SOIL:	Sandy, well-drained loam, adaptable to poor, dry soil
CARE:	You may choose to deadhead it for neatness.
USES:	Cut flower, dye, winter color, rock garden
PROBLEMS:	Rots out in heavy clay soils
INSIDER'S TIPS:	Brooms are often seen in European gardens, but only rarely in America. Because of the size of 'Royal Gold', it should be considered for the rock garden, where it will have excellent drainage.
COMBINES WITH:	*Salvia* x *superba* 'Blue Hill', *Paeonia officinalis* 'Golly', *Leucanthemum* x *superbum* 'Becky'

Indigofera kirilowii
KIRILOW INDIGO

PLANT TYPE:	Deciduous shrub
ZONE:	4–7
FLOWER/FRUIT:	Rose-pink spikes are packed with up to 30 individual flowers
HABIT/FOLIAGE:	Low, dense suckering shrub; light green compound leaves have a very delicate texture and turn yellow in fall
HEIGHT:	2–3 feet
WIDTH/SPREAD:	2–3 feet
LIGHT:	Full sun
SOIL:	Average to rich, evenly moist
CARE:	This will be a dieback shrub in the North, and cutting it down to the ground will not affect the bloom. Watch for any suckering, or use other plants that can withstand invasion of root space.
USES:	Groundcover, textural contrast, small space
PROBLEMS:	Has a tendency to sucker
INSIDER'S TIPS:	To show off this plant in the landscape, try to use plants with bolder texture, not as in the picture above.
COMBINES WITH:	*Stachys byzantina* 'Helene von Stein', *Hibiscus* 'Kopper King', *Weigela florida* 'Midnight Wine'

Itea virginica 'Henry's Garnet'

VIRGINIA SWEETSPIRE

PLANT TYPE:	Deciduous shrub
ZONE:	5–9
FLOWER/FRUIT:	Drooping chains of tiny white fragrant flowers
HABIT/FOLIAGE:	Mounds of widely arching stems; glossy, light green foliage turns wine red in fall
HEIGHT:	3–4 feet
WIDTH/SPREAD:	3–4 feet
LIGHT:	Sun, part shade, shade
SOIL:	Rich, moist—wet tolerant
CARE:	Use composted leaves to open heavy clay soils.
USES:	Unusual flower, fragrance, wet tolerant, fall color
PROBLEMS:	Must maintain consistent soil moisture; becomes chlorotic in heavy clay soils
INSIDER'S TIPS:	Discovered by Josephine Henry, Henry Foundation, Gladwyn, Pennsylvania.
COMBINES WITH:	*Lamium maculatum* 'White Nancy', *Lysimachia nummularia* 'Aurea', *Dryopteris marginalis*

Itea virginica 'Little Henry', 'Sprich'

'LITTLE HENRY' SWEETSPIRE

PLANT TYPE:	Deciduous shrub
ZONE:	5–9
FLOWER/FRUIT:	White fragrant drooping spires; flowers are shorter than the flowers on 'Henry's Garnet'
HABIT/FOLIAGE:	Compact, rounded mound created with arching branches; glossy, light green leaves turn red and burgundy in fall
HEIGHT:	18–24 inches
WIDTH/SPREAD:	3 feet
LIGHT:	Sun, part shade, shade
SOIL:	Rich, moist—somewhat wet tolerant
CARE:	It may hold leaves through winter; remove them in early spring so as to not detract from new growth. Very little pruning is needed on this slow grower.
USES:	Unusual flower, fragrance, wet tolerant, fall color, small space
PROBLEMS:	If fall leaves color up late in the season, the leaves may hold on until spring.
INSIDER'S TIPS:	Because this plant is so adaptable, I have used it in shade a lot—but don't forget to site it where you will enjoy the fragrance. 'Little Henry' is repeated in the fall color chapter.
COMBINES WITH:	*Pulmonaria* 'Majeste', *Hosta* 'Diamond Tiara', *Astilbe* x *arendsii* 'Fanal', *Lobelia cardinalis*

Syringa pekinensis 'China Snow', 'Morton'

'CHINA SNOW' PEKING LILAC

© Jim Ault

PLANT TYPE:	Deciduous tree
ZONE:	3–8
FLOWER/FRUIT:	Large, creamy-white, fragrant panicles
HABIT/FOLIAGE:	Upright, small tree with a rounded top; has peeling, cherry-like bark; dark green, pointed oval leaves with no fall color
HEIGHT:	10–12 feet
WIDTH/SPREAD:	7–8 feet
LIGHT:	Full sun
SOIL:	Rich, moist, well-drained, slightly acidic but adaptable
CARE:	Size may require some pruning—see insider's tip on 80-year-old parent tree.
USES:	Specimen, fragrant, winter interest, architectural anchor
PROBLEMS:	None; is disease resistant
INSIDER'S TIPS:	A Chicagoland Grows Inc. selection. The parent tree, which measures 35 feet in height with a 30-foot spread, originated from seed collected in Gansu, China, by Joseph Rock during the 1920s. *Syringa pekinensis* 'Beijing Gold' is a newer cultivar with primrose yellow flowers.
COMBINES WITH:	*Hosta* 'Patriot' or 'Pilgrim', *Brunnera macrophylla* 'Dawson's White', *Lamium maculatum* 'White Nancy', *Astilbe* x *arendsii* 'Bressingham Beauty'

Syringa reticulata 'Summer Snow'

'SUMMER SNOW' JAPANESE TREE LILAC

PLANT TYPE:	Deciduous tree
ZONE:	3–7
FLOWER/FRUIT:	Large, lightly fragrant, creamy white panicles
HABIT/FOLIAGE:	Upright, oval form with glossy, red-brown, cherry-like bark; dark green, pointed oval leaves without good fall color
HEIGHT:	15–20 feet
WIDTH/SPREAD:	12–15 feet
LIGHT:	Sun to light shade
SOIL:	Rich, moist, well-drained
CARE:	Pruning for size control should be done right after blooming. It will come back from renovative pruning.
USES:	Architectural anchor, background, showy in bloom, winter interest
PROBLEMS:	"The most trouble-free of the lilacs," says Michael Dirr.
INSIDER'S TIPS:	If you are working on progression of bloom, this is the last lilac to start blooming.
COMBINES WITH:	*Chamaecyparis pisifera* 'Golden Mop', *Hakonechloa macra* 'Aureola', *Phlox paniculata* 'Bright Eyes', *Hibiscus* 'Kopper King'

Cotinus coggygria 'Young Lady'

'YOUNG LADY' SMOKE SHRUB

PLANT TYPE:	Deciduous shrub
ZONE:	4–8
FLOWER/FRUIT:	Non-showy yellow flowers are followed by smoky-pink "hairs" in rounded panicles giving the impression of smoke; blooms at an early age
HABIT/FOLIAGE:	Irregularly rounded habit; medium-green oval leaves emerge lime green then become orange-red in fall
HEIGHT:	8–10 feet
WIDTH/SPREAD:	8–10 feet
LIGHT:	Sun to light shade
SOIL:	Rich, moist, well-drained
CARE:	Pruning early in the season will eliminate the "smoke."
USES:	Long season of interest, textural background, foundation, fall color
PROBLEMS:	Difficult to propagate
INSIDER'S TIPS:	I have long been in love with the deep, purple-burgundy leafed smoke shrubs, but after watching 'Young Lady' throughout an entire season, I was impressed with its many changes in each season. By the way, the marketing on 'Young Lady' (so named because it blooms at an early age even in a nursery container) calls it a "poodle in a pot."
COMBINES WITH:	*Aster* x *frikartii* 'The Monk', *Echinacea purpurea* 'Magnus', *Monarda didyma* 'Marshall's Delight'

Vitex agnus-castus

CHASTE TREE

Plant type:	Deciduous shrub
Zone:	(5) 6–9
Flower/fruit:	Flowers are long, thin spikes of violet-blue often in clusters at the branch tips
Habit/foliage:	Upright rounded form; gray-green leaves have up to seven leaflets giving it a feathery texture, no fall color
Height:	5–10 feet
Width/spread:	5–10 feet
Light:	Full sun
Soil:	Any soil with good drainage!
Care:	It blooms on new wood so cutting it back to the ground in early spring does not affect the blooms. People in Georgia and Alabama report plants that are nearly tree-like at 10 feet!
Uses:	Long blooming, textural background, disease free
Problems:	Marginally hardy in the North; a dieback shrub in Zone 5
Insider's tips:	This Mediterranean plant is usually rated for Zones 6–9! Currently *Vitex* is being trialed for cold hardiness at the Chicago Botanic Garden, and I have observed plants of 4–5 feet growing at Olbrich Botanical Garden in Madison, Wisconsin. One other tidbit: *Vitex* is one of the oldest phytomedicines (herbals) dating back to the ancient Greek physician Hypocrates.
Combines with:	*Artemisia ludoviciana* 'Valerie Finnis', *Physocarpus opulifolius* 'Diabolo', *Achillea* x 'Anthea'

Hydrangea arborescens 'Annabelle'

'ANNABELLE' HYDRANGEA

PLANT TYPE:	Deciduous shrub
ZONE:	3–9
FLOWER/FRUIT:	Dull white clusters form huge 8–10-inch-diameter balls; flowers age to chartreuse by summer's end
HABIT/FOLIAGE:	Clump forming rounded shrub; stems are weak and will arch with the weight of the large flower heads; dark green heart-shaped leaves; occasional yellow fall color
HEIGHT:	3–5 feet
WIDTH/SPREAD:	3–5 feet, suckers
LIGHT:	Part shade, shade
SOIL:	Rich, moist, well-drained
CARE:	Cut back to the ground at the end of winter. You also may choose to cut it back by half in May to help slow down the "floppiness." Please notice that this gardener has used a "cat's cradle" to support the plant.
USES:	Long blooming, dried flower, shade tolerant, winter interest
PROBLEMS:	Proliferates in rich soils; needs extra watering in hot, dry summers
INSIDER'S TIPS:	I really do prefer the straight species to 'Annabelle'. It has a more refined look to it instead of the big, blowzy flower heads, which cause 'Annabelle' to flop over.
COMBINES WITH:	*Hosta* 'Queen Josephine', *Polygonatum odoratum* 'Variegatum, *Athyrium nipponicum* 'Pictum', *Astilbe japonica* 'Red Sentinel'

Hydrangea arborescens 'Dardom', 'White Dome'

'WHITE DOME' HYDRANGEA

© ColorChoicePlants.com

PLANT TYPE:	Deciduous shrub
ZONE:	3–9
FLOWER/FRUIT:	Large domed clusters of tiny white flowers edged in intermittent sterile flowers
HABIT/FOLIAGE:	Densely mounded form with strong, up-standing stems; dark green leaves have a bluish cast but stand out all season long but have no fall color
HEIGHT:	4–6 feet
WIDTH/SPREAD:	4–6 feet
LIGHT:	Sun, part shade, shade
SOIL:	Average to rich, moist but not wet
CARE:	No need to cut back to keep from flopping over, as 'Annabelle' does.
USES:	Long blooming, dried flower, shade tolerant, Victorian garden, background
PROBLEMS:	Not available in many local garden centers
INSIDER'S TIPS:	The dried flower has a nice chartreuse color for winter arrangements.
COMBINES WITH:	*Narcissus* 'Ice Follies', *Rudbeckia fulgida* 'Goldsturm', *Hosta* 'Robert Frost'

Hydrangea quercifolia

Oakleaf Hydrangea

PLANT TYPE:	Deciduous shrub, native to the South
ZONE:	4–9
FLOWER/FRUIT:	Cone-shaped cluster of creamy white flowers age to tan
HABIT/FOLIAGE:	Upright, multistemmed, coarse-textured, exfoliating brown bark; dark green lobed leaves become burgundy in fall persisting into December.
HEIGHT:	6–8 feet
WIDTH/SPREAD:	6+ feet
LIGHT:	Sun to part shade
SOIL:	Rich, moist, well-drained—tolerates occasional standing water
CARE:	Prune after blooming.
USES:	Naturalistic, fall color, background, long blooming
PROBLEMS:	Less fall color and less flowering in shade
INSIDER'S TIPS:	'Snow Queen' has denser flower heads. 'Sikes Dwarf' is only 3–4 feet.
COMBINES WITH:	*Aruncus dioicus, Athyrium nipponicum* 'Pictum', *Heuchera* 'Plum Pudding'

CHAPTER 5

July
ALL-STARS
IN THE GARDEN

Cephalanthus occidentalis

BUTTONBUSH

PLANT TYPE:	Native, deciduous shrub
ZONE:	4–10
FLOWER/FRUIT:	White, fragrant ball-like flowers attract butterflies, become a persistent cluster of "nutlets"
HABIT/FOLIAGE:	Large, gangly shrub; glossy green leaves becomes yellow in fall
HEIGHT:	6–12 feet
WIDTH/SPREAD:	12+ feet
LIGHT:	Sun to part shade
SOIL:	Rich, moist
CARE:	Cut down close to ground in spring to keep in bounds.
USES:	Naturalistic, attracts butterflies and honeybees, wet garden
PROBLEMS:	Leaves are late to emerge; plant may look dead until the end of May
INSIDER'S TIPS:	Often found in wet areas
COMBINES WITH:	*Baptisia australis, Phlox paniculata* 'Eva Cullum', *Buddleia davidii* 'Summer Beauty', *Monarda didyma* 'Colrain Red'

Clethra alnifolia
SUMMERSWEET

PLANT TYPE:	Native, deciduous shrub, found in swamps and woodlands
ZONE:	4–9
FLOWER/FRUIT:	4–6 inch white spires; spicy fragrance
HABIT/FOLIAGE:	Upright oval, densely branched, spreading by underground stems; glossy, medium green, lancelike leaves turn yellow to gold in fall
HEIGHT:	3–8 feet
WIDTH/SPREAD:	4–6 feet
LIGHT:	Sun to part shade—tolerates more shade
SOIL:	Moist, acid organic soil
CARE:	If the plant becomes leggy, cutback a third of the stems to cause lower growth. I grow summersweets in clay soil that has been amended with composted leaf mold and mulched with more compost.
USES:	Naturalistic, wet garden, fragrant
PROBLEMS:	Spider mites are a problem when plants get too dry
INSIDER'S TIPS:	Summersweets bloom late in summer and should be planted near decks or patios, where the fragrance during a warm evening can be enjoyed. It withstands coastal salt spray. 'Pink Spires' (3–8-foot rounded habit with pink to rose flowers) and 'Hummingbird' (3–4 feet) tolerate heavy shade. 'Ruby Spice' is very compact (3–4 feet) with longer-blooming pink flowers.
COMBINES WITH:	*Echinacea purpurea* 'Magnus', *Hemerocallis* 'Hall's Pink', *Hosta* 'Brim Cup'

Clethra alnifolia 'Hummingbird'

'HUMMINGBIRD' COMPACT SUMMERSWEET

PLANT TYPE:	Deciduous shrub
ZONE:	3–9
FLOWER/FRUIT:	4–6 inch white spires; spicy fragrance
HABIT/FOLIAGE:	Compact, roundy-moundy form; glossy, medium green leaves turn yellow to gold in fall
HEIGHT:	To 30 inches
WIDTH/SPREAD:	30–36 inches
LIGHT:	Part shade to sun
SOIL:	Moist, acid organic soil
CARE:	Easy! It holds its compact smaller shape well.
USES:	Wet garden, fragrant, fall color, small space
PROBLEMS:	Spider mites appear when shrub is too dry; difficult to transplant; it spreads by runners
INSIDER'S TIPS:	I grow it in my "leaf mold"—amended clay soils without extra acidity.
COMBINES WITH:	*Phlox paniculata* 'Eva Cullum', *Kirengeshoma palmata, Lobelia* x 'Grape Knee High'

Clethra alnifolia 'Ruby Spice'

'RUBY SPICE' SUMMERSWEET

© Jenny Lee

PLANT TYPE:	Deciduous shrub
ZONE:	4–9
FLOWER/FRUIT:	From ruby colored buds, fragrant flowers open to deep pink, non-fading, upright panicles
HABIT/FOLIAGE:	Upright oval, densely branched; glossy medium green leaves turn yellow in fall
HEIGHT:	3–6 feet
WIDTH/SPREAD:	3–6 feet
LIGHT:	Part shade to sun
SOIL:	Rich, moist
CARE:	Easy! Responds well to pruning because of its dense branching habit. The one shown here is a young plant, so it is shorter than the average growth. But notice the amount of bloom at an early age.
USES:	Wet tolerant, fragrant, fall color, foundation, mixed border
PROBLEMS:	No diseases
INSIDER'S TIPS:	For late season bloom and fragrance, this is a must-have plant. You may choose any summersweet by the bloom color, but remember that 'Ruby Spice' will be the best non-fading pink.
COMBINES WITH:	*Echinacea purpurea* 'White Swan', *Tradescantia* x *andersoniana* 'Concord Grape', *Viola cornuta* 'Rebecca'

Rhododendron prunifolium

PLUMLEAF AZALEA

PLANT TYPE:	Native, deciduous shrub
ZONE:	5–8
FLOWER/FRUIT:	Orange-red clusters of trumpet-like flowers
HABIT/FOLIAGE:	Large and very open, widely spreading shape; deciduous, dark green leaves similar to plum trees
HEIGHT:	10–15 feet
WIDTH/SPREAD:	10–12 feet
LIGHT:	Open shade, part shade—needs more shade in the South
SOIL:	Rich, moist, well-drained, acidic
CARE:	Attention to siting is the most critical issue for this native. I envy those who have the acidic soils to support the native azaleas.
USES:	Late-blooming azalea, naturalistic garden, woodland edge
PROBLEMS:	None
INSIDER'S TIPS:	Dirr says, "Grows in sandy ravines along stream banks." My picture was taken in the Philadelphia area and was a great brightener for the woods with its open, naturalistic look. I suspect it grows more densely in the South. There are other summer-blooming azaleas worth trying, such as 'Weston's Lemon Drop'.
COMBINES WITH:	*Heuchera* villosa 'Purpurea', *Gaultheria procumbens, Cimicifuga americana, Asarum canadense*

Hydrangea macrophylla 'Pia'

'PIA' MOPHEAD HYDRANGEA

PLANT TYPE:	Deciduous shrub
ZONE:	(5) 6–9
FLOWER/FRUIT:	Profusion of bright rosy-pink mopheads
HABIT/FOLIAGE:	Compact rounded mound; dark green leaves with no fall color
HEIGHT:	2–3 feet
WIDTH/SPREAD:	2–3 feet
LIGHT:	Part shade, shade—no afternoon sun
SOIL:	Rich, moist
CARE:	From www.hydrangeasplus.com: "Prune in early fall. With young plants, be sure to prune enough growth to form them into a good 'shape.' This is generally 10 to 20 percent of the growth."
USES:	Color accent, long blooming, small space
PROBLEMS:	Winter temperatures below 10°F will kill flowering buds and cause dieback of stems.
INSIDER'S TIPS:	Lacecap and mophead hydrangeas are not fully "bud hardy" in Zone 5. Gardeners who successfully get flowers use insulating mulches and/or plant on the north side of their houses.
COMBINES WITH:	*Astilbe* 'Avalanche', *Aster divaricatus*, *Hosta montana* 'Aureomarginata'

Hydrangea serrata 'Shirofuji'

'SHIROFUJI' (SNOW-CAPPED MT. FUJI) SAWTOOTH HYDRANGEA

PLANT TYPE:	Deciduous shrub
ZONE:	(5) 6–7
FLOWER/FRUIT:	Cluster of pendulous snowflakes
HABIT/FOLIAGE:	Compact, rounded form; unusually fine textured, small, medium green leaves
HEIGHT:	3–4 feet
WIDTH/SPREAD:	3–4 feet
LIGHT:	Part shade
SOIL:	Rich, moist
CARE:	In the North, you may have to insulate the buds over winter until no likelihood of late spring freeze. It could be pruned back if you want an even smaller plant. Prune after flowering, as it will bloom on old wood (plant shown is 2 feet tall)
USES:	Textural contrast, small space, long blooming
PROBLEMS:	Questionable bud hardiness in colder regions
INSIDER'S TIPS:	Planting this one in a protected garden site is likely to increase the chances for flowers.
COMBINES WITH:	*Hemerocallis* 'Toyland', *Heucherella* x 'Bridget Bloom', *Cimicifuga simplex* 'Black Negligee'

Hibiscus x 'Tosca'

'TOSCA' ROSE OF SHARON

PLANT TYPE:	Deciduous shrub
ZONE:	5–8 (9)
FLOWER/FRUIT:	Large, five-petaled pink flowers look like saucers with a carmine eye
HABIT/FOLIAGE:	Dense, upright vase shape; bold, dark green leaves have no fall color
HEIGHT:	8–10 feet
WIDTH/SPREAD:	5–6 feet
LIGHT:	Sun to part shade
SOIL:	Rich, moist, well-drained
CARE:	To increase bloom as well as to shape, prune each branch back to two or three buds in early spring.
USES:	Accent, long blooming, background
PROBLEMS:	None
INSIDER'S TIPS:	The Spring Meadow Nursery trial gardens have a collection of hibiscus. Both the flowers and the leaves of 'Tosca' are showier when compared to other shrubby hibiscus.
COMBINES WITH:	*Amsonia hubrectii*, *Physostegia virginiana* 'Miss Manners', *Paeonia lactiflora* 'Flame', *Knautia macedonica*

Hydrangea paniculata 'Kyushu'

'KYUSHU' PANICLED HYDRANGEA

PLANT TYPE:	Deciduous shrub
ZONE:	3–8
FLOWER/FRUIT:	White, 12-inch, cone-shaped flowers look like a tiered lacecap; late to have pinkish fall tinge
HABIT/FOLIAGE:	Upright habit, somewhat arching, stems do not flop; dark green leaves sometimes tinged yellow in fall
HEIGHT:	6–8 feet
WIDTH/SPREAD:	6 feet
LIGHT:	Sun to part shade
SOIL:	Rich, moist
CARE:	Leave flowers for winter interest, and prune in early spring.
USES:	Long blooming, bold background, foundation
PROBLEMS:	None
INSIDER'S TIPS:	I like hydrangeas for their late-season bloom over a long period of time. 'Kyushu' flowers earlier and at a younger age than 'Tardiva' does. In the picture, 'Kyushu' is the one with the longest, most-open panicles in the back. Hydrangea *paniculata* 'Little Dot' is the shorter one with flowers already turning pink at the end of July.
COMBINES WITH:	*Rudbeckia nitida* 'Herbstsonne', *Hemerocallis* 'Tetriana's Daughter', *Astilbe* x *arendsii* 'Bressingham Beauty'

Hydrangea paniculata 'Little Lamb'
'LITTLE LAMB' HYDRANGEA

PLANT TYPE:	Deciduous shrub
ZONE:	4–8
FLOWER/FRUIT:	Small, white cones start lime-green give a nice fresh bicolor look, then in late September the panicles are blushed pink
HABIT/FOLIAGE:	Smaller, compact vase shape; dark green leaves are tinged in blue
HEIGHT:	4–6 feet
WIDTH/SPREAD:	4 feet
LIGHT:	Sun to part shade
SOIL:	Average to rich, moist but not wet
CARE:	If flower heads are left up over winter, deadheading in spring will improve the appearance.
USES:	Profuse bloom, winter interest, small space
PROBLEMS:	None
INSIDER'S TIPS:	Another cultivar worth trying is *Hydrangea paniculata* 'Limelight'. The blossoms are an unusual creamy lime color, but overall it's a larger plant with larger flowers than 'Little Lamb' has.
COMBINES WITH:	*Astilbe simplicifolia* 'Sprite', *Amsonia hubrectii, Anemone hupehensis* 'September Charm'

Hydrangea serrata 'Preziosa'

SAWTOOTH HYDRANGEA

PLANT TYPE:	Deciduous shrub
ZONE:	(5) 6–7
FLOWER/FRUIT:	Light pink rounded clusters age to crimson then purple-tinged
HABIT/FOLIAGE:	Compact, upright rounded form with purple-tinted stems when young; dark green leaves have reddish-purple fall color
HEIGHT:	4–5 feet
WIDTH/SPREAD:	4 feet
LIGHT:	Sun to part shade
SOIL:	Average to rich, moist but not wet
CARE:	Must have consistent moisture. Mounding with leaves or wood chips or perhaps wrapping to keep "frozen" until last spring frosts.
USES:	Late summer bloom, long season of interest
PROBLEMS:	While the plant is hardy, the buds are not; you would need to added insulating material
INSIDER'S TIPS:	In the last five years we have not had extreme winters in my Zone 5 garden, and my 'Preziosa' has bloomed reliably each year without any extra precautions. I am fascinated by the progression of change in flower and leaf color.
COMBINES WITH:	*Phlox paniculata* 'Bright Eyes', *Heucherella* x 'Viking Ship', *Hemerocallis* 'Bama Music'

Hypericum erectum 'Gemo'

'GEMO' ST. JOHN'S WORT

PLANT TYPE:	Deciduous shrub
ZONE:	5–8
FLOWER/FRUIT:	Bright yellow buttercup with fluffy centers that have showy tan seed capsules for fall then brown in winter
HABIT/FOLIAGE:	A very tightly mounded ball shape; glossy, dark green, tinged blue, willow-like leaves that turn yellow-gold in very late fall
HEIGHT:	2–3 feet
WIDTH/SPREAD:	2–3 feet
LIGHT:	Full sun
SOIL:	Average, well-drained
CARE:	Very little care needed!
USES:	Small space, long blooming, foliage color, all-season interest
PROBLEMS:	None
INSIDER'S TIPS:	The glossy leaves on 'Gemo' almost seem to be evergreen because the fall color is so late. *Hypericum kalmianum* 'Ames' (a 2–3 foot cultivar from Iowa) is said to be hardy to Zone 4.
COMBINES WITH:	*Rosa* 'Starry Night', *Hemerocallis* 'Joan Senior', *Phlox paniculata* 'Blue Paradise'

Hypericum x 'Hidcote'

'HIDCOTE' ST. JOHN'S WORT

PLANT TYPE:	Deciduous shrub
ZONE:	(5) 6–8
FLOWER/FRUIT:	Large golden-yellow, five-petaled flowers are fragrant; fruit is a red-brown capsule in fall
HABIT/FOLIAGE:	Low-growing with wider spreading branches; blue-green ovals displayed in a nicely textural opposite pattern turning golden brown in fall
HEIGHT:	3–5 feet
WIDTH/SPREAD:	3–5 feet
LIGHT:	Sun to part shade
SOIL:	Average, well-drained
CARE:	Prune in late winter or early spring. Remove oldest and woodiest stems. Tip-cut or headback longer branches to encourage dense growth.
USES:	Foliage color, long blooming, mixed border, groundcover
PROBLEMS:	Tends to be a dieback shrub in my Zone 5 garden, but it comes back to begin bloom in July
INSIDER'S TIPS:	In northern zones it can be killed to the ground in severe winters, but it can be evergreen to semi-evergreen in zones with milder winters.
COMBINES WITH:	*Nepeta mussinii* 'Blue Wonder', *Leucanthemum* x *superbum* 'Becky', *Veronica spicata* 'Royal Candles'

96

Leptodermis oblonga

CHINESE LEPTODERMIS

© Steve VarderWoude

PLANT TYPE:	Deciduous shrub
ZONE:	5–7
FLOWER/FRUIT:	Tiny clusters of tubular lilac flowers bloom in the leaf axils
HABIT/FOLIAGE:	Compact, upright oval, densely twiggy; small, medium-green leaves give a texture similar to boxwood; no fall color
HEIGHT:	2–3 feet
WIDTH/SPREAD:	3–4 feet
LIGHT:	Sun to light shade
SOIL:	Average to rich, moist but not wet
CARE:	Easy
USES:	Long blooming, textural contrast, small space, hedge
PROBLEMS:	Hard to find (probably because it is so new)
INSIDER'S TIPS:	The blooms are most profuse in July and August, then sporadic through October. Friend Steve VanderWoude thinks this would be nice used as a short hedge, as boxwoods are used.
COMBINES WITH:	*Paeonia officinalis* 'Krinkled White', *Geranium wallichianum* 'Buxton's Blue', *Phlox paniculata* 'Blue Paradise'

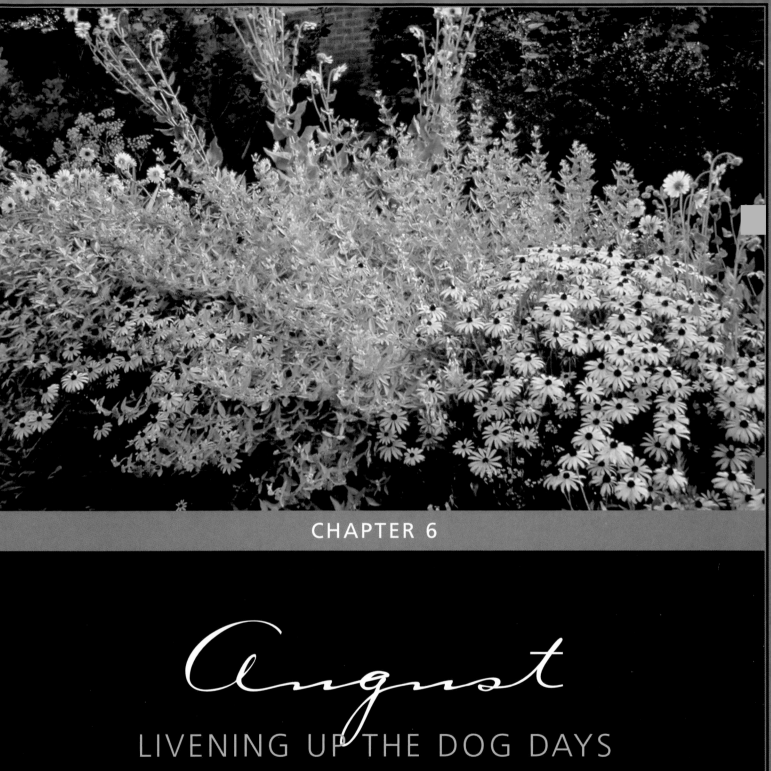

CHAPTER 6

August

LIVENING UP THE DOG DAYS OF SUMMER

Caryopteris × *clandonensis* 'First Choice'

'FIRST CHOICE' BLUE MIST SHRUB, BLUEBEARD

PLANT TYPE:	Deciduous shrub
ZONE:	5–8
FLOWER/FRUIT:	Deeper, rich blue clusters in the leaf axils; seed pods are tan "puffs" all winter long
HABIT/FOLIAGE:	More compact roundy-moundy form with tan stems; silvery, willowlike leaves emerge gray-blue
HEIGHT:	2–4 feet
WIDTH/SPREAD:	2–4 feet
LIGHT:	Full sun
SOIL:	Average, well-drained
CARE:	Cut to the ground in spring just as new growth emerges.
USES:	Late blooming, disease free, easy care, deer resistant
PROBLEMS:	No pests
INSIDER'S TIPS:	After milder winters, this plant may not need to be cutback. This has proven to be one of the best dieback shrubs because it has a showy winter presence.
COMBINES WITH:	*Geum coccineum* 'Borisii', *Rosa* 'Knockout', *Echinacea purpurea* 'White Swan', *Berberis thunbergii* 'Concorde'

Lespedeza thunbergii 'Pink Fountain'

'PINK FOUNTAIN' BUSH CLOVER

PLANT TYPE:	Deciduous shrub
ZONE:	5–8
FLOWER/FRUIT:	Rosy-pink pealike flowers
HABIT/FOLIAGE:	Upright, but with arching branches that cascades as a fountain; unusual trifoliate, soft green leaves with occasional yellow fall color
HEIGHT:	4–5 feet
WIDTH/SPREAD:	4–5 feet
LIGHT:	Sun to light shade
SOIL:	Average, well-drained, tolerates poor soil
CARE:	Can be cut back yearly. After cold winters, plants may dieback and resprout from the roots. Not to worry—they will bloom in that same season.
USES:	Late flowering, background, textural accent
PROBLEMS:	May dieback; gets leggy with too much shade
INSIDER'S TIPS:	This shrub blooms when few others are in bloom! Emerging stems and leaves are quite striking. Japanese selection 'Edo Shibori' has two-tone lilac-and-white flowers. 'Spring Grove' is the best purple-flowered selection, and 'Avalanche' is white. This is a dieback shrub in Zone 5.
COMBINES WITH:	*Pennisetum setaceum* 'Rubrum', *Heuchera* x 'Plum Pudding', *Anemone* x *hybrida* 'Honorine Jobert', *Helianthus helianthoides* 'Lemon Queen'

Heptacodium miconioides

SEVEN-SONS FLOWER

PLANT TYPE:	Deciduous tree
ZONE:	(4) 5–8
FLOWER/FRUIT:	Fragrant, creamy-white, seven-tiered panicles in August and September, followed by persistent rosy-pink sepals
HABIT/FOLIAGE:	Upright, open very irregular shape with exfoliating light brown bark; glossy dark green leaves tinged purple in fall
HEIGHT:	10–20 feet
WIDTH/SPREAD:	8–12 feet
LIGHT:	Sun to part shade
SOIL:	Rich, moist, well-drained, tolerates drier conditions and some acid
CARE:	Prune to maintain height. I have seen this cut way back to the ground ("stooled") to regenerate a better habit.
USES:	Late blooming, exfoliating bark, fragrance, background
PROBLEMS:	Gets very big and ungainly if allowed to grow unchecked
INSIDER'S TIPS:	In October, this large shrub looks like it is having a second bloom. It's called "the crape myrtle of the North." This picture highlights its colorful rosy sepals.
COMBINES WITH:	*Eupatorium maculatum* 'Gateway', *Schizachyrium scoparium* 'The Blues', *Panicum virgatum* 'Northwind', *Physocarpus opulifolius* 'Diabolo'

CHAPTER 7

Foliage

FOR SUMMERTIME COLOR

Acer palmatum 'Bloodgood'

BLOODLEAF JAPANESE MAPLE

PLANT TYPE:	Deciduous
ZONE:	5–8
FLOWER/FRUIT:	Small clusters of red purple flowers are difficult to see because of emerging leaves; red samaras (winged seeds) appear September–October.
HABIT/FOLIAGE:	Rounded habit with layered branching; deeply cut, rich reddish purple leaves brightening to deep red in fall
HEIGHT:	15–25 feet
WIDTH/SPREAD:	10 feet
LIGHT:	Sun to light shade
SOIL:	Rich, moist, well-drained, somewhat acidic
CARE:	This maple is easily pruned to maintain smaller height.
USES:	Specimen, foliage color, winter architecture
PROBLEMS:	Plant in protected site; watch for sunscald
INSIDER'S TIPS:	The coral-bark maple, *Acer palmatum* 'Sango-Kako', is currently available in my area but is not as hardy as 'Bloodgood'. Other Japanese maples will have stems with red color in winter but are not as showy as 'Sango-Kako'.
COMBINES WITH:	*Iris sibirica* 'Caesar's Brother', *Paeonia lactiflora* 'Flame', *Platycodon grandiflorus* 'Mariesii', *Aconitum napellus*

Acer palmatum 'Crimson Queen'

'CRIMSON QUEEN' JAPANESE MAPLE

PLANT TYPE:	Deciduous tree
ZONE:	5–8
FLOWER/FRUIT:	Small red-purple flowers in May–June; samaras turn red in September through October
HABIT/FOLIAGE:	Compact, rounded form with cascading branches; newer branches are wine red in winter; ferny (finely dissected) foliage is crimson-red, becoming scarlet in fall
HEIGHT:	6–10 feet
WIDTH/SPREAD:	6–10 feet
LIGHT:	Sun to part shade, morning sun is best
SOIL:	Rich, moist, well-drained, neutral to slightly acidic
CARE:	Grow in a protected area away from winter winds. You may need to protect from sun scald in winter by wrapping the trunk and largest branches.
USES:	Container, specimen, color accent, suitable for bonsai, architecture
PROBLEMS:	In the South, the foliage is often more bronze-green than red
INSIDER'S TIPS:	'Crimson Queen' is currently one of the most popular in the dissectum group. This finely dissected maple is a very slow grower and is easily managed in any protected site.
COMBINES WITH:	*Geranium wallichianum* 'Buxton's Blue', *Aquilegia alpina*, *Astilbe* x *arendsii* 'Fanal', *Campanula carpatica* 'Samantha'

Acer palmatum 'Emperor I'

'EMPEROR I' JAPANESE MAPLE

PLANT TYPE:	Deciduous tree
ZONE:	4–8
FLOWER/FRUIT:	Small, red-purple flowers in May–June, samaras turn red in September through October
HABIT/FOLIAGE:	Very upright vase shape from a single trunk; deep crimson-purple leaves are palmate and not finely dissected; they turn deep red in fall
HEIGHT:	12–15 feet
WIDTH/SPREAD:	5–8 feet
LIGHT:	Sun to part shade
SOIL:	Rich, moist, well-drained, neutral to slightly acidic
CARE:	Pruning is best done in late summer or early fall. Supplement clay soils with composted organic material.
USES:	Architecture accent, background color accent
PROBLEMS:	None
INSIDER'S TIPS:	Try 'Emperor I' for a diversity of form in Japanese maples. It is one of the hardiest, as reported from friends living in Minneapolis, Minnesota. Because it leafs-out nearly two weeks later than 'Bloodgood' Japanese maple, there is less chance of frost damage.
COMBINES WITH:	*Astilbe* x *arendsii* 'Bressingham Spire', *Eupatorium maculatum* 'Gateway', *Miscanthus sinensis* 'Blooming Wonder', *Aconitum carmichaelii* 'Arendsii'

Acer shirasawanum 'Aureum'

GOLDEN FULL MOON MAPLE

PLANT TYPE:	Deciduous tree
ZONE:	5–7
FLOWER/FRUIT:	Red-purple flowers in April, followed by red samaras
HABIT/FOLIAGE:	Vase-shaped with branches "suspended in cloudlike strata," according to Michael Dirr; showy yellow leaves turn bright red in fall
HEIGHT:	10–12 feet
WIDTH/SPREAD:	8–10 feet
LIGHT:	Light to part shade, does best with morning sun only
SOIL:	Rich, moist, well-drained, somewhat acidic
CARE:	Easily pruned to maintain smaller height. Incorporate leaf mold when planting in clay soils.
USES:	Accent, foliage color, winter architecture
PROBLEMS:	Leaves will turn brown at edges; becomes "crisp" in too much sun
INSIDER'S TIPS:	A slow-growing tree that is often narrower than it is wide at maturity, it fits easily into the mixed border.
COMBINES WITH:	*Delphinium elatum, Caryopteris* x *clandonensis* 'First Choice', *Hydrangea paniculata* 'Limelight'

Aralia elata 'Variegata'

VARIEGATED JAPANESE ANGELICA TREE

PLANT TYPE:	Deciduous tree
ZONE:	4–9
FLOWER/FRUIT:	White 18-inch-long clusters look like astilbe plumes, followed by purplish fruit
HABIT/FOLIAGE:	Gives appearance of a layered umbrella, but only main stem is left for winter; very large compound leaves are glossy green with white edges, becoming red-orange in fall
HEIGHT:	Slowly to 15 feet
WIDTH/SPREAD:	10 feet
LIGHT:	Part shade to sun
SOIL:	Rich, moist, well-drained
CARE:	Soil should not be allowed to dry out.
USES:	Tropical look, all-summer color, specimen, late flowering
PROBLEMS:	No winter interest—only the main stalk or trunk is left for winter
INSIDER'S TIPS:	This plant is very difficult to find in the trade—mine came from a grower in New Zealand! But it is worth tracking down. I also grow it behind other "shrubbier" plants to hide the barren look in winter
COMBINES WITH:	*Delphinium elatum*, *Rosa* 'Knockout', *Hydrangea serrata* 'Preziosa'

Berberis thunbergii 'Aurea'

YELLOW BARBERRY

PLANT TYPE:	Deciduous shrub
ZONE:	5–8
FLOWER/FRUIT:	Tiny yellow flowers appear in April are not profuse, followed in October by few red berries
HABIT/FOLIAGE:	Stiff, densely mounded; red-tinged black stems; small bright golden yellow ovals tend to hold this color in fall
HEIGHT:	3–4 feet
WIDTH/SPREAD:	3–4 feet
LIGHT:	Sun to part shade
SOIL:	Average, well-drained
CARE:	Prune to a natural shape and not into a big ball!
USES:	Bright accent, highlight, fine texture
PROBLEMS:	With too much shade, foliage becomes more green
INSIDER'S TIPS:	Until *Berberis thunbergii* cultivars have been evaluated for invasiveness in your region, it is best not to use this plant if you live close to a natural area, such as a forest preserve or prairie.
COMBINES WITH:	*Lilium tigrinum, Verbascum chaixii* 'Album', *Coreopsis verticillata* 'Zagreb', *Crambe cordifolia*

Berberis thunbergii 'Bonanza Gold', 'Bogozam'

'BONANZA GOLD' BARBERRY

PLANT TYPE:	Deciduous shrub
ZONE:	4–8
FLOWER/FRUIT:	Tiny white flowers become very few bright red fruits in fall
HABIT/FOLIAGE:	Densely rounded; small golden yellow leaves
HEIGHT:	18 inches
WIDTH/SPREAD:	24–36 inches
LIGHT:	Sun to part shade
SOIL:	Average to rich, moist but not wet
CARE:	Needs little to no care
USES:	Contrast, color accent, small space, formal garden
PROBLEMS:	Non-scorching, has not been reported to seed about
INSIDER'S TIPS:	Use this where you need an accent with a very globular shape.
COMBINES WITH:	*Tulipa* 'Electra', *Alchemilla mollis*, *Geranium wallichianum* 'Buxton's Blue', *Veronica spicata* 'Royal Candles'

Berberis thunbergii 'Concorde' (var. *atropurpurea*)

'CONCORDE' BARBERRY

PLANT TYPE:	Deciduous shrub
ZONE:	4–8
FLOWER/FRUIT:	Non-flowering and non-fruiting
HABIT/FOLIAGE:	Dwarf, dense ball shape; stems black-purple; velvety, deep purple foliage
HEIGHT:	18 inches
WIDTH/SPREAD:	2 feet
LIGHT:	Full sun
SOIL:	Average to rich, moist but not wet
CARE:	Needs little to no pruning. It holds its nice "roundy-moundy" shape.
USES:	Contrast, color accent, small space, formal garden
PROBLEMS:	None; it's a rust-free barberry
INSIDER'S TIPS:	Because the foliage is not glossy, it has a velvety, more color-saturated appearance.
COMBINES WITH:	*Rosa* 'Knockout', *Campanula carpatica* 'Samantha', *Platycodon grandiflorus* 'Mariesii'

Berberis thunbergii 'Crimson Pygmy' (var. *atropurpurea*)

'CRIMSON PYGMY' BARBERRY

PLANT TYPE:	Deciduous shrub
ZONE:	4–8
FLOWER/FRUIT:	Varies in flower and fruit production
HABIT/FOLIAGE:	Low, dense mound; dark red-back stems; red-purple, tiny, glossy leaves
HEIGHT:	18–24 inches
WIDTH/SPREAD:	3–5 feet
LIGHT:	Full sun
SOIL:	Average to rich, moist but not wet
CARE:	Easily trained to a short hedge or parterre.
USES:	Hedge, knot garden, color accent, easy care
PROBLEMS:	Until evaluated for invasiveness, do not use near a natural area
INSIDER'S TIPS:	This is the most popular Japanese barberry. It looks smashing with its orange-colored flowers. This barberry in particular has been found to seed about—and not necessarily close to the parent plant. Seeds are carried by birds that eat the fruit.
COMBINES WITH:	*Hemerocallis* 'Rocket City', *Tulipa* 'Orange Triumph', *Aster novae-angliae* 'Purple Dome'

Berberis thunbergii 'Helmond's Pillar' (var. *atropurpurea*)

'HELMOND'S PILLAR' BARBERRY

PLANT TYPE:	Deciduous shrub
ZONE:	4–8
FLOWER/FRUIT:	Small, yellow-tinged red flowers; few brilliant red berries
HABIT/FOLIAGE:	Columnar, narrow shape; small red-purple leave becomes redder in fall
HEIGHT:	4–5 feet
WIDTH/SPREAD:	2 feet
LIGHT:	Full sun
SOIL:	Average, well-drained, not tolerant of wet soil
CARE:	Prune any branches damaged in winter.
USES:	Accent, architecture, small space
PROBLEMS:	Leaf color fades in summer's heat
INSIDER'S TIPS:	Use like an exclamation point in the garden. I have not heard of this barberry seeding itself where not wanted.
COMBINES WITH:	*Knautia macedonica, Alchemilla mollis, Astilbe japonica* 'Red Sentinel', *Phlox paniculata* 'Bright Eyes'

Berberis thunbergii 'Rose Glow' (var. *atropurpurea*)

'ROSE GLOW' BARBERRY

PLANT TYPE:	Deciduous shrub
ZONE:	4–8
FLOWER/FRUIT:	Clusters of yellow flowers are not showy; bead-like orange-red berries add some winter interest
HABIT/FOLIAGE:	Rounded, upright form; red-tinged black stems showy in winter; rosey pink new foliage suffuses into deep red-purple that "glows" brighter in fall
HEIGHT:	4–6 feet
WIDTH/SPREAD:	5 feet
LIGHT:	Full sun to light shade
SOIL:	Average, well-drained
CARE:	Allow this to grow into a natural form unless used as hedging. If grown as a hedge, shearing should be kept to a minimum, or there will be bald spots.
USES:	Hedge, showy color, mixed border, background
PROBLEMS:	Until evaluated for invasiveness, do not use near a natural area
INSIDER'S TIPS:	Barberries, in general, tend to collect fall leaves and trash in the winter. Shown here with ladybells (which has been invasive for me) and annual snapdragons.
COMBINES WITH:	*Campanula persicifolia* 'Telham Beauty', *Geranium endressii* 'Wargrave Pink', *Malva alcea* 'Fastigiata'

Berberis thunbergii 'Royal Cloak'

'ROYAL CLOAK' BARBERRY

PLANT TYPE:	Deciduous shrub
ZONE:	4–7
FLOWER/FRUIT:	Insignificant yellow flowers with little to no fruit
HABIT/FOLIAGE:	Bold, arching to almost cascading form; stems are black-red; bolder-sized burgundy-purple foliage; holds this color into late fall, when it becomes highlighted in yellow
HEIGHT:	3–4 feet
WIDTH/SPREAD:	4–5 feet
LIGHT:	Full sun
SOIL:	Rich, moist, well-drained
CARE:	Little pruning will be needed if this barberry is given space to mature. If used as a hedge, prune before new growth begins.
USES:	Color accent, hedge, barrier, fall color
PROBLEMS:	Not on the federal rust-free barberry list
INSIDER'S TIPS:	'Royal Cloak' has the look of a more refined smokebush, as used in gardens in England and Scotland. And like *Berberis thunbergii* 'Concorde', the foliage is not glossy, but has a velvety, more color-saturated appearance. Most of the plants I have observed also have no fruit, which may eliminate the concern over invasiveness.
COMBINES WITH:	*Artemisia ludoviciana* 'Valerie Finnis', *Alchemilla mollis, Lilium tigrinum, Heliopsis helianthoides* 'Prairie Sunset', *Aster laevis* 'Blue Bird'

Cercis canadensis 'Forest Pansy'

'FOREST PANSY' REDBUD

PLANT TYPE:	Deciduous tree
ZONE:	5–8
FLOWER/FRUIT:	Deep rose-purple in May; fruit is a pendulous seedpod
HABIT/FOLIAGE:	Rounded small tree, could be multistemmed; heart-shaped leaves are burgundy-red, often fading to dark green in summer heat and yellowish in fall
HEIGHT:	15–25 feet
WIDTH/SPREAD:	15–25 feet
LIGHT:	Sun to part shade
SOIL:	Rich, moist, well-drained
CARE:	Needs consistent water and fertile soils.
USES:	Specimen, background, foliage color
PROBLEMS:	Does not hold its color well in heat
INSIDER'S TIPS:	This redbud is not reliably hardy in Zone 5.
COMBINES WITH:	*Rosa* 'Blanc Double de Coubert', *Miscanthus sinensis* 'Morning Light', *Hemerocallis* 'Joan Senior' or 'Summer Wine'

Cornus alba 'Ivory Halo', 'Bailhalo'

'IVORY HALO' RED-STEMMED DOGWOOD

PLANT TYPE:	Deciduous shrub
ZONE:	3–7
FLOWER/FRUIT:	Yellowish-white, flat-topped clusters in May–June are followed by barely noticeable white fruits
HABIT/FOLIAGE:	Compact rounded form with many red stems in winter; green-centered leaves have showy white edges, only lightly tinged reddish purple in fall
HEIGHT:	5–6 feet
WIDTH/SPREAD:	5–6 feet
LIGHT:	Part shade
SOIL:	Rich, moist, well-drained
CARE:	Renewal prune a third of oldest stems each year to maintain stem color. As with all dogwoods, pay attention to good soil fertility and moisture.
USES:	Showy summer foliage, winter stems, specimen, accent
PROBLEMS:	Possible canker, powdery mildew, and borers if plant is stressed
INSIDER'S TIPS:	I think this is the cleanest white variegation of the red-stemmed dogwoods, when compared to 'Argenteo-marginata' and 'Elegantissima'.
COMBINES WITH:	*Heuchera* 'Plum Pudding', *Astilbe* x *arendsii* 'Glow', *Aconitum* x *cammarum* 'Bressingham Spires'

Cornus alternifolia 'Golden Shadows'

'GOLDEN SHADOWS' PAGODA DOGWOOD

PLANT TYPE:	Deciduous tree
ZONE:	3–7
FLOWER/FRUIT:	Fragrant yellowish-green clusters become clusters of deep blue fruits quickly eaten by birds
HABIT/FOLIAGE:	Spreading, horizontally branching gives a tiered effect; medium-green leaves are edged in yellow-green and tinged red-purple in fall
HEIGHT:	10–15 feet
WIDTH/SPREAD:	10–15 feet
LIGHT:	Part shade
SOIL:	Rich, consistently moist, slightly acidic
CARE:	Heavy clay soils must be amended with organic matter. A mulch of composted material will help keep the soil moist through the summer.
USES:	Specimen, showy summer foliage, winter branching pattern, attracts birds
PROBLEMS:	Problems with canker can occur when plants are drought- or nutrient-stressed
INSIDER'S TIPS:	This is a newly introduced cultivar developed by William Stackman and Peter Linzer in northern Illinois. I would grow showy, golden-leaved hostas as an underplanting in the shade of the canopy, and hot pink or purple flowers in front, where there is no shade (facing south).
COMBINES WITH:	*Lilium* 'Star Gazer', *Hosta* 'Birchwood Parky's Gold', *Gaura lindheimeri* 'Siskyou Pink', *Phlox paniculata* 'Eva Cullum', *Aster novae-angliae* 'Purple Dome'

Cornus controversa 'Variegata'

VARIEGATED GIANT DOGWOOD

PLANT TYPE:	Deciduous tree
ZONE:	(4) 5–7
FLOWER/FRUIT:	Large, creamy-white, flat-topped cymes become red to blue-black fruit in September
HABIT/FOLIAGE:	Horizontally branching and wide-spreading; very pointed, narrow leaves with creamy edges; may turn pinkish red in fall
HEIGHT:	30–45 feet!
WIDTH/SPREAD:	30 feet
LIGHT:	Part shade
SOIL:	Rich, moist, well-drained, acidic
CARE:	Prune to manage ultimate size or grow in a large garden space.
USES:	Specimen, summer foliage color, bright accent, structural branches
PROBLEMS:	Neither heat nor drought tolerant; more vigorous than *Cornus alternifolia* 'Variegata'
INSIDER'S TIPS:	While most often seen in England, I have seen this growing in American gardens, particularly in the East—but they have yet to reach giant size! With the foreknowledge of the ultimate size of this plant, one must work early with pruners or grow in a very large space.
COMBINES WITH:	*Papaver orientale* 'Prince of Orange', *Hemerocallis* 'Rocket City', *Polemonium reptans*

Cornus kousa 'Snowboy'

JAPANESE KOUSA DOGWOOD

© Charles Price

PLANT TYPE:	Deciduous tree
ZONE:	5–8
FLOWER/FRUIT:	Flowers are made up of four greenish-white bracts; fruits are raspberry-like globes in August–September
HABIT/FOLIAGE:	Vase-shaped when young, becoming more horizontally branched as it matures; dark green pointed oval leaves are heavily edged in white and turn red-purple in fall
HEIGHT:	12–15 feet
WIDTH/SPREAD:	8–10 feet
LIGHT:	Part shade, shade
SOIL:	Rich, moist, well-drained, somewhat acidic
CARE:	Sun is likely to scorch the variegated leaves. The addition of organic material (compost) will improve alkaline soils.
USES:	Summer color, accent, winter structure, shade brightener
PROBLEMS:	More resistant to anthracnose than *Cornus florida* is
INSIDER'S TIPS:	I fell in love with 'Snowboy' when I visited the Dunn Garden in Seattle (thanks to hosts Charles Price and Glenn Withey). Without experience in growing it myself, I would recommend paying close attention to soil and light conditions. Other variegated and more shrubby kousa dogwoods to consider are 'Wolf's Eyes' and 'Lemon Ripple'.
COMBINES WITH:	*Hosta* 'Blue Angel', *Astilbe* x *arendsii* 'Bridal Veil', *Anemone sylvestris*, *Polystichum braunii*

Cornus sericea 'Silver and Gold'

'SILVER AND GOLD' YELLOW-STEMMED DOGWOOD

PLANT TYPE:	Deciduous shrub
ZONE:	2–8
FLOWER/FRUIT:	Flat-topped white clusters become bluish-white berries in fall, which are not always noticeable
HABIT/FOLIAGE:	Vase-shaped form with yellow-green stems throughout winter and early spring; medium-green leaves have creamy irregular edges; edges of leaves brown in fall
HEIGHT:	6–8 feet
WIDTH/SPREAD:	6–8 feet
LIGHT:	Tolerates both sun and shade, best in part shade
SOIL:	Rich, moist
CARE:	Easily pruned to desired height and width and to maintain stem color. Mulch annually with organic matter, and water during dry periods.
USES:	Accent, showy leaf variegation, backdrop for perennials, winter stems
PROBLEMS:	A little suckering is possible; tip dieback signals canker due to lack of sufficient water
INSIDER'S TIPS:	Maintaining soil moisture and good fertility will decrease the incidence of canker. For this reason, a mulch of composted organic material should be applied on an annual basis.
COMBINES WITH:	*Rosa* 'Carefree Sunshine', *Hemerocallis* 'Rocket City', *Lysimachia nummularia* 'Aurea', *Tradescantia* 'Sweet Kate', *Campanula lactiflora* 'Pouffe'

Cotinus coggygria 'Royal Purple'

'ROYAL PURPLE' SMOKE BUSH

PLANT TYPE:	Deciduous shrub
ZONE:	(4) 5–8
FLOWER/FRUIT:	Loose clusters with purple hairs that look like puffs of lavender smoke
HABIT/FOLIAGE:	Broad, loose, open form, multistemmed; darkest purple-leaved form; spoon-shaped oval leaves
HEIGHT:	10–12 feet
WIDTH/SPREAD:	10–12 feet
LIGHT:	Full sun
SOIL:	Rich, moist, well-drained
CARE:	Stooling is a technique used to keep plant size small by cutting it down close to the ground in early spring. The resulting densely smaller plant (perhaps to 4 or 5 feet) will have larger, more richly colored foliage but *no* blooms or "smoke."
USES:	Accent, focal point, foliage color, mixed border
PROBLEMS:	No serious pests or disease
INSIDER'S TIPS:	The purple-leaved smokebushes tend to be less hardy than green types. They are also very slow to leaf out in April or early May, so don't give up on them too early.
COMBINES WITH:	*Rosa* 'All that Jazz', *Lilium* (orange-flowered), *Achillea* 'Moonshine', *Allium* 'Giganteum', *Digitalis grandiflora, Delphinium elatum*

Daphne x *burkwoodii* 'Carol Mackie'

'CAROL MACKIE' DAPHNE

PLANT TYPE:	Scmi-evergreen
ZONE:	4–8
FLOWER/FRUIT:	Fragrant clusters of pale pink tubular flowers
HABIT/FOLIAGE:	Densely mounded shape; semi-evergreen elliptical leaves are edged in cream
HEIGHT:	2–4 feet
WIDTH/SPREAD:	2–4 feet
LIGHT:	Sun to part shade
SOIL:	Rich, moist, well-drained
CARE:	Does not do well in heavy clay soils. Take time in preparing the soil, and you will be rewarded with foliage that is showy all season. Little to no pruning is needed.
USES:	Foliage color, fragrance, small space, specimen
PROBLEMS:	Slow to difficult to establish
INSIDER'S TIPS:	Choose your site well (also consider a raised bed) because all daphnes resent transplanting or any disturbance of soil around their roots.
COMBINES WITH:	*Coreopsis verticillata* 'Zagreb', *Knautia macedonica*, *Asclepias tuberosa* (shown with annual *Melampodium*)

123

Deutzia crenata 'Variegatus'

VARIEGATED DEUTZIA

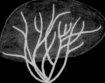

PLANT TYPE:	Deciduous shrub
ZONE:	4–8
FLOWER/FRUIT:	Profuse clusters of white starry flowers bloom along the stems, nearly covering entire bush
HABIT/FOLIAGE:	Arching branches form a medium tall mound; lancelike, medium-green leaves are blotched silvery-white
HEIGHT:	4–6 feet
WIDTH/SPREAD:	4–6 feet
LIGHT:	Part shade to sun
SOIL:	Average, well-drained
CARE:	Prune any dead wood to maintain attractiveness. Prune out any stems that might have reverted to having green leaves.
USES:	Specimen, shade tolerant, background
PROBLEMS:	Variegation may revert to mostly green leaves
INSIDER'S TIPS:	This is a quietly different variegated plant to lighten up a shadier site. Will highlight bright-colored flowers planted in front of it.
COMBINES WITH:	*Hosta* 'Patriot', *Rudbeckia fulgida* 'Goldsturm', *Hemerocallis* 'Baja'

Eleutherococcus sieboldianus 'Variegatus'

VARIEGATED FIVELEAF ARALIA

PLANT TYPE:	Deciduous shrub
ZONE:	4–8
FLOWER/FRUIT:	Greenish-white flowers are inconspicuous, as is the black fruit
HABIT/FOLIAGE:	Upright oval shape; each leaf is "five fingered" and has showy, wide, creamy edges on bright green
HEIGHT:	6–8 feet
WIDTH/SPREAD:	6–8 feet
LIGHT:	Sun to part shade
SOIL:	Rich, moist, tolerates dry shade
CARE:	Easy to prune and to grow
USES:	Specimen, urban garden, variegated foliage, shade brightener
PROBLEMS:	Leaf spot
INSIDER'S TIPS:	This has been such a slow grower for me (perhaps because I am pushing the shade tolerance) that I have had very little need to prune it. I like to make this plant standout by using green-leafed plants around it.
COMBINES WITH:	*Hosta* 'Green Piecrust', *Anemonella thalictroides, Polystichum acrostichoides, Hemerocallis* 'Frans Hals'

Euonymus fortunei 'Emerald 'n Gold'

'EMERALD 'N GOLD' WINTER CREEPER

PLANT TYPE:	Evergreen shrub
ZONE:	5–8
FLOWER/FRUIT:	Tiny white clusters
HABIT/FOLIAGE:	Roundy-moundy, but I have seen this climbing; glossy dark green with yellow margins, turns pink-red in fall
HEIGHT:	12–18 inches
WIDTH/SPREAD:	12–18 inches
LIGHT:	Sun, part shade, shade
SOIL:	Average to rich, evenly moist
CARE:	Most euonymus want to climb—pruning will curb that tendency. Keeping it pruned especially after flowering will also discourage seed set.
USES:	Color accent, highlighter, evergreen, edger
PROBLEMS:	The species is on the invasives list for the Midwest—cultivars are being evaluated
INSIDER'S TIPS:	To re-enervate this evergreen, I give it a "spring tonic" of Epsom salts—just sprinkle a handful around the plant in early May.
COMBINES WITH:	*Hemerocallis* 'Hyperion' or 'Happy Returns', *Hosta fortunei* 'Gold Standard', *Potentilla fruticosa* 'Primrose Beauty'

Euonymus fortunei 'Gold Splash'

'GOLD SPLASH' EUONYMUS

PLANT TYPE:	Deciduous shrub
ZONE:	5–8
FLOWER/FRUIT:	Tiny white clusters
HABIT/FOLIAGE:	Roundy-moundy; glossy dark green with broad golden-yellow margins that are very showy
HEIGHT:	18–24 inches
WIDTH/SPREAD:	18–24 inches
LIGHT:	Sun, part shade, shade
SOIL:	Average to rich, evenly moist
CARE:	I would keep this pruned because it could climb. Pruning will also discourage seed set.
USES:	Edger, color accent, groundcover, evergreen
PROBLEMS:	The species is on the invasives list for the Midwest—cultivars are being evaluated
INSIDER'S TIPS:	In the landscape, 'Gold Splash' and 'Emerald 'n Gold' are just different enough to both be used nearby. 'Gold Splash' has a bolder presence, but 'Emerald 'n Gold' will be more readily available. At the end of winter, use the Epsom salts as a "spring tonic."
COMBINES WITH:	*Myosotis sylvatica* 'Victoria Dark Blue', *Forsythia* x 'Gold Tide', *Platycodon grandiflorus* 'Sentimental Blue'

Fagus sylvatica 'Dawyck Gold'

'DAWYCK GOLD' COLUMNAR BEECH

© Ed Lyon/Stonewall

PLANT TYPE:	Deciduous tree
ZONE:	4–7 (8)
FLOWER/FRUIT:	Flowers occur when plant is leafing out and are not showy
HABIT/FOLIAGE:	Columnar form with branches that reach upward, almost hugging the main trunk; oval-pointed leaves emerge chartreuse, then turn golden yellow in summer, yellow in fall, tan in winter
HEIGHT:	10–12 feet in 10 years, 20 feet in 20 years
WIDTH/SPREAD:	2–4 feet
LIGHT:	Sun to light shade
SOIL:	Average to rich, moist but not wet
CARE:	Easy
USES:	Architectural accent, small space, colorful specimen, all-season interest
PROBLEMS:	None
INSIDER'S TIPS:	This is one of the most interesting specimen trees for every season. Texture, color and form are standouts and there is a progression of change with each season. This beech does not scorch in the sun.
COMBINES WITH:	*Hemerocallis* 'Rocket City', *Aconitum napellus*, *Rudbeckia nitida* 'Herbstsonne', *Picea pungens* 'Montgomery'

Fagus sylvatica 'Purple Fountain'

'PURPLE FOUNTAIN' WEEPING BEECH

PLANT TYPE:	Deciduous tree
ZONE:	4–7 (8)
FLOWER/FRUIT:	Not ornamental
HABIT/FOLIAGE:	Tall, narrow form with pendulous branches; arches down at the top; purple-bronze leaves are more bronzed green in summer
HEIGHT:	12–20 feet
WIDTH/SPREAD:	3–6 feet
LIGHT:	Sun to part shade
SOIL:	Average to rich, evenly moist
CARE:	Very little pruning is necessary.
USES:	Specimen, foundation, architectural accent
PROBLEMS:	None
INSIDER'S TIPS:	I have seen some specimens that have an occasional branch that grows outward instead of being pendulous—but it adds "character"!
COMBINES WITH:	*Hemerocallis* 'Tetrina's Daughter', *Malva alcea* 'Fastigiata', *Boltonia asteroides, Perovskia atriplicifolia*

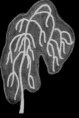

Fagus sylvatica 'Purpurea Pendula'

PURPLE WEEPING EUROPEAN BEECH

PLANT TYPE:	Deciduous tree
ZONE:	4–7 (8)
FLOWER/FRUIT:	Not ornamental
HABIT/FOLIAGE:	Slow-growing mounded form created by smooth gray branches that cascade to the ground; purple-bronze leaves become green-tinged in summer
HEIGHT:	8–10 feet (the one pictured here is 4 feet tall)
WIDTH/SPREAD:	5–7 feet
LIGHT:	Sun to light shade
SOIL:	Average to rich, evenly moist
CARE:	It will not tolerate wet or compacted soils. Take care to not plant too closely anything that is likely to shade the weeping branches.
USES:	Specimen, foundation, color accent
PROBLEMS:	None
INSIDER'S TIPS:	Many purple weeping beeches are labeled 'Purpurea Pendula', but if they have a central leader, they are not the true form.
COMBINES WITH:	*Pachysandra terminalis*, *Veronica spicata* 'Royal Candles', *Geranium sanguineum* var. *striatum*

Fagus sylvatica 'Roseomarginata'

ROSE-MARGINED BEECH

PLANT TYPE:	Deciduous tree
ZONE:	4–7
FLOWER/FRUIT:	Not showy
HABIT/FOLIAGE:	Upright oval shape with ascending branches that begin close to the ground; bronze purple leaves have irregular rose and light pink margins
HEIGHT:	9–12 feet in 10 years, ultimately could grow to 25–30 feet
WIDTH/SPREAD:	7–10 feet in 10 years
LIGHT:	Part shade
SOIL:	Average to rich, moist but not wet
CARE:	This is a very slow grower but has the potential for pruning to maintain size.
USES:	Color accent, background, specimen
PROBLEMS:	Leaves scorch with too much sun
INSIDER'S TIPS:	This picture is taken in friend Lee Rhandhava's garden, where she has it growing with *Syringa meyeri* 'Palibin' and 'Montgomery' blue spruce.
Combines with:	*Hosta* 'Sum and Substance', *Chelone lyonii* 'Hot Lips', *Aruncus dioicus, Lobelia* x *gerardii* 'Vedrariensis'

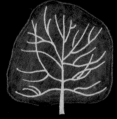

Forsythia × *intermedia* 'Gold Leaf'

'GOLD LEAF' FORSYTHIA

PLANT TYPE:	Deciduous shrub
ZONE:	5–8
FLOWER/FRUIT:	Drooping four-petaled bells; not a profuse bloomer
HABIT/FOLIAGE:	Somewhat upright with arching branches, which create a rounded top; vivid yellow leaves throughout the growing season
HEIGHT:	3–4 feet
WIDTH/SPREAD:	3–4 feet
LIGHT:	Part shade, shade
SOIL:	Average, well-drained
CARE:	Any pruning should be done right after flowering. Prune only oldest stems.
USES:	Foliage color, accent, shade brightener
PROBLEMS:	Difficult to find in the trade
INSIDER'S TIPS:	This Arnold Arboretum introduction will scorch in full sun.
COMBINES WITH:	*Astilbe* × *arendsii* 'Ellie', *Hosta montana* 'Aureomarginata', *Corydalis lutea, Scilla sibirica*

Hydrangea macrophylla 'Lemon Wave'

'LEMON WAVE' VARIEGATED HYDRANGEA

PLANT TYPE:	Deciduous shrub
ZONE:	(4) 5–9
FLOWER/FRUIT:	Light blue lacecaps in acid soils, otherwise more of a mauve color
HABIT/FOLIAGE:	Compact rounded form; medium-green leaves variegated in white, cream, and yellow in varying degrees
HEIGHT:	4–6 feet
WIDTH/SPREAD:	4–6 feet
LIGHT:	Part shade, shade
SOIL:	Rich, moist
CARE:	All hydrangeas need consistent moisture throughout the season.
USES:	Foliage color, accent, shade brightener
PROBLEMS:	Not bud-hardy in the North
INSIDER'S TIPS:	In Zones 5 and lower, grow this one as a dieback shrub. The showy foliage will come back each year, but the flower buds are not likely to be hardy unless very well insulated. It is still worth growing for its foliage alone!
COMBINES WITH:	*Phlox divaricata, Polemonium reptans, Carex elata* 'Bowles Golden'

Hypericum frondosum 'Sunburst'

'SUNBURST' ST. JOHN'S WORT

© Jenny Lee

PLANT TYPE:	Deciduous shrub
ZONE:	5–8
FLOWER/FRUIT:	Bright yellow buttercup flowers with fluffy centers bloom off and on July–September
HABIT/FOLIAGE:	Densely mounded shape with reddish-brown stems; small blue-green ovals are closely spaced along stems
HEIGHT:	2–3 feet
WIDTH/SPREAD:	3 feet
LIGHT:	Sun to part shade
SOIL:	Average, well-drained
CARE:	Prune in late winter or early spring. Remove oldest and woodiest stems. Tip-cut or headback longer branches to encourage dense growth.
USES:	Foliage color, long blooming, small space
PROBLEMS:	Old, browning flowers may detract from floral display
INSIDER'S TIPS:	The blue textural foliage blends with everything in the garden, and it's a great way to add a spot of color in the mixed border.
COMBINES WITH:	*Rosa* 'Henry Kelsey', *Hemerocallis* 'Janice Brown', *Hibiscus* 'Kopper King'

Kerria japonica 'Picta'

VARIEGATED JAPANESE KERRIA

PLANT TYPE:	Deciduous shrub
ZONE:	4b–9
FLOWER/FRUIT:	Tiny, golden yellow, single rose-like flowers
HABIT/FOLIAGE:	Loosely upright but rounded habit with arching yellow-green stems that provide winter color; gray-green leaves are edged in creamy white with a delicate to lacy texture
HEIGHT:	3–4 feet
WIDTH/SPREAD:	3–4 feet
LIGHT:	Shade, part shade
SOIL:	Average, well-drained
CARE:	Because this variegated form is not as vigorous as the species, very little pruning is necessary.
USES:	All-season color, winter interest, easy care, textural background, shade tolerant
PROBLEMS:	Some stems may revert to green leaves—just prune out
INSIDER'S TIPS:	This shrub is not what I would call a show-stopper, but a more subtle filler or enhancer of other plants, especially in the shade.
COMBINES WITH:	*Rudbeckia hirta*, *Hemerocallis* 'Hall's Pink', *Hosta* 'Krossa Regal'

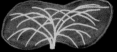

Larix decidua 'Pendula'

WEEPING EUROPEAN LARCH

PLANT TYPE:	Deciduous conifer
ZONE:	3–6 (7)
FLOWER/FRUIT:	Male and female flowers in spring, but they'll only develop on mature plants; female flowers can become small purple cones, but again, only on mature plants
HABIT/FOLIAGE:	Weeping or pendulous branches cascade like a fountain, usually grafted on a standard; bright green and soft clusters of needles become darker green then turn yellow in fall
HEIGHT:	Usually 6–9, feet but dependent on the height of the standard
WIDTH/SPREAD:	2–4 feet
LIGHT:	Full sun
SOIL:	Rich, moist, well-drained
CARE:	In the first year planted, it must have consistent soil moisture.
USES:	Architectural accent, small space, fall color
PROBLEMS:	Shallow rooted—could be blown over in a wind storm
INSIDER'S TIPS:	Even the experts have difficulty telling the difference between this weeping larch and *Larix kaempferi* 'Pendula', as they look very similar. It doesn't matter that they are mixed in the trade, as either may be interchanged in the landscape.
COMBINES WITH:	*Chamaecyparis pisifera* 'Golden Mop', *Geranium wallichianum* 'Buxton's Blue', *Phlox paniculata* 'Laura'

Ligustrum x *vicaryi*

GOLDEN VICARY PRIVET

PLANT TYPE:	Semi-evergreen
ZONE:	5–8
FLOWER/FRUIT:	Tiny white tubular flowers appear in the leaf axils in spring
HABIT/FOLIAGE:	Compact, upright oval shape; bright glossy yellow leaves throughout the growing season
HEIGHT:	4–6 feet (maybe taller?)
WIDTH/SPREAD:	3–4 feet
LIGHT:	Sun to part shade
SOIL:	Average to poor, well-drained
CARE:	Can be kept under 6 feet with careful, consistent pruning.
USES:	Accent, specimen, background brightener, salt tolerant
PROBLEMS:	Some references suggest this plant grows to 10 or 12 feet! I have yet to see one that size.
INSIDER'S TIPS:	Highly tolerant of difficult soils, even salt. Pollution tolerant. This is a "little dab will do ya" plant—one plant alone can brighten up a planting combination, but a whole hedge is overwhelming.
COMBINES WITH:	*Narcissus* 'Filly', *Platycodon grandiflorus* 'Mariesii', *Physostegia virginiana* 'Miss Manners', *Baptisia australis*

Philadelphus coronarius 'Aureus', 'Variegatus'

GOLDEN MOCK ORANGE

PLANT TYPE:	Deciduous shrub
ZONE:	4–8
FLOWER/FRUIT:	Fragrant single white flowers in June
HABIT/FOLIAGE:	Neat, compact, somewhat upright with lateral branching habit; bark is reddish brown; yellow or white-edged medium-green leaves give all-season color (yellow leaves may become more green during the heat of summer)
HEIGHT:	3–6 feet
WIDTH/SPREAD:	4–5 feet
LIGHT:	Part shade, needs afternoon shade
SOIL:	Rich, moist
CARE:	Easily pruned right after blooming.
USES:	Color accent, three-season color, shade brightener
PROBLEMS:	Can scorch in too much hot sun
INSIDER'S TIPS:	Use mock oranges for their foliage color, highlighting other surrounding plants.
COMBINES WITH:	*Geranium wallichianum* 'Buxton's Blue', *Veronica spicata* 'Royal Candles', *Hemerocallis* 'Rosy Returns', *Juniperus sabina* 'Calgary Carpet'

Physocarpus opulifolius 'Dart's Gold'

'DART'S GOLD' NINEBARK

PLANT TYPE:	Deciduous shrub
ZONE:	3–7
FLOWER/FRUIT:	Creamy white ball-like clusters in June
HABIT/FOLIAGE:	Upright, rounded; three-lobed bright yellow leaves become light green in summer and back to yellow in fall
HEIGHT:	4–5 feet
WIDTH/SPREAD:	4–5 feet
LIGHT:	Sun to part shade
SOIL:	Average to rich, moist but not wet
CARE:	Renew by cutting to the ground in late winter
USES:	Adaptable, shade brightener, small space
PROBLEMS:	Foliage color may not hold
INSIDER'S TIPS:	I have only seen 'Dart's Gold' at 5 feet high in England. I suspect that it is often overlooked in the U.S. because the color is not so reliable. There is a newer introduction from South Dakota University called *Physocarpus opulifolius* 'Nugget'.
COMBINES WITH:	*Dicentra spectabilis* 'Alba', *Primula* 'Pacific Hybrids', *Alchemilla mollis, Aster dumosus* 'Woods Light Blue'

Physocarpus opulifolius 'Monlo', 'Diabolo'

'DIABOLO' NINEBARK

PLANT TYPE:	Deciduous shrub
ZONE:	2–7
FLOWER/FRUIT:	Cream-white and pink-tinged clusters bloom in May into June, followed by clusterd red fruit
HABIT/FOLIAGE:	Upright, rounded habit is noticeably narrower than tall; peeling bark on older stems is only noticeable in winter; dark purple-burgundy, maplelike leaves
HEIGHT:	8–10 feet
WIDTH/SPREAD:	4–6 feet
LIGHT:	Sun to part shade
SOIL:	Average to rich, moist but not wet
CARE:	Don't allow this plant to dry out! It will show powdery mildew if the soil is too dry. Mulch around the roots to conserve soil moisture.
USES:	Color accent or background, hedge, bold contrast, profuse bloom
PROBLEMS:	Japanese beetles affect the species, but it doesn't seem to be the case with dark foliage
INSIDER'S TIPS:	A good substitute for *Prunus* x *cistena* in hardiness and durability (from Monrovia Nursery). It's incredible how popular this colored shrub has become! I think we are finally learning how important that different colored foliage is to the mixed border.
COMBINES WITH:	*Hemerocallis* 'Cramer's Amazon', *Hibiscus* 'Fantasia', *Miscanthus sinensis* 'Huron Sunrise'

Pyrus salicifolia 'Silver Frost'

'SILVER FROST' WILLOWLEAF WEEPING PEAR

PLANT TYPE:	Deciduous tree
ZONE:	4–7
FLOWER/FRUIT:	Small greenish-white flowers become small green pears
HABIT/FOLIAGE:	Upright oval shape with pendulous branching; silver-gray willowlike leaves
HEIGHT:	12–15 feet
WIDTH/SPREAD:	10–12 feet
LIGHT:	Sun to light shade
SOIL:	Average to rich, moist but not wet
CARE:	You may need to prune to fit your garden space.
USES:	Background, soft color, weeping form
PROBLEMS:	Difficult to find in the trade
INSIDER'S TIPS:	*Pyrus salicifolia* gets pretty big at 25 feet and is susceptible to fire blight. 'Silver Frost' and 'Pendulous' are smaller, with a pendulous habit. They may even be the same plant.
COMBINES WITH:	*Rosa rugosa, Nepeta sibirica, Penstemon digitalis* 'Husker's Red', *Sedum* X 'Autumn Joy', *Berberis thunbergii* 'Rosy Glow'

Rhamnus frangula 'Fine Line', 'Ron Williams'

'FINE LINE' ALDER BUCKTHORN

© ColorChoicePlants.com

PLANT TYPE:	Deciduous shrub
ZONE:	2–8
FLOWER/FRUIT:	Rarely fruits and never produces viable seed
HABIT/FOLIAGE:	Narrowly, upright column; medium-green, finely textured leaves are very narrow and willowlike; leaves become butter yellow in fall
HEIGHT:	5–6 feet
WIDTH/SPREAD:	2–3 feet
LIGHT:	Sun to part shade
SOIL:	Average to rich, evenly moist
CARE:	Sheers easily.
USES:	Hedge, small space, textural and architectural accent, container
PROBLEMS:	None
INSIDER'S TIPS:	A new and unusual shrub addition that I believe will find its way into many gardens. Show off its texture and columnar habit by contrasting the plant material grown in close proximity.
COMBINES WITH:	*Perovskia atriplicifolia, Malva alcea* 'Fastigiata', *Oenothera tetragona* 'Summer Solstice', *Physocarpus opulifolius* 'Diabolo'

Salix integra 'Hakuro Nishiki'

JAPANESE DAPPLED WILLOW

PLANT TYPE:	Deciduous shrub
ZONE:	3–6 (7)
FLOWER/FRUIT:	I haven't seen it on this plant, but most willows have catkins prior to leafing out
HABIT/FOLIAGE:	Medium-sized rounded dome, often seen in a "standard" form; soft gray leaves are splashed with white; newest growth is tipped in pink
HEIGHT:	3–5 feet
WIDTH/SPREAD:	3–5 feet
LIGHT:	Sun to light shade
SOIL:	Average to rich, evenly moist
CARE:	I have seen this willow sucker—this could be a nightmare when grown on a standard unless the understock used is a non-suckering form.
USES:	Color accent, specimen, small space, wet garden
PROBLEMS:	Foliage color fades as season progresses
INSIDER'S TIPS:	All willows can be used in wet but sunny sites, even along stream banks and ponds.
COMBINES WITH:	*Iris germanica* 'Dusky Challenger', *Weigela florida* 'Briant's Rubidor', *Hemerocallis* 'Cherry Cheeks' or 'Lullaby Baby', *Schizachyrium scoparium* 'The Blues'

143

Salix purpurea 'Nana'

DWARF ARCTIC BLUE-LEAF WILLOW

PLANT TYPE:	Deciduous shrub
ZONE:	3–6 (7)
FLOWER/FRUIT:	Small catkins before plant leafs out
HABIT/FOLIAGE:	Small to medium mounded shape, with smoky purple stems; narrow blue-gray foliage gives a soft texture
HEIGHT:	3–5 feet
WIDTH/SPREAD:	3–5 feet
LIGHT:	Sun to light shade
SOIL:	Rich, moist, well-drained
CARE:	In very early spring, prune out any stems that have lost the soft purple color
USES:	Background, small hedge, foliage color, winter color
PROBLEMS:	Disease free
INSIDER'S TIPS:	Five feet in height and width is not what I would call a "dwarf" in the mixed border, so do not be misled by the terminology. Either give it the space or be tied to annual pruning.
COMBINES WITH:	*Lobelia cardinalis* 'Purple Towers' or *Lobelia* x *gerardii* 'Vedrariensis', *Phlox paniculata* 'Blue Paradise', *Knautia macedonica*

Salix repens var. *argentea*

CREEPING WILLOW

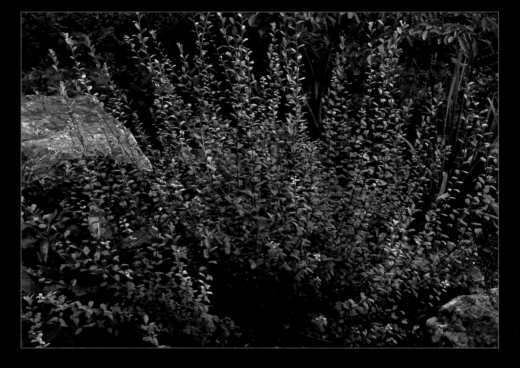

PLANT TYPE:	Deciduous shrub
ZONE:	4–9
FLOWER/FRUIT:	Tiny catkins before the plant leafs out
HABIT/FOLIAGE:	Low, roundy-moundy but open form with dark brown stems that set off the leaves; leaves are silvery blue "mouse ears" that do not change color in fall
HEIGHT:	2–3 feet
WIDTH/SPREAD:	3–5 feet
LIGHT:	Sun to light shade
SOIL:	Average to rich, evenly moist
CARE:	Easy. May need to prune out old stems occasionally.
USES:	Small space, textural contrast, wet tolerant
PROBLEMS:	Hard to find in the trade—in 2003 I found it in the Joy Creek catalog
INSIDER'S TIPS:	A new texture for a willow! Easy to grow anywhere that is sunny— even in wet soils.
COMBINES WITH:	*Monarda didyma* 'Colrain Red', *Phlox paniculata* 'Laura', *Heliopsis helianthoides* 'Prairie Sunset', *Heuchera* x 'Plum Pudding', *Coreopsis* x 'Limerock Ruby'

Sambucus nigra 'Black Beauty', 'Gerda'

'BLACK BEAUTY' ELDERBERRY

© ColorChoicePlants.com

PLANT TYPE:	Deciduous shrub
ZONE:	4–7
FLOWER/FRUIT:	Lemon-scented, pink, flat-topped cymes in June become black edible fruit
HABIT/FOLIAGE:	Tends toward a wide-spreading, flat-topped shape; foliage is dark purple, almost black, but becomes greenish if shaded
HEIGHT:	6–8 feet
WIDTH/SPREAD:	8–10 feet
LIGHT:	Sun to part shade
SOIL:	Average to rich, evenly moist
CARE:	Be prepared to shape this beauty' to fit your garden. It may also be "stooled" or cut down to the ground in early spring. Don't allow soil to dry out.
USES:	Stunning foliage color, backdrop for bright perennials, fragrant
PROBLEMS:	Somewhat rangy habit—prune to reshape
INSIDER'S TIPS:	Pruning or cutting back will change the degree of flowering and fruiting, but it is the foliage that is the main feature of 'Black Beauty'.
COMBINES WITH:	*Gaura lindheimeri, Hemerocallis* 'Janice Brown' followed by 'Hall's Pink', *Lobelia siphilitica, Phlox paniculata* 'Katherine'

146

Sambucus nigra 'Linearis'

'LINEARIS' ELDERBERRY

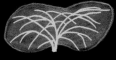

PLANT TYPE:	Deciduous shrub
ZONE:	4–7
FLOWER/FRUIT:	Creamy white flowers in June, black berries in September; both are limited
HABIT/FOLIAGE:	Dense roundy-moundy shape; tan stems show in winter; unusual thin, twisted, gray-green leaves with threadlike tips—very textural
HEIGHT:	3–5 feet
WIDTH/SPREAD:	3–5 feet
LIGHT:	Sun to part shade
SOIL:	Rich, moist
CARE:	Requires very little care other than to water during drought.
USES:	Fine texture, specimen, unusual
PROBLEMS:	Difficult to find
INSIDER'S TIPS:	If you are looking for a smaller, low-maintenance elderberry with an unusual textural contrast, try *Sambucus nigra* 'Linearis'. Contrast it with bolder foliage.
COMBINES WITH:	*Brunnera macrophylla, Trollius chinensis, Astilbe x arendsii* 'Glow', *Heuchera* x 'Stormy Seas', *Canna* 'Rose Futurity' or 'Black Knight'

147

Sambucus nigra 'Madonna'

'MADONNA' EUROPEAN ELDER

PLANT TYPE:	Deciduous shrub
ZONE:	5–6 (7)
FLOWER/FRUIT:	Creamy white cymes in June become black fruit in September, except when hard-pruned in early spring
HABIT/FOLIAGE:	Multi-stemmed, shrubby, and rounded habit; leaves are mottled shades of yellow along the leaf edges with green centers; yellow fades to cream in fall
HEIGHT:	4–8 feet
WIDTH/SPREAD:	4–8 feet
LIGHT:	Part shade, light shade
SOIL:	Rich, moist
CARE:	Jeff Epping, Olbrich Botanical Gardens, says, "Prune it very hard each spring. First we renewal prune it by taking out a quarter to half of the oldest wood at ground level and then 'head back' all of the remaining canes to about 2–3 feet long, creating a dome shape. They respond extremely well and quickly—fast and full. We planted a 1 gallon pot and after the second season it was the size that you saw—about 6 by 6 feet."
USES:	Color accent, specimen, foundation
PROBLEMS:	Slow to establish
INSIDER'S TIPS:	I was amazed at the differences in heights recorded for 'Madonna' elderberry! Dan Hinkley at Heronswood Nursery, Washington, reports his at only 4 feet. Some literature suggests a height of 10 feet. The one photographed here was 6 feet.
COMBINES WITH:	*Lysimachia nummularia* 'Aurea', *Miscanthus sinensis* 'Strictus', *Helianthus helianthoides* 'Lemon Queen', *Hemerocallis* 'Autumn Minaret'

Sambucus nigra 'Pulverulenta'

WHITE-VARIEGATED ELDERBERRY

PLANT TYPE:	Deciduous shrub
ZONE:	5–6 (7)
FLOWER/FRUIT:	White typical elder-flowers in June and blue-black fruit in September (I have never seen flowers/fruit, probably because plants have been cutback after winter)
HABIT/FOLIAGE:	Multi-stemmed, upright oval habit; leaves are splashed and splotched in variable amounts of white, with some even all white
HEIGHT:	5–8 feet
WIDTH/SPREAD:	5–6 feet
LIGHT:	Sun, part shade, shade
SOIL:	Average to rich, evenly moist
CARE:	All elderberries seem to benefit from pruning on an annual basis. If the plant you start with is only 1-foot tall , I suggest you wait until the second year allowing, it an extra year to get established.
USES:	Fine texture, showy variegation, background, shade tolerant
PROBLEMS:	None
INSIDER'S TIPS:	A slower-growing elderberry with a presence all its own, particularly in the shade garden. And the combinations are endless! I can't even think of a plant it wouldn't go with. This plant was photographed at Heronswood Nursery on Bainbridge Island, Washington. Many thanks to Dan Hinkley for introducing me to this plant!
COMBINES WITH:	*Cimicifuga simplex* 'Black Negligee', *Chelone lyonii* 'Hot Lips', *Astilbe* x *arendsii* 'Maggie Daley', *Berberis thunbergii* 'Rosy Glow'

Sambucus racemosa 'Sutherland's Gold'

'SUTHERLAND'S GOLD' ELDERBERRY

PLANT TYPE:	Deciduous shrub
ZONE:	4–6 (7)
FLOWER/FRUIT:	Umbels of tiny, fragrant, yellowish-white flowers in May, followed by red berries, but only if the plant is *not* cut back
HABIT/FOLIAGE:	Upright, vase-shaped; finely cut yellow foliage that does not scorch in sun; in fall the edges become bronzed
HEIGHT:	8–12 feet
WIDTH/SPREAD:	6–8 feet
LIGHT:	Sun, part shade, shade
SOIL:	Rich, moist
CARE:	It must have consistently moist soil. You may also "stool" or cut it down to the ground in early spring.
USES:	Background, color accent, finely textured
PROBLEMS:	It is likely to defoliate in drought situations
INSIDER'S TIPS:	Only in England and Scotland have I seen 'Sutherland's Gold' in a tree form to nearly 10 feet tall.
COMBINES WITH:	*Rosa* 'Knockout' or 'Carefree Wonder', *Artemisia ludoviciana* 'Valerie Finnis', *Picea glauca* 'Montgomery', *Weigela florida* 'Wine & Roses'

Spiraea japonica 'Mertyann', 'Dakota Goldcharm

'DAKOTA GOLDCHARM' SPIREA

PLANT TYPE:	Deciduous shrub
ZONE:	4–8
FLOWER/FRUIT:	Small, pink "buttons" for much of the summer without shearing
HABIT/FOLIAGE:	Dwarf roundy-moundy form; red-brown stems for winter; yellow leaves with bronze tips turn orange-red in fall—even the leaves are smaller on this dwarf
HEIGHT:	12–15 inches
WIDTH/SPREAD:	12–15 inches
LIGHT:	Sun to light shade
SOIL:	Average to rich, moist but not wet
CARE:	Shearing is not necessary for repeat bloom
USES:	Groundcover, edger, all-season foliage color
PROBLEMS:	Does not hold yellow color through the summer in warmer climates
INSIDER'S TIPS:	Most descriptions call this a "smaller" *Spiraea* 'Goldflame', but I don't think that the new leaf tips are as orangy-red, nor are the flowers purple-pink—a combination that is often hard to fit into the garden! 'Dakota Goldcharm' is so similar to *Spiraea* x *bumalda* 'Magic Carpet' that I cannot tell the difference in foliage. 'Magic Carpet' may grow to 18 inches.
COMBINES WITH:	*Salvia* x *superba* 'May Night', *Iris sibirica* 'Caesar's Brother', *Sedum* x 'Autumn Joy'

Spiraea x *bumalda* 'Golden Carpet'

'GOLDEN CARPET' SPIREA

PLANT TYPE:	Deciduous shrub
ZONE:	3–7
FLOWER/FRUIT:	Very few light pink
HABIT/FOLIAGE:	Ground-hugging spreader; small golden leaves may turn lime green in mid-summer and will hold color into fall, with some bronzing on the edges
HEIGHT:	3–6 inches
WIDTH/SPREAD:	8–12 inches
LIGHT:	Sun to light shade
SOIL:	Must be well drained
CARE:	Easy
USES:	Rock garden, foliage color, edger
PROBLEMS:	Stems root where they touch the ground; difficult to find—try the specialty mail order catalogs.
INSIDER'S TIPS:	This spirea is reported to have few flowers, but the finely textured, bright golden yellow leaves are the main feature. They add pizzazz to any combination planting!
COMBINES WITH:	Shown here with *Delosperma, Dianthus* x *allwoodii* 'Doris', *Festuca glauca, Echinacea purpurea* 'Cygnet White', *Veronica alpina* 'Goodness Grows' or 'Royal Candles'

Weigela florida 'Midnight Wine'

'MIDNIGHT WINE' WEIGELA

PLANT TYPE:	Dwarf, deciduous shrub
ZONE:	4–8
FLOWER/FRUIT:	Deep rosy-red tubular flowers in May and June
HABIT/FOLIAGE:	Low mounding dwarf; dark, burgundy-purple lancelike foliage deepens with summer heat
HEIGHT:	18–24 inches
WIDTH/SPREAD:	18–24 inches
LIGHT:	Full sun
SOIL:	Average, well-drained
CARE:	Less care due to dwarf size
USES:	Groundcover, edger, foliage color, small accent
PROBLEMS:	None
INSIDER'S TIPS:	'Midnight Wine' is my favorite because it so easily fits into the perennial garden and perks up any planting combination. Shown here in my garden, blending in the "stray" *Geranium sanguineum* with its magenta flowers.
COMBINES WITH:	*Geranium sanguineum* var. *striatum, Stachys byzantina* 'Helene von Stein', *Salvia* x *superba* 'May Night', *Rosa* 'Betty Prior', *Leucanthemum* x *superbum* 'Becky' (just budded)

Weigela florida 'Variegata'

VARIEGATED WEIGELA

PLANT TYPE:	Deciduous shrub
ZONE:	5–8
FLOWER/FRUIT:	Flowers are profuse; trumpets are the palest pink on the inside and darker pink on the outside
HABIT/FOLIAGE:	Rounded form with more broadly arching stems
HEIGHT:	4–5 feet
WIDTH/SPREAD:	6–7 feet
LIGHT:	Sun to part shade
SOIL:	Average, well-drained
CARE:	To maintain a more tightly mounded habit, the stems should be cut back by half after blooming. It will also benefit from renovation pruning, selectively cutting a third of the oldest stems right to the ground. This can be done anytime if you aren't concerned with losing flowers.
USES:	Three-season interest, color accent, background
PROBLEMS:	Leggy with age
INSIDER'S TIPS:	The cultivar 'Variegata' may be incorrect—others listed with the same name have deep rose flowers. To me the flowers are not as important as the foliage, so I have no problem hard pruning to prevent the leggy tendency.
COMBINES WITH:	*Sedum* 'Brilliant', *Coreopsis* x 'Limerock Ruby', *Hibiscus* 'Sweet Caroline', *Buddleia davidii* 'Potter's Purple'

154

CHAPTER 8

Fall BLOOMERS

Callicarpa dichotoma 'Issai'

'ISSAI' PURPLE BEAUTYBERRY

PLANT TYPE:	Deciduous shrub
ZONE:	5–8
FLOWER/FRUIT:	Pinkish lavender, fluffy clusters become lilac-violet berries in October that persist through winter, becoming bronze
HABIT/FOLIAGE:	Arching branches to a graceful rounded form; bright green, pointed leaves are opposite and form a nice lacy pattern
HEIGHT:	3–4 feet
WIDTH/SPREAD:	4–5 feet
LIGHT:	Sun to light shade
SOIL:	Average, well-drained
CARE:	Do not fertilize, or it may become leggy. This is the hardiest beautyberry, but it may need cutting back after an unusually cold winter.
USES:	Late blooming, unusual fruit, hedge, specimen
PROBLEMS:	No pests or diseases
INSIDER'S TIPS:	All season long this is a great textural backdrop with bright green leaves. Its late-season bloom followed by unusual fruit is a real treat entering the fall season!
COMBINES WITH:	*Ajuga reptans* 'Burgundy Glow', *Phlox paniculata* 'Fairest One', *Delphinium grandiflorum* 'Blue Butterfly', *Hemerocallis* 'Rosy Returns'

Hamamelis virginiana

COMMON WITCH HAZEL

PLANT TYPE:	Deciduous tree
ZONE:	3–8
FLOWER/FRUIT:	Yellow, fragrant wispy stars or spiders
HABIT/FOLIAGE:	Rounded and somewhat spreading small tree; medium-green leaves turn golden yellow in fall before dropping to the ground to expose the already blooming flowers
HEIGHT:	15–20 feet
WIDTH/SPREAD:	15–20 feet
LIGHT:	Sun, part shade, shade
SOIL:	Rich, moist
CARE:	Will need pruning to maintain a smaller size in the mixed border; in a naturalized shrub border it requires little or no pruning.
USES:	Widely adaptable, fall color, fragrant, shade tolerant
PROBLEMS:	Fall foliage often hides the fall blooms, which are identical in color
INSIDER'S TIPS:	Yes, I waited and waited until after the leaves had fallen to take this picture! This is the hardiest and most shade tolerant of the witch hazels. The astringent witch hazel is made by distilling bark of young stems and roots. Shown here with *Hydrangea paniculata* 'Tardiva'; try it with 'Pink Diamond' or 'Limelight'.
COMBINES WITH:	*Hosta montana* 'Aureomarginata', *Aconitum carmichaelii* 'Arendsii', *Alchemilla mollis, Astilbe simplicifolia* 'Darwin's Snow Sprite'

CHAPTER 9

Fall Fruit
PROVIDES ADDITIONAL COLOR

Aronia melanocarpa 'Viking'

'VIKING' BLACK CHOKEBERRY

PLANT TYPE:	Deciduous shrub
ZONE:	4–8
FLOWER/FRUIT:	Fragrant, white flower clusters with profuse purple-black berries
HABIT/FOLIAGE:	Upright, rounded shape, not as leggy as the species; glossy, green leaves with bright, red-orange fall color
HEIGHT:	3–6 feet
WIDTH/SPREAD:	5–6 feet
LIGHT:	Sun to part shade
SOIL:	Tolerant of most soil types
CARE:	Easy
USES:	Attracts birds, hedge, fall color, fruit jelly
PROBLEMS:	None
INSIDER'S TIPS:	As soon as the leaves fall, the birds are busily "harvesting" the fruits, removing any chance for winter interest! This one was hybridized for the fruit set and is used in jelly-making.
COMBINES WITH:	*Solidago rugosa* 'Fireworks', *Caryopteris* x *clandonensis* 'First Choice', *Heliopsis helianthoides* 'Prairie Sunset', *Aster laevis* 'Blue Bird'

Callicarpa americana

AMERICAN BEAUTYBERRY

PLANT TYPE:	Native, deciduous shrub
ZONE:	6–9
FLOWER/FRUIT:	Pale lavender-pink flowers in the leaf axils from June–August become dense clusters of violet-magenta fruit in fall
HABIT/FOLIAGE:	Upright with stems that flare out rather than arch; medium-green, pointed ovals that are opposite; has a coarser appearance than other beautyberries
HEIGHT:	3–8 feet
WIDTH/SPREAD:	5–8 feet
LIGHT:	Sun to part shade
SOIL:	Average, well-drained
CARE:	Do not over fertilize
USES:	Naturalizes, fall fruit, background
PROBLEMS:	Not zone hardy for me!
INSIDER'S TIPS:	Because the fruit is larger and more prolific, this is a very showy plant for a native shrub. *Callicarpa americana* 'Lactea' is a white-fruited form and also has white flowers.
COMBINES WITH:	*Digitalis purpurea, Phlox paniculata* 'Katherine' and 'Laura', *Heuchera* 'Midnight Claret'

Callicarpa bodinieri 'Profusion'

'PROFUSION' BEAUTYBERRY

PLANT TYPE:	Deciduous shrub
ZONE:	(5) 6–8
FLOWER/FRUIT:	Fluffy lavender flowers in leaf axles become clusters of lavender purple berries in October
HABIT/FOLIAGE:	Upright, arching stems; dark green opposite leaves tinged purple when new and are not as delicate or lacy looking as *Callicarpa dichotoma*
HEIGHT:	4–10 feet
WIDTH/SPREAD:	5 feet
LIGHT:	Sun to light shade
SOIL:	Average, well-drained
CARE:	Easily cut back to avoid legginess. In the North, treat as a perennial by cutting to the ground each year. It will still make 4–5 feet in height.
USES:	Hedge, late blooming, background, fruit
PROBLEMS:	Fruit is not as persistent as *Callicarpa dichotoma*
INSIDER'S TIPS:	Beautyberries are important for their late-season bloom followed by lavender-purple berries. For spring, clusters of *Narcissus* will deflect attention from the cutback plant trying to put on growth. Treated as a dieback shrub in Zone 5.
COMBINES WITH:	*Aster novae-angliae* 'Purple Dome', *Hemerocallis* 'Stella d'Oro', *Echinacea purpurea* 'White Swan'

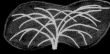

Cornus mas 'Golden Glory'

'GOLDEN GLORY' CORNELIAN CHERRY

PLANT TYPE:	Deciduous tree
ZONE:	4–7 (8)
FLOWER/FRUIT:	Profuse clusters of fuzzy yellow puffs along the stems become bright red cherries in late August through fall
HABIT/FOLIAGE:	Oval to almost pyramidal, multistemmed; rich, dark green, pointed oval leaves turn purple-bronze in fall
HEIGHT:	To 20 feet
WIDTH/SPREAD:	15 feet
LIGHT:	Sun, part shade, shade
SOIL:	Average, well-drained
CARE:	'Golden Glory' is a multi-use large shrub or tree—it may also be kept pruned as a hedge! It withstands even hard pruning. The tree can be trained to a single trunk, otherwise it tends to be very low-branched. The leaves are so dense that it makes an excellent screen.
USES:	Screen, hedge, early blooming, fall fruit, attracts birds, shade garden
PROBLEMS:	Difficult to see the fruits through the leaves
INSIDER'S TIPS:	'Golden Glory' is a preferred cultivar in the North for its profuse bloom and fruit. Because the leaves are so dense, they tend to hide the fruit, hence the reason for getting inside the plant to take a picture of the cherries.
COMBINES WITH:	*Lysimachia nummularia* 'Aurea', *Hosta* 'Patriot', *Anthyrium nipponicum* 'Pictum'

163

Crataegus crus-galli var. *inermis*

THORNLESS COCKSPUR HAWTHORN

PLANT TYPE:	Deciduous tree
ZONE:	3–7
FLOWER/FRUIT:	White flower clusters in May smell "sickly sweet"; profuse orange fruit starts in September and persists well into January
HABIT/FOLIAGE:	Wide-spreading horizontal branching; is usually low-branched with one to three trunks; dense masses of glossy, dark green, oval leaves turn bronze-red in fall
HEIGHT:	20–30 feet
WIDTH/SPREAD:	20–35 feet
LIGHT:	Full sun
SOIL:	Average, well-drained, slightly acidic
CARE:	The hawthorn shown in this picture is about 15 feet and probably could be maintained at a smaller size with annual pruning. So either choose a larger space or be prepared to spend time in pruning.
USES:	Fall fruit, winter architecture, screen, specimen
PROBLEMS:	Occasionally cedar hawthorn rust
INSIDER'S TIPS:	Until you have tried planting bulbs under a cockspur hawthorn and been "skewered" by thorns, you may not appreciate having a tree without thorns!
COMBINES WITH:	*Lamium maculatum* 'White Nancy', *Brunnera macrophylla* 'Dawson's White', *Hosta* 'Summer Music' or 'Remember Me'

Ilex verticillata 'Afterglow'

'AFTERGLOW' WINTERBERRY

PLANT TYPE:	Deciduous shrub
ZONE:	4–9
FLOWER/FRUIT:	White-but-not-showy flowers; prolific orange-red fruit starts in September
HABIT/FOLIAGE:	Compact, slow-growing, rounded oval; dark green, glossy leaves turn yellow in fall
HEIGHT:	4–6 feet
WIDTH/SPREAD:	3–5 feet
LIGHT:	Sun to light shade
SOIL:	Rich, moist, well-drained
CARE:	Must have a male pollinator such as 'Jim Dandy' for fruit set. Prepare soil with organic compost.
USES:	Background, showy fruit
PROBLEMS:	Not tolerant of compacted clay soils
INSIDER'S TIPS:	After the foliage has dropped, I am amazed at the diversity of fruit colors (gold, orange, and red). 'Afterglow', as observed in the Chicago Botanic Garden, had the most prolific fruits along the stems. Two other new introductions with similar habits and red berries are 'Berry Nice' and 'Berry Heavy'.
COMBINES WITH:	*Calamagrostis* x *acutiflora* 'Karl Foerster', *Schizachyrium scoparium* 'The Blues', *Asclepias tuberosa*

Ilex verticillata 'Red Sprite'

WINTERBERRY HOLLY

PLANT TYPE:	Deciduous shrub
ZONE:	4
FLOWER/FRUIT:	Small white flowers become red fruit in September, persistent until January
HABIT/FOLIAGE:	Slow-growing compact mound; glossy, bright green foliage turns purple-bronze in fall
HEIGHT:	3–4 feet
WIDTH/SPREAD:	4–5 feet
LIGHT:	Sun to part shade
SOIL:	Rich, moist, well-drained
CARE:	Must have a male pollinator such as 'Jim Dandy' or 'Appolo' for fruit set. Prepare soil with organic compost.
USES:	Small space, persistent fruit, easy care
PROBLEMS:	Not tolerant of compacted clay soils
INSIDER'S TIPS:	This picture was taken shortly after the fruit had ripened in September, so the leaves had not yet changed. I am still looking for the name of a winterberry that I have seen with red fall color—I can't find a reference on it anywhere.
COMBINES WITH:	*Stachys byzantina* 'Helene von Stein', *Hemerocallis* 'Pardon Me', *Echinacea purpurea* 'White Swan'

Ilex x *meserveae* 'Blue Princess'

BLUE MAID HOLLY

© Ec Hasselkus

PLANT TYPE:	Broadlef evergreen
ZONE:	4–9
FLOWER/FRUIT:	Creamy white flower clusters in spring become large red berrries by August
HABIT/FOLIAGE:	Broadly pyramidal; blue-purple stems compliment red berries; evergreen mounds of glossy sharp leaves
HEIGHT:	8–10 feet, Dirr even mentions some to 15 feet
WIDTH/SPREAD:	6–8 feet
LIGHT:	Sun to light shade
SOIL:	Rich, moist, well-drained, slightly acidic
CARE:	Leaf dessication due to winter wind and sun may occur when the ground is frozen and roots cannot take up enough soil moisture. Prepare soil as you would for rhododendrons, and grow in a site protected from winter winds.
USES:	Hedge, screening, foundation, evergreen
PROBLEMS:	Prone to *Phytophthora* in wet clay soil
INSIDER'S TIPS:	Use *Ilex* x *meserveae* 'Blue Prince' as a pollinator. The "blue" hollies in the North are often grown in too much shade, which tends to make them become very lanky. I have never seen these grow to 15 feet in Zone 5—most are under 5 feet. For southern gardens, I like *Ilex cornuta* 'Rotunda' with the typical holly leaf and very compact habit.
COMBINES WITH:	*Monarda didyma* 'Jacob Cline', *Hemerocallis* 'Christmas Carol', *Tulipa* 'Leen van der Mark'

Malus 'Chrishozam', 'Christmas Holly'

'CHRISTMAS HOLLY' CRABAPPLE

PLANT TYPE:	Deciduous tree
ZONE:	4–8
FLOWER/FRUIT:	Red buds open to white flowers; bright red, persistent fruit is displayed in clusters
HABIT/FOLIAGE:	Densely rounded form—main trunk is short (the mass of the tree is closer to the ground); dark green, cupped foliage
HEIGHT:	10–15 feet
WIDTH/SPREAD:	10 feet
LIGHT:	Full sun
SOIL:	Rich, moist, well-drained
CARE:	May choose to prune to "open up" the densely branching habit
USES:	Persistent fruit
PROBLEMS:	Slightly susceptible to apple scab but does not defoliate
INSIDER'S TIPS:	The fall fruit gives the impression of Christmas holly and is showy with fall-blooming perennials.
COMBINES WITH:	*Pennisetum alopecuroides* 'Hameln', *Anemone* x *hybrida* 'Honorine Jobert', *Aster novae-angliae* 'Hella Lacey'

Malus 'Molten Lava', 'Molazam'

'MOLTEN LAVA' CRABAPPLE

© Lake County Nursery, Perry, Ohio

PLANT TYPE:	Deciduous tree
ZONE:	4–8
FLOWER/FRUIT:	Dark red buds open to single, white flowers; small, persistent red-orange fruit
HABIT/FOLIAGE:	Broadly horizontal weeper, yellow winter bark; medium-green leaves
HEIGHT:	15 feet
WIDTH/SPREAD:	12–15 feet
LIGHT:	Full sun
SOIL:	Rich, moist, well-drained
CARE:	Can be maintained in a smaller form with pruning—use the above picture as an example of what your pruning might look like.
USES:	Weeping form, disease resistant, four-season interest
PROBLEMS:	None; is resistant to apple scab and has excellent resistance to Japanese beetles
INSIDER'S TIPS:	Many new crabapples are coming from Lake County Nursery, Perry, Ohio, as did this Father Fiala introduction. As America's favorite ornamental tree, there are more choices than ever! My thanks to the Zampini family for sending this picture.
COMBINES WITH:	*Lobelia cardinalis, Knautia macedonica, Hemerocallis* 'Christmas Carol'

Malus 'Snowdrift'

'SNOWDRIFT' CRABAPPLE

PLANT TYPE:	Deciduous tree
ZONE:	4–8
FLOWER/FRUIT:	Pink buds open to a profusion of white flowers; small orange-red fruit are loved by birds
HABIT/FOLIAGE:	Densely rounded form with a more upright look from multistemmed trunk; medium green foliage drops early in the fall
HEIGHT:	15–20 feet
WIDTH/SPREAD:	15–20 feet
LIGHT:	Full sun
SOIL:	Rich, moist, well-drained
CARE:	All crabs can be kept smaller by "heading back" limbs right after the tree has bloomed.
USES:	Flowers profusely, attracts birds
PROBLEMS:	May have some susceptibility to fire blight
INSIDER'S TIPS:	For city gardens where fruit dropping on sidewalks is a problem, look for the non-fruiting cultivar *Malus* 'Spring Sensation', which is similar to the habit and profuse bloom of 'Snowdrift'.
COMBINES WITH:	*Gaura lindheimeri*a, *Miscanthus sinensis* 'Morning Light', *Pennisetum alopecuroides* 'Hameln'

Myrica pensylvanica 'Silver Sprite', 'Morton'

'SILVER SPRITE' NORTHERN BAYBERRY

© Chicagoland Grows Inc.

PLANT TYPE:	Native, deciduous shrub, semi-evergreen in warmer climate
ZONE:	3–7
FLOWER/FRUIT:	Yellow-green flowers are not showy; waxy blue-gray fruit on female plants only, used in making candles
HABIT/FOLIAGE:	A new selection with a denser, broadly oval habit (it will be wider than it is high); aromatic (when crushed) dark green leaves become bronzed in fall
HEIGHT:	3–5 feet
WIDTH/SPREAD:	5–7 feet
LIGHT:	Sun to part shade
SOIL:	Average to poor, well-drained—even sandy
CARE:	In heavy clay soil, iron may be added to prevent chlorosis. Composted material added annually to heavy soils will improve the drainage.
USES:	Naturalizes, salt tolerant, seaside, winter interest
PROBLEMS:	No diseases, may become chlorotic in heavy clay soils
INSIDER'S TIPS:	Both male and female plants are needed for fruit set. This selection of the native bayberry was made by Kris Bachtell of the Morton Arboretum and is a part of the Chicagoland Grows introductions program.
COMBINES WITH:	*Stachys byzantina* 'Silver Carpet', *Euphorbia myrsinites*, *Campanula glomerata* 'Joan Elliott', *Caryopteris* x *clandonensis* 'First Choice'

Nandina domestica 'Harbor Dwarf'

HEAVENLY BAMBOO

PLANT TYPE:	Evergreen
ZONE:	6–9
FLOWER/FRUIT:	Panicles of tiny white flowers in May–June; sprays of red berries in late September-persistent
HABIT/FOLIAGE:	Dense mound of arching stems; leaves are glossy, blue-green, tri-pinnately compound at the ends of stems giving a lacy texture; evergreen winter color is red-green
HEIGHT:	2–3 feet
WIDTH/SPREAD:	2–4 feet, spreading
LIGHT:	Sun, part shade, shade
SOIL:	Rich, moist, well-drained
CARE:	Prune any dead wood. Curb spreading of rhizomatous root system.
USES:	Edger, four-season interest, evergreen, textural contrast
PROBLEMS:	Spreads too easily
INSIDER'S TIPS:	This is one of those plants that I have yet to try in my Zone 5 garden. It has so many interesting attributes for fall and winter, but I have only seen it growing where winter temperatures do not dip below –15°F.
COMBINES WITH:	*Anemome* x *hybrida* 'Honorine Jobert', *Rodgersia pinnata* 'Superba', *Hosta* 'Shade Fanfare'

Rhus typhina 'Laciniata'

CUTLEAF SUMAC

PLANT TYPE:	Deciduous shrub
ZONE:	4–8
FLOWER/FRUIT:	From yellow-green flowers in July come the red-orange "staghorn" fruit
HABIT/FOLIAGE:	Upright but spreading and multi-stemmed—it also gives a flat-topped appearance; green, deeply cut leaves turn red, orange, yellow in fall
HEIGHT:	10–12 feet
WIDTH/SPREAD:	10–12 feet, spreading
LIGHT:	Sun to light shade
SOIL:	Average, well-drained—even dry
CARE:	Curb the spreading habit, or grow sumacs where they will have plenty of space to naturalize. Not for the small garden!
USES:	Fall fruit, architecture, fall color, naturalistic garden
PROBLEMS:	Suckering
INSIDER'S TIPS:	The root-run can be contained by walls and sidewalks. This is the English Walled Garden at the Chicago Botanic Garden; and besides watching for "errant" roots, the horticulturists prune this on a regular basis to improve the architecture.
COMBINES WITH:	Whatever you use as an underplanting, you will most likely lose! Let it stand on its own.

Rosa glauca

REDLEAF ROSE

PLANT TYPE:	Deciduous shrub
ZONE:	2–7 (8)
FLOWER/FRUIT:	Deep pink, five-petaled flower blooms with white eyes in June; the fruits are profuse clusters of orange hips that begin in September
HABIT/FOLIAGE:	Upright vase-shaped with arching stems at the ends, stems have a purple cast; typical rose leaves are blue, blushed purple-rose, yellowing in the fall but dropping quickly, better displaying the orange hips
HEIGHT:	5–7 feet
WIDTH/SPREAD:	3–5 feet
LIGHT:	Sun to light shade
SOIL:	Average to rich, evenly moist
CARE:	I prune mine when it starts "grabbing" passersby! And don't be afraid to "renovate" prune right above the lowest growth in the spring.
USES:	Profuse fall fruit, color accent, specimen
PROBLEMS:	Old-age decline
INSIDER'S TIPS:	In 2002, my *Rosa glauca* developed canker on several of its canes. I waited until spring before cutting out the diseased stems because I could not easily see the canker and I wanted to see if at least some of the plant would survive. If it doesn't pull through, I certainly will replace it, as it has been a show-stopper for twelve years.
COMBINES WITH:	*Paeonia officinalis* 'Mrs. Wilder Bancroft', *Iris germanica* 'Red at Night', *Hemerocallis* 'Dad's Best White'

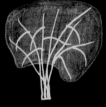

Sambucus canadensis

Elderberry

PLANT TYPE:	Native, deciduous shrub
ZONE:	(3) 4–9
FLOWER/FRUIT:	Fragrant white lacecap flower becomes purple edible fruit in August–September
HABIT/FOLIAGE:	Rounded, multi-stemmed with arching branches—stoloniferous; leafs-out early, dark green but not much fall color
HEIGHT:	6–12 feet
WIDTH/SPREAD:	6–12 feet
LIGHT:	Sun, part shade, shade
SOIL:	Average to rich, evenly moist, tolerates dry soils
CARE:	Please consider your site for this spreading shrub and the amount of root-pruning that may be required to curb its lateral growth. Naturalize in spaces where other plants don't grow as well, and if you have the space.
USES:	Naturalizes, attracts birds, wet tolerant, background, fragrant, showy fruit
PROBLEMS:	Stoloniferous—must be managed; also susceptible to borers and powdery mildew
INSIDER'S TIPS:	I have included this plant because of its fruit, but you will find six other elderberries in this book that are better suited to the mixed border because they are not vigorous spreaders. For *Sambucus canadensis,* use planting combinations that won't be overwhelmed.
COMBINES WITH:	*Hosta* 'Piedmont Gold' or 'Sum and Substance', *Monarda didyma* 'Jacob Cline' or 'Raspberry Wine'

Viburnum dentatum 'Blue Muffin', 'Chistom'

'BLUE MUFFIN' ARROWWOOD

PLANT TYPE:	Deciduous shrub
ZONE:	3–8
FLOWER/FRUIT:	Creamy white clusters (not a likeable fragrance); blue berries in October persist if not eaten by birds
HABIT/FOLIAGE:	Rounded, somewhat compact habit, not as upright as the species; dark green coarsely dentate leaves become red, orange, and golden yellow late in the fall
HEIGHT:	5–7 feet
WIDTH/SPREAD:	5–7 feet
LIGHT:	Sun to part shade
SOIL:	Average, well-drained
CARE:	Prune to maintain muffin-like habit.
USES:	Hedge, foundation, showy fruit, attracts birds
PROBLEMS:	Watch for suckering, which is common for the species
INSIDER'S TIPS:	My experience is that arrowwood viburnums want to grow more upright, and they become leggy, vase shapes with too much shade. 'Blue Muffin' is a newer selection about half the size of the species, with very show fruit.
COMBINES WITH:	*Aster divaricatus, Schizachyrium scoparium* 'The Blues', *Phlox paniculata* 'Laura', *Alchemilla mollis*

Viburnum dilatatum 'Cardinal Candy'

'CARDINAL CANDY' LINDEN VIBURNUM

PLANT TYPE:	Deciduous shrub
ZONE:	(4) 5–7, maybe 8 in shade
FLOWER/FRUIT:	Profuse creamy-white mounds to 5 inches in May; large clusters of red berries from August—October
HABIT/FOLIAGE:	Upright and nicely rounded; dark green, oval leaves become red and orange in fall and drop later than most
HEIGHT:	5–6 feet
WIDTH/SPREAD:	5–6 feet
LIGHT:	Sun to part shade, perhaps even shadier
SOIL:	Average to rich, evenly moist
CARE:	Many will recommend this viburnum for slightly acidic soils. I have it growing in my garden in regularly compost-amended soils.
USES:	Outstanding fruit, showy flowers, three-season interest, screening, hedge
PROBLEMS:	May need a clone for fruiting
INSIDER'S TIPS:	The cultivar 'Erie' does not hold its fruit as long (perhaps the birds enjoy the fruit of this cultivar more than others?).
COMBINES WITH:	*Buddleia davidii* 'Ellen's Blue', *Tradescantia* x *andersoniana* 'Bilberry Ice', *Aruncus dioicus*

Viburnum dilatatum 'Michael Dodge'

YELLOW-FRUITED LINDEN VIBURNUM

PLANT TYPE:	Deciduous shrub
ZONE:	5–7
FLOWER/FRUIT:	Large, creamy-white dome-shaped flower clusters in May; yellow fruit in fall
HABIT/FOLIAGE:	Smaller and a little more roundy-moundy than 'Cardinal Candy' viburnum; leaves are dark green ovals with scarlet (orange-red) fall color
HEIGHT:	4–5 feet
WIDTH/SPREAD:	5–6 feet
LIGHT:	Sun to part shade
SOIL:	Average to rich, evenly moist
CARE:	If you prune after blooming (which really is the best time), you will decrease the amount of fruit.
USES:	Outstanding fruit, showy flowers, three-season interest, foundation
PROBLEMS:	Needs a clone to pollinate
INSIDER'S TIPS:	Viburnum 'Cardinal Candy' may be used as a pollinator.
COMBINES WITH:	*Sporobolus heterolepis, Helictotrichon sempervirens, Stylophorum diphyllum, Trollius chinensis* 'Lemon Queen'

Viburnum trilobum 'J.N. Select', 'Redwing'

'REDWING' AMERICAN CRANBERRY VIBURNUM

© Chicagoland Grows Inc.

PLANT TYPE:	Deciduous shrub
ZONE:	2–7
FLOWER/FRUIT:	Fragrant white clusters in May and June; red cranberry-like fruit in fall, persisting until the following spring
HABIT/FOLIAGE:	Upright rounded form; three-lobed green leaves emerge reddish (like redwings) and turn bright red in fall; leaf petioles are red all season
HEIGHT:	8–10 feet
WIDTH/SPREAD:	6–8 feet
LIGHT:	Sun to part shade
SOIL:	Rich, moist, well-drained
CARE:	Prune if necessary right after bloom.
USES:	Persistent fruit, hedge, background, fall color
PROBLEMS:	None
INSIDER'S TIPS:	A Chicagoland Grows introduction for 2003. The red coloration on new growth and red leaf petioles make this cranberry viburnum a little different than others in the market.
COMBINES WITH:	*Sporobolus heterolepis*, *Schizachyrium scoparium* 'The Blues', *Pinus parviflora* (or any blue-needled conifer)

Viburnum trilobum 'Wentworth'

'WENTWORTH' CRANBERRY VIBURNUM

PLANT TYPE:	Deciduous shrub
ZONE:	2–7
FLOWER/FRUIT:	Fragrant white lacecaps in May become clusters of early, large, glossy red "cranberries" that persist into the following spring (if not grazed by cedar waxwings)
HABIT/FOLIAGE:	Large, densely-rounded habit; bright green, maple-like leaves turn red in fall
HEIGHT:	10–12 feet
WIDTH/SPREAD:	10–12 feet
LIGHT:	Sun to part shade
SOIL:	Rich, moist, well-drained
CARE:	Prune to maintain desired height
USES:	Showy fruit, fragrant flowers, dense screen, fall color, attracts birds
PROBLEMS:	Lose some fruit with pruning
INSIDER'S TIPS:	By now you have discovered my love affair with viburnums! And you will find three cranberry viburnums in the book because they have fruit that persists through winter. 'Wentworth' viburnum is most distinct from the others because its fruit is larger and ripens earlier in August.
COMBINES WITH:	*Monarda didyma* 'Jacob Cline', *Miscanthus sinensis* 'Yaku Jima', *Gaillardia* x *grandiflora* 'Goblin'

CHAPTER 10

Fall Color

ANOTHER TOOL
FOR GOOD COMBINATIONS

Acer palmatum dissectum 'Atropurpureum'

RED FERNLEAF JAPANESE MAPLE

PLANT TYPE:	Deciduous shrub
ZONE:	5–7 (8)
FLOWER/FRUIT:	Small red-purple flowers overshadowed by foliage; fruit are red samaras in September
HABIT/FOLIAGE:	Broadly rounded, cascades to the ground, branches layered and twisted; ferny (finely dissected) foliage is purple-red, becoming a blaze of orange in the fall
HEIGHT:	6–8 feet
WIDTH/SPREAD:	6–8 feet
LIGHT:	Part shade or dappled shade—fries in hot summer sun
SOIL:	Rich, moist, well-drained
CARE:	Mulch to maintain soil moisture during dry summers. Plant in a site protected from late spring frost—new leaves are very sensitive to cold!
USES:	Fall color, all-season color, winter structure, specimen
PROBLEMS:	Not suitable for underplanting
INSIDER'S TIPS:	Site also to protect from winter winds. Do not closely plant around this maple. Branches will be lost to shading.
COMBINES WITH:	*Aster novae-angliae* 'Purple Dome', *Platycodon grandiflorus* 'Sentimental Blue', *Tiarella* 'Iron Butterfly', *Rodgersia pinnata* 'Superba'

Acer palmatum dissectum 'Ever Red'

'EVER RED' LACELEAF JAPANESE MAPLE

PLANT TYPE:	Deciduous shrub
ZONE:	5–7 (8)
FLOWER/FRUIT:	Small red-purple flowers are overshadowed by foliage; fruit are red samaras in September
HABIT/FOLIAGE:	Small, cascading weeper, seems to be as wide as it is tall; newest branches wine-red in winter; lacy, purple-red leaves may fade to bronze-green in summer heat but ignite to fiery red in fall
HEIGHT:	8–12 feet
WIDTH/SPREAD:	8–12 feet
LIGHT:	Part shade or dappled shade—fries in hot summer sun
SOIL:	Rich, moist, well-drained
CARE:	Mulch to maintain soil moisture during dry summers. Plant in site protected from late spring frost—new leaves are very sensitive to cold.
USES:	Fall color, all-season color, winter structure, specimen
PROBLEMS:	Can scorch in unprotected sites
INSIDER'S TIPS:	In Zone 5, it rarely gets above 8 feet. This maple is very slow growing. Site also to protect from winter winds. Do not closely plant around this maple. Branches will be lost to shading.
COMBINES WITH:	*Playtcodon grandiflorus* 'Mariesii', *Sedum* 'Bertram Anderson', *Pulmonaria longifolia* ssp. *cevennensis, Iris tectorum*

Acer shirasawanum 'Aureum'

GOLDEN FULL MOON MAPLE

PLANT TYPE:	Deciduous tree
ZONE:	5–7
FLOWER/FRUIT:	Red-purple flowers in April followed by red samaras
HABIT/FOLIAGE:	Vase-shaped with branches "suspended in cloudlike strata," according to Dirr; showy yellow leaves turn bright red in fall
HEIGHT:	10–12 feet
WIDTH/SPREAD:	8–10 feet
LIGHT:	Light to part shade, does best with morning sun only
SOIL:	Rich, moist, well-drained, somewhat acidic
CARE:	Easily pruned to maintain smaller height. Incorporate leaf mold when planting in clay soils.
USES:	Accent, fall color, winter architecture
PROBLEMS:	Leaves will turn brown at edges, or crisp, in too much sun
INSIDER'S TIPS:	I couldn't resist showing this Japanese maple twice because I like both its summer foliage color and its progression to an even showier fall color.
COMBINES WITH:	*Delphinium elatum, Aconitum* x *cammarum* 'Bressingham Spire', *Caryopteris* x *clandonensis* 'First Choice', *Hydrangea paniculata* 'Limelight'

Amelanchier x *grandiflora* 'Forest Prince'

'FOREST PRINCE' SERVICEBERRY

PLANT TYPE:	Deciduous tree
ZONE:	3–8
FLOWER/FRUIT:	Fragrant, lacy five-petalled flowers become edible red berries by June
HABIT/FOLIAGE:	Densely rounded shape, most often seen multi-stemmed; dark green leaves are golden orange to red-orange in more sunlight
HEIGHT:	15–20 feet
WIDTH/SPREAD:	10–15 feet
LIGHT:	Sun to part shade
SOIL:	Rich, moist, somewhat acidic
CARE:	Because of moderate growth rate, easily prune this for height control.
USES:	Fruit, flower, fall color, woodland edge, naturalistic garden
PROBLEMS:	All serviceberries can get an occasional powdery mildew
INSIDER'S TIPS:	The serviceberry species is often seen along streambanks. As to soils, it seems to tolerate most—but be sure to read in the back of the book about how I improve my heavy clay soils. 'Forest Prince' is a Klehm Nursery introduction.
COMBINES WITH:	*Aconitum napellus* 'Arendsii', *Astilbe simplicifolia* 'Praecox Alba', *Aster novae-angliae* 'Purple Dome'

Aronia arbutifolia 'Brilliantissima'

VERY BRILLIANT RED CHOKEBERRY

© Roy Klehm

PLANT TYPE:	Native, deciduous shrub
ZONE:	4–8
FLOWER/FRUIT:	Fragrant white flowers; red glossy berries persist well into winter
HABIT/FOLIAGE:	Upright, somewhat leggy form, which can grow into a suckering colony; glossy, dark green foliage turns brilliant red in fall
HEIGHT:	6–8 feet
WIDTH/SPREAD:	3–5 feet
LIGHT:	Sun to part shade
SOIL:	Widely adaptable, native to wetlands
CARE:	Renewal prune to keep plants more compact.
USES:	Massing, naturalizes, fall-into-winter color
PROBLEMS:	May need to "curb" the suckering habit
INSIDER'S TIPS:	Although this may not be a good choice for the mixed border, as a naturalizer and given adequate space, it works well in a larger garden or on a woodland edge.
COMBINES WITH:	*Aster oblongifolius* 'October Skies', *Calamagrostis brachytricha*, *Gaura lindheimeri* 'Whirling Butterflies'

Calycanthus floridus 'Athens'

'ATHENS' CAROLINA ALLSPICE

PLANT TYPE:	Deciduous shrub
ZONE:	4–9
FLOWER/FRUIT:	Fragrant, light yellow-green flowers smell like pineapple; fruit not ornamental
HABIT/FOLIAGE:	Dense, rounded form or upright, spreading in a more shaded spot; aromatic bark; gray-green leaves turn golden yellow in fall
HEIGHT:	5–9 feet
WIDTH/SPREAD:	8+ feet
LIGHT:	Sun, part shade, shade
SOIL:	Rich, moist, well-drained, acid but tolerates others
CARE:	Prune after flowering to shape plant or if plant becomes leggy. Renewal prune if needed.
USES:	Fall color, fragrant, trouble-free, shade tolerant
PROBLEMS:	None
INSIDER'S TIPS:	Plants are more compact in sun. Scott Arboretum selection 'Edith Wilder' has wine-scented and wine-colored flowers.
COMBINES WITH:	*Chrysanthemum* x *morifolium, Agastache* x 'Blue Fortune', *Chelone lyonii* 'Hot Lips', *Heucherella* 'Viking Ship'

Cercis canadensis
REDBUD

PLANT TYPE:	Native, deciduous tree
ZONE:	5–9
FLOWER/FRUIT:	Purple-pink pea-shaped flowers, almost buds; brown seedpods in fall
HABIT/FOLIAGE:	Rounded crown over branches that are spreading and layered; heart-shaped, medium-green leaves turn golden-yellow in fall
HEIGHT:	20–30 feet
WIDTH/SPREAD:	30 feet
LIGHT:	Part shade to sun, okay with afternoon sun
SOIL:	Rich, moist, well-drained
CARE:	Prune to maintain desired size. Watch soil's moisture content— it should not be too wet or overly dry.
USES:	Fall color, focal point, open woodland, winter architecture
PROBLEMS:	When stressed by drought or wet soils, canker and verticillium wilt can develop
INSIDER'S TIPS:	The extra bonus with redbuds is that they turn to gold in fall and shine again.
COMBINES WITH:	*Aster ptarmicoides, Astilbe chinensis* 'Visions', *Brunnera macrophylla* 'Jack Frost'

Clethra alnifolia 'Rosea'

PINK-FLOWERED SUMMERSWEET

PLANT TYPE:	Deciduous shrub
ZONE:	4–9
FLOWER/FRUIT:	Fragrant, pink tubes fade to pinkish-white
HABIT/FOLIAGE:	Upright oval shape; stems are very dark; glossy, dark green leaves become golden yellow in fall
HEIGHT:	3–6 feet
WIDTH/SPREAD:	3–4 feet
LIGHT:	Part shade to sun
SOIL:	Rich, moist
CARE:	Becomes more leggy in deep shade and will need some pruning.
USES:	Fall color, late blooming, fragrant, wet tolerant
PROBLEMS:	Difficult to transplant
INSIDER'S TIPS:	The pink flowers are not very showy, but as with all the summersweets, the fall color is outstanding! The spired seedheads are also showy through winter.
COMBINES WITH:	I like the contrast with shade tolerant, low-growing evergreens in fall: *Taxus* x *media* 'Tauntonii', *Cephalotaxus harringtonia* 'Prostrata'

Cornus stolonifera 'Hedgerow's Gold'

'HEDGEROW'S GOLD' DOGWOOD

© Steve VanderWoude

PLANT TYPE:	Deciduous shrub
ZONE:	4–7
FLOWER/FRUIT:	Flat-topped white clusters in June–July, not the main feature of this plant; seldom-seen, bluish-white fruit
HABIT/FOLIAGE:	Upright, rounded form accented in winter with red stems; medium-green leaves have golden yellow irregular margins slowly turning rosy-red in fall
HEIGHT:	6–7 feet
WIDTH/SPREAD:	6–7 feet
LIGHT:	Sun to part shade
SOIL:	Rich, moist
CARE:	As with most dogwoods, mulch annually to maintain soil moisture and fertility. Renovation pruning will result in showier foliage and young red stems.
USES:	Fall color, winter stems, all-season foliage color
PROBLEMS:	A little suckering is possible; tip die-back signals canker due to insufficient water
INSIDER'S TIPS:	This dogwood is a real stand out in the fall and holds its colorful leaves longer than other dogwoods. Maintaining soil moisture and good fertility will decrease the incidence of canker.
COMBINES WITH:	*Boltonia asteroides* 'Nana', *Geranium wallichianum* 'Buxton's Blue', *Chelone lyonii* 'Hot Lips'

Cotoneaster apiculatus 'Nana'

DWARF CRANBERRY COTONEASTER

PLANT TYPE:	Deciduous shrub
ZONE:	4–7
FLOWER/FRUIT:	Tiny light pink flowers in May; small, red "cranberries" August–September
HABIT/FOLIAGE:	Compact, dwarf, roundy-moundy with neatly arching light brown stems; dark, glossy green leaves are tiny, becoming bronzed purple in fall and holding on into November
HEIGHT:	8–12 inches
WIDTH/SPREAD:	1–3 feet
LIGHT:	Full sun
SOIL:	Average to rich, moist but not wet
CARE:	Needs little to no pruning.
USES:	Drought resistant, rock garden, small space, fall color, architecture
PROBLEMS:	Fruit does not last long (pictured here in late October)
INSIDER'S TIPS:	Another dwarf, *Cotoneaster adpressus* 'Tom Thumb', may be more readily available at nurseries. It is supposed to be even smaller, at only 6 inches high! Both will provide winter architecture.
COMBINES WITH:	*Campanula carpatica* 'Samantha', *Arabis caucasica* 'Snowcap', *Veronica incana*

FALL COLOR: ANOTHER TOOL FOR GOOD COMBINATIONS

Cotoneaster lucidus

HEDGE COTONEASTER

PLANT TYPE:	Deciduous shrub
ZONE:	3–7
FLOWER/FRUIT:	Tiny white slightly pink flowers; inconspicuous black fruit
HABIT/FOLIAGE:	Dense upright vase shape, stems are noticeably black; glossy, green oval leaves turn outstanding shades of orange to red in fall
HEIGHT:	6–10 feet
WIDTH/SPREAD:	6–10 feet
LIGHT:	Sun to part shade, tolerant of more shade
SOIL:	Average, well-drained
CARE:	Easily sheared
USES:	Hedge, screening, background, fall color
PROBLEMS:	Occasional mites, scale, or fireblight
INSIDER'S TIPS:	Often confused with Peking cotoneaster, *Cotoneaster acutifolius*, which has dull green leaves. This is a useful background plant all summer long, particularly in a more shady spot, and then is a blaze of color in fall. Shown here with *Berberis thunbergii* 'Crimson Pygmy'.
COMBINES WITH:	*Hemerocallis* 'Tetrina's Daughter', *Aster tataricus* 'Jin-Dai', *Rosa* 'Carefree Sunshine', *Veronica spicata* 'Royal Candles' or 'Heraud'

Deutzia gracilis 'Nikko'

'NIKKO' SLENDER DEUTZIA

PLANT TYPE:	Deciduous shrub
ZONE:	5–8
FLOWER/FRUIT:	Clusters of white bells in May into June
HABIT/FOLIAGE:	Low-growing, dwarf mound with slender, twiggy stems; medium-green, lancelike leaves become burgundy in fall
HEIGHT:	12–18 inches
WIDTH/SPREAD:	3–4 feet
LIGHT:	Sun to light shade
SOIL:	Average to rich, moist but not wet
CARE:	Do not plant in soggy soils.
USES:	Groundcover, rock garden, fall color, profuse bloom
PROBLEMS:	Often marginal in Zone 5, but this is likely due to overly wet soils in winter
INSIDER'S TIPS:	I particularly like 'Nikko' over other deutzias because of its burgundy fall color.
COMBINES WITH:	*Campanula lactiflora* 'Pouffe', *Dianthus gratianopolitanus* 'Spotty', *Aster oblongifolius* 'October Skies'

Fothergilla gardenii

DWARF FOTHERGILLA, BOTTLEBRUSH BUSH

PLANT TYPE:	Deciduous shrub
ZONE:	4–8
FLOWER/FRUIT:	Fragrant, white bottlebrushes
HABIT/FOLIAGE:	Low, densely mounded form; leaves blue-green to dark green, turning orange & red in fall, becoming more yellow in shadier sites
HEIGHT:	2–3 feet
WIDTH/SPREAD:	3–4 feet
LIGHT:	Sun, part shade, shade
SOIL:	Rich, moist, well-drained, slightly acidic
CARE:	Easy
USES:	Fragrant, small space, fall color, disease free
PROBLEMS:	No pests or diseases
INSIDER'S TIPS:	'Blue Mist' has foliage that is bluer than the species but does not have as good a fall color.
COMBINES WITH:	*Polystichum polyblepharum, Hosta* 'Minuteman', *Chelone obliqua* 'Alba', *Physostegia virginiana* 'Miss Manners'

Hamamelis vernalis 'Autumn Embers'

'AUTUMN EMBERS' VERNAL WITCH HAZEL

© Roy Klehm

PLANT TYPE:	Deciduous shrub
ZONE:	4–8
FLOWER/FRUIT:	Yellow-orange fragrant flowers which look like wispy spiders appear January–March dependent on early warm temperatures for your zone
HABIT/FOLIAGE:	Upright oval shape; leaves are dark green, crinkled ovals turning to red-purple where temperatures are colder in fall
HEIGHT:	6–8 feet
WIDTH/SPREAD:	4–6 feet
LIGHT:	Sun to part shade—perhaps to three-quarters shade
SOIL:	Rich, moist, tolerates poorly drained heavy soils
CARE:	It's smaller size requires little maintenance.
USES:	Hedge, screen, fall color, fragrant
PROBLEMS:	May miss the fragrance unless planted in an area where it's easily passed
INSIDER'S TIPS:	The fall color of this Klehm Nursery selection adds another seasonal interest in witch hazels. The common witch hazel (*Hamamelis virginiana*) has golden yellow leaves. Because the stunning color does not appear until fall, plant with companions that are colorful all summer and one with purple fall flowers.
COMBINES WITH:	*Hemerocallis* 'Happy Returns', *Geranium* 'Rozanne', *Leucanthemum* x *superbum* 'Ryan's White', *Aster novae-angliae* 'Purple Dome'

Hydrangea arborescens

SMOOTH HYDRANGEA

PLANT TYPE:	Deciduous shrub
ZONE:	(3) 4–9
FLOWER/FRUIT:	Creamy-white globes become greenish to chartreuse by late August
HABIT/FOLIAGE:	Arching, rounded habit; very twiggy, tan stems; dark green leaves have occasional yellow-green fall color
HEIGHT:	3–5 feet
WIDTH/SPREAD:	3–5 feet
LIGHT:	Sun, part shade, shade
SOIL:	Rich, moist
CARE:	Leave the flower heads for winter interest.
USES:	Woodland garden, winter interest, long blooming, background
PROBLEMS:	None
INSIDER'S TIPS:	The species of smooth hydrangea has a more upstanding habit than the cultivar 'Annabelle', but it still is a riot of bloom, even in shade.
COMBINES WITH:	*Rudbeckia fulgida* 'Goldsturm', *Hosta undulata* 'Albo-marginata', *Hemerocallis* 'Tetrina's Daughter'

Hydrangea paniculata 'Pink Diamond'

'PINK DIAMOND' PANICLED HYDRANGEA

PLANT TYPE:	Deciduous shrub
ZONE:	4–9
FLOWER/FRUIT:	White panicled or cone-shaped flowers change to rich pink in fall and hold this color into October
HABIT/FOLIAGE:	Upright, rounded form; dark green leave with no fall color
HEIGHT:	6–8 feet
WIDTH/SPREAD:	6–8 feet
LIGHT:	Sun to part shade
SOIL:	Rich, moist
CARE:	Prune in spring to accommodate the size needed for your garden.
USES:	Fall color, long blooming, winter interest, background
PROBLEMS:	*Hydrangea paniculata* blooms on new wood, so there is no difficulty with being bud hardy
INSIDER'S TIPS:	It's fun to watch the progression of change in these flowers—they open to white in July, then turn a clear rosy-pink in August, and finally a tan "dried" flower for winter.
COMBINES WITH:	*Solidago rugosa* 'Fireworks', *Miscanthus sinensis* 'Huron Sunrise', *Aster tataricus* 'Jin-Dai'

Hydrangea quercifolia 'Sykes Dwarf'

'SYKES DWARF' OAKLEAF HYDRANGEA

PLANT TYPE:	Deciduous shrub
ZONE:	5–9
FLOWER/FRUIT:	Small white cones turn pink to tan in fall
HABIT/FOLIAGE:	Compact, upright and rounded form; dark green oaklike leaves turn burgundy and red in fall
HEIGHT:	3–4 feet
WIDTH/SPREAD:	3 feet
LIGHT:	Sun, part shade, shade
SOIL:	Rich, moist, well-drained
CARE:	Little pruning is needed with this more compact habit.
USES:	Four-season interest, long blooming, shade tolerant
PROBLEMS:	None
INSIDER'S TIPS:	Peeling cinnamon-colored bark and dried flowers provide winter interest.
COMBINES WITH:	*Geranium sanguineum* var. *striatum, Hemerocallis* 'Hall's Pink', *Astilbe chinensis* 'Veronica Klose'

Itea virginica 'Little Henry', 'Sprich'

'LITTLE HENRY' SWEETSPIRE

PLANT TYPE:	Deciduous shrub
ZONE:	5–9
FLOWER/FRUIT:	White fragrant drooping spires, shorter than flowers on 'Henry's Garnet'
HABIT/FOLIAGE:	Compact, rounded mound created with arching branches; glossy, light green leaves turn red and burgundy in fall
HEIGHT:	18–24 inches
WIDTH/SPREAD:	3 feet
LIGHT:	Sun, part shade, shade
SOIL:	Rich, moist, somewhat wet tolerant
CARE:	May hold leaves through winter; if so, remove them in early spring so as to not detract from new growth. Very little pruning is needed on this slow grower.
USES:	Unusual flower, fragrance, wet tolerant, fall color, small space
PROBLEMS:	If fall leaves color up late in the season, the leaves may hold on until spring
INSIDER'S TIPS:	The fall color is spectacular on *Itea* and works well with red-fruited shrubs nearby. In January, the foliage color was still showy.
COMBINES WITH:	*Ilex verticillata* 'Afterglow', *Viburnum trilobum* 'Redwing', *Chasmanthium latifolium*

Leucothoë axillaris

COASTAL LEUCOTHOË, FETTERBUSH

PLANT TYPE:	Native broadleaf evergreen shrub
ZONE:	5–8
FLOWER/FRUIT:	Drooping racemes of white fragrant flowers at the leaf axils in April and May
HABIT/FOLIAGE:	Horizontal oval shape with arching branches that seem to zig-zag at the ends; glossy, dark green leaves emerge red-tinged, then turn bronze-purple in winter
HEIGHT:	3–4 feet
WIDTH/SPREAD:	3–4 feet
LIGHT:	Light shade to full shade
SOIL:	Rich, moist, well-drained, acidic
CARE:	Selectively prune older stems each year.
USES:	Winter color, fragrance, evergreen, woodland
PROBLEMS:	Fragile in exposed sites; may get leaf spot
INSIDER'S TIPS:	In my first experiment with this plant, it died! I believe the problem was getting established in my heavy-alkaline clay soil at that time. Over the years, I have improved the drainage with yearly additions of composted leaf mold, so that it is time to try again.
COMBINES WITH:	*Sedum* x 'Autumn Joy', *Aster divaricatus*, *Phlox divaricata*, *Primula vulgaris*

Malus 'Prairifire'

'PRAIRIFIRE' CRABAPPLE

PLANT TYPE:	Deciduous tree
ZONE:	4–8
FLOWER/FRUIT:	Red-purple in bud and flower; deep purple-red fruit persistent to early spring
HABIT/FOLIAGE:	Rounded but somewhat irregular growth habit, also available with multi-stemmed trunk; new leaves are burgundy-tinged, turning very dark green in summer then rich burgundy and red in fall
HEIGHT:	15–20 feet
WIDTH/SPREAD:	15–20 feet
LIGHT:	Full sun
SOIL:	Rich, moist, well-drained
CARE:	Prune to maintain a desired size. Pruning should be done in early June.
USES:	Persistent fruit, fall color, attracts birds, specimen, disease resistant
PROBLEMS:	Irregular, open habit often needs pruning
INSIDER'S TIPS:	For leaves that hold the purple-green color during summer, try *Malus* 'Purple Prince'. Also there is a new, purple cut-leafed crab from J. Frank Schmidt & Son in Boring, Oregon, called *Malus* 'Royal Raindrops'.
COMBINES WITH:	*Pennisetum orientale* 'Karley Rose', *Echinacea purpurea* 'White Swan', *Hemerocallis* 'Fairy Tale Pink'

Malus 'Satin Clouds'

'SATIN CLOUDS' CRABAPPLE

© Roy Klehm

PLANT TYPE:	Deciduous tree
ZONE:	4–8
FLOWER/FRUIT:	White flowers are cinnamon scented in May; small yellow fruit in fall
HABIT/FOLIAGE:	Dwarf rounded form; dark green, disease-resistant leaves become bright red in fall
HEIGHT:	6–8 feet
WIDTH/SPREAD:	6–8 feet
LIGHT:	Full sun
SOIL:	Rich, moist, well-drained
CARE:	Easy—it's a much smaller crabapple selection.
USES:	Fall color, small stature, fragrant, disease resistant, low maintenance, background
PROBLEMS:	No foliar disease problems
INSIDER'S TIPS:	Finally, a crabapple with outstanding fall color. A Father Fiala selection that looks a bit like a shrub. Many thanks to Roy Klehm—owner of Klehm's Nursery, Barrington, Illinois, and Song Sparrow Nursery (mailorder)—for providing this picture.
COMBINES WITH:	*Hemerocallis* 'Rocket City' or 'Ice Carnival', *Caryopteris* x *clandonensis* 'First Choice', *Rosa* 'Carefree Sunshine'

Pseudolarix amabilis

GOLDEN LARCH

PLANT TYPE:	Deciduous conifer
ZONE:	(4) 5–7
FLOWER/FRUIT:	Small, glaucous green cones mature to golden brown in fall
HABIT/FOLIAGE:	Broadly pyramidal deciduous conifer; silver bark and shape are showy in winter; distinctly soft fans of light-green needles turn golden yellow in fall
HEIGHT:	More that 15 feet in 10–15 years (ACS classification: Large)
WIDTH/SPREAD:	Can be as wide as it is high
LIGHT:	Full sun
SOIL:	Slightly acidic, light, moist, well-drained
CARE:	Protect from wind. Pruning for size control should be done in late winter or early spring. Rich Eyre, owner of Rich's Foxwillow Pines, suggests pruning a stem back to a branching fork, being careful to leave two branches.
USES:	Textural, fall color, winter outline, specimen
PROBLEMS:	Slowly could outgrow the mixed border
INSIDER'S TIPS:	The golden larch is mostly available as very small specimens— usually only 2–3 feet tall. For this reason, it might be grown until it has "outgrown" its space in the garden, or you can get in there and prune it on a regular basis.
COMBINES WITH:	*Phlox paniculata* 'Fairest One', *Iris pumila* 'Manhattan Blues', *Geranium* 'Brookside'

Rhododendron dauricum 'Madison Snow'

'MADISON SNOW' DAURIAN RHODODENDRON

PLANT TYPE:	Evergreen in the South, semi-evergreen in the North
ZONE:	4–6
FLOWER/FRUIT:	White clusters of trumpets with yellow spots bloom profusely in March and April
HABIT/FOLIAGE:	Compact mounded form; glossy, green, small ovals turn golden yellow in fall—lepidote
HEIGHT:	3–4 feet
WIDTH/SPREAD:	3–4 feet
LIGHT:	Sun to part shade
SOIL:	Rich, moist, well-drained
CARE:	Good drainage is a must! It cannot stand in water at anytime.
USES:	Early blooming, winter hardiness, fall color
PROBLEMS:	None
INSIDER'S TIPS:	Besides being one of the earliest rhododendrons to bloom, it has golden yellow fall color. Other rhododendrons with this yellow fall color are the cultivars starting with the name 'April', which are also early blooming. Notice that the 'Madison Snow' shown in the above picture are growing in a full-sun nursery bed.
COMBINES WITH:	*Aster dumosus* 'Woods Purple', *Chelone obliqua* 'Alba', *Viola cornuta* 'Rebecca'

Rhododendron 'Ginny Gee'

'GINNY GEE' RHODODENDRON

PLANT TYPE:	Broadleaf evergreen
ZONE:	5–7
FLOWER/FRUIT:	Light purple clusters (trusses) in April and May
HABIT/FOLIAGE:	Very compact mound; very small, glossy blue-green ovals become dark maroon in fall—lepidote
HEIGHT:	18 inches
WIDTH/SPREAD:	30 inches
LIGHT:	Part shade to sun
SOIL:	Rich, moist, well-drained, acidic
CARE:	As for any rhododendron, provide loose, well-draining soils with good availability of iron.
USES:	Fall-into-winter color, small space, heat/cold resistant
PROBLEMS:	None
INSIDER'S TIPS:	Mahogany-to-purple fall foliage color adds another dimension to using rhododendrons. 'Ginny Gee' holds that foliage color until the following early spring and still looks good with the early-flowering bulbs.
COMBINES WITH:	*Galanthus elwesii, Scilla sibirica, Anemonella thalictroides*

Rhododendron 'Staccato'

'STACCATO' RHODODENDRON

PLANT TYPE:	Broadleaf evergreen to semi-evergreen in the North
ZONE:	4–7
FLOWER/FRUIT:	Hot pink clusters of semi-double, flared, and ruffled bells
HABIT/FOLIAGE:	Vase-shaped with rounded top; glossy, medium-green, small-leaf type (lepidote) turns deep red in fall until spring, when new foliage emerges
HEIGHT:	3–5 feet
WIDTH/SPREAD:	2–4 feet
LIGHT:	Sun to light shade
SOIL:	Rich, moist, well-drained, not so acid specific
CARE:	Tip prune after blooming to maintain compact shape. Lepidotes (rhododendrons with smaller leaves and more compact habits) do best in a sunnier site with mulch to conserve soil moisture.
USES:	Fall color, profuse bloomer, winter interest, small space
PROBLEMS:	Needs good drainage; may be a problem in clay soil
INSIDER'S TIPS:	Highly recommended by Roy Klehm, who has grown it in his Barrington, Illinois, garden for 10 years. With interest in color throughout the seasons, try to remember that rhododendrons and azaleas may have outstanding fall color.
COMBINES WITH:	*Aster novae-angliae* 'Purple Dome', *Ceratostigma plumbaginoides*, *Hydrangea serrata* 'Preziosa'

Rhododendron yedoense var. *poukhanense* 'Compacta'

COMPACT KOREAN AZALEA

PLANT TYPE:	Evergreen in the South, semi-evergreen in the North
ZONE:	4–8
FLOWER/FRUIT:	Lightly fragrant, lavender, single flowers in May
HABIT/FOLIAGE:	Low spreading, mounded; dark green foliage turns orange to red-purple in fall
HEIGHT:	2–3 feet
WIDTH/SPREAD:	3 feet
LIGHT:	Part shade
SOIL:	Rich, moist, well-drained, acidic
CARE:	See rhododendron/azalea hints at the back of this book or visit: www.rhododendron.org.
USES:	Fall color, fragrant, small space, Japanese garden
PROBLEMS:	Very difficult to get the light just right for this azalea
INSIDER'S TIPS:	Remember that even the deciduous azaleas have good fall color. For both rhododendrons and azaleas, choose ones that have more than one season of interest.
COMBINES WITH:	*Polygonatum odoratum* 'Variegatum', *Physostegia virginiana* 'Miss Manners', *Persicaria amplexicaulis* 'Firetail'

Rhus copallina var. *latifolia* 'Morton', 'Prairie Flame'

'PRAIRIE FLAME' SHINING SUMAC

PLANT TYPE:	Deciduous shrub
ZONE:	4–8
FLOWER/FRUIT:	Yellow-green flowers in pyramidal clusters in July and August, followed by red fruit
HABIT/FOLIAGE:	Low suckering, irregular mound, more compact than the species; glossy trifoliate green leaves become crimson to orange in fall
HEIGHT:	5–7 feet
WIDTH/SPREAD:	5–7 feet, spreading
LIGHT:	Sun to light shade
SOIL:	Average, well-drained, very tolerant of dry soils
CARE:	Be prepared to curb the spreading tendency or plant where that does not matter.
USES:	Fall color, holding soil, naturalistic garden, pest-free
PROBLEMS:	Suckering
INSIDER'S TIPS:	The fall color and texture is outstanding! The planting shown is at The Morton Arboretum in Lisle, Illinois. The suckering roots will be stopped by the building in the background and a cement sidewalk that you do not see in the foreground!
COMBINES WITH:	*Geranium* x *cantabrigiense, Vinca minor, Aster novi-belgii* 'Professor Kippenburg', *Aster oblongifolius* 'Raydon's Favorite'

Spiraea betulifolia 'Tor'

'TOR' BIRCH-LEAF SPIREA

PLANT TYPE:	Deciduous shrub
ZONE:	(3) 4–6
FLOWER/FRUIT:	Small puffs of white
HABIT/FOLIAGE:	Compact mounded with purple-tinged stems; iridescent green leaves with a hint of blue, turning varying shades of plum or orange in fall
HEIGHT:	2–3 feet
WIDTH/SPREAD:	2–3 feet
LIGHT:	Sun to light shade
SOIL:	Average to rich, moist but not wet
CARE:	Easy; stays very small—prune only if you want it shorter. You may choose to thin a third of stems selectively to thin plant.
USES:	Four-season interest, small space, easy care, trouble-free
PROBLEMS:	No pests; reported to not do well in the South (Zone 7)
INSIDER'S TIPS:	Leaves have a bolder texture (mini-birch-like) than other spireas do, which makes it standout in the mixed border. As for fall color, it varies. I have seen some plants with light plum leaves and others with orange to gold hues. No matter what the fall color, this plant seems to go with everything in the garden.
COMBINES WITH:	*Aster novae-angliae* 'Purple Dome', *Hemerocallis* 'Rosy Returns', *Rosa* 'Carefree Sunshine'

Spiraea thunbergii 'Ogon'

'OGON' GOLDEN SPIREA

© Steve VanderWoude

PLANT TYPE:	Deciduous shrub
ZONE:	4–8
FLOWER/FRUIT:	White, domed buttons bloom early—April into May
HABIT/FOLIAGE:	Consistent, mounded form; thin, red-brown stems in winter; thin, willow-like leaves are yellow to chartreuse and turn to burnt orange in fall
HEIGHT:	3–4 feet
WIDTH/SPREAD:	3–4 feet
LIGHT:	Sun to light shade
SOIL:	Average, well-drained
CARE:	Shear spent flowers so that they don't detract from foliage color.
USES:	Four-season interest, small space, color accent
PROBLEMS:	None
INSIDER'S TIPS:	Great textural change in the mixed border at all seasons of the year! White-flowered spireas are easier to mix with other bloom colors in the garden. 'Ogon' is resistant to powdery mildew.
COMBINES WITH:	*Helictotrichon sempervirens, Aconitum* x *cammarum* 'Bressingham Spire', *Callirhoë involucrata*

Spiraea x *bumalda* 'Everblooming'

'EVERBLOOMING' BUMALD SPIREA

PLANT TYPE:	Deciduous shrub
ZONE:	3–8
FLOWER/FRUIT:	Carmine flowers bloom June–September
HABIT/FOLIAGE:	Mounded form of dense red brown stems; dark green leaves turn wine-red in fall
HEIGHT:	2–3 feet
WIDTH/SPREAD:	3–4 feet
LIGHT:	Sun to light shade
SOIL:	Average to rich, moist but not wet
CARE:	Easy
USES:	Fall color, long blooming, small space
PROBLEMS:	None
INSIDER'S TIPS:	Spireas are often overused in the landscape, so choose wisely the ones that fit best into your garden combinations. And don't forget all the choices in fall foliage color. This one has amazing wine-red fall color, which holds on till December.
COMBINES WITH:	*Aster novae-angliae* 'Purple Dome', *Schizachyrium scoparium* 'The Blues', *Boltonia asteroides*, *Anemone japonica* 'Whirlwind'

Spiraea x *bumalda* 'Magic Carpet'

'MAGIC CARPET' SPIREA

PLANT TYPE:	Deciduous shrub
ZONE:	3–8
FLOWER/FRUIT:	Purplish-pink rounded clusters
HABIT/FOLIAGE:	Very compact, low mound, looks like a miniature 'Gold Flame'; golden yellow leaves with red leaf tips turn bronzed orange in fall
HEIGHT:	12–18 inches
WIDTH/SPREAD:	12–18 inches
LIGHT:	Sun to light shade
SOIL:	Rich, moist, well-drained
CARE:	In winter, cut out the oldest branches.
USES:	Groundcover, fall color, all-season color
PROBLEMS:	None
INSIDER'S TIPS:	If you feel that the purple-pink flowers clash with the red-tipped yellow leaves, shear the plant. This also encourages repeat bloom. And as with 'Gold Flame', think of combinations with orange. Orange daylilies, geums, or tulips work well with the foliage color and make for a very bright garden.
COMBINES WITH:	*Schizachyrium scoparium* 'The Blues', *Aster novae-angliae* 'Purple Dome', *Picea pungens* 'Montgomery', *Hemerocallis* 'Rocket City'

Syringa patula 'Miss Kim'

'MISS KIM' LILAC

PLANT TYPE:	Deciduous shrub
ZONE:	3–7
FLOWER/FRUIT:	Soft lavender-blue panicles
HABIT/FOLIAGE:	Upright oval form; dark green leaves turn bronze-purple over gold in fall
HEIGHT:	4–6 feet
WIDTH/SPREAD:	4–5 feet
LIGHT:	Full sun
SOIL:	Rich, moist, well-drained
CARE:	Prune right after blooming to control size
USES:	Fall color, hedge, fragrant, mildew-resistant
PROBLEMS:	None
INSIDER'S TIPS:	'Miss Kim' adds one more season of interest that most other lilacs are lacking: fall.
COMBINES WITH:	*Miscanthus sinensis* 'Variegatus', *Phlox paniculata* 'Katherine', *Chelone lyonii* 'Hot Lips', *Amelanchier canadensis* 'Grandiflora' (in the background of this photo)

Viburnum nudum 'Winterthur'

'WINTERTHUR' POSSUM-HAW, SMOOTH WITHEROD VIBURNUM

PLANT TYPE:	Deciduous shrub
ZONE:	5–9
FLOWER/FRUIT:	White, flat-topped flower clusters in May and June; whitish-pink to red and blue fruit, often all on the same cluster
HABIT/FOLIAGE:	Upright, rounded, many stemmed; glossy green leaves turn red and red-purple in fall and hold for an extended period (mine into December in 2002)
HEIGHT:	5–6 feet
WIDTH/SPREAD:	4–5 feet
LIGHT:	Sun to part shade
SOIL:	Rich, moist, slightly acidic
CARE:	This was another of those plants I thought I couldn't grow because I do not have acidic soil. But close attention to soil moisture so far has worked for me. Do not allow plants to dry out.
USES:	Fall color, colorful fruit, attracts birds, clean foliage
PROBLEMS:	Fruit is hidden under the leaves
INSIDER'S TIPS:	'Winterthur' viburnum has glossy foliage, which reflects light and seems to sparkle throughout the entire season. At Winterthur Garden in Delaware I have seen this viburnum in a woodsy, filtered light situation—they were at least 8 feet tall! A native species, *Viburnum cassinoides,* is a very similar viburnum but is difficult to find in Chicagoland.
COMBINES WITH:	*Hemerocallis* 'Pink Embers' and 'Hall's Pink', *Salvia* x *superba* 'May Night', *Astilbe* x *arendsii* 'Bressingham Beauty'

Viburnum prunifolium

BLACKHAW VIBURNUM

PLANT TYPE:	Native deciduous shrub or tree
ZONE:	3–9
FLOWER/FRUIT:	4-inch clusters of cream in May; fruit starts pink, turning blue-black
HABIT/FOLIAGE:	Rounded with horizontal branching similar to a hawthorn; dark, glossy finely toothed green leaves turn red-purple to bronze-red (in shade) in fall
HEIGHT:	12–15 feet
WIDTH/SPREAD:	8–12 feet
LIGHT:	Sun, part shade, shade
SOIL:	Average to rich, evenly moist, tolerates dry soil
CARE:	Pruning is only necessary on dead wood or for maintaining a tree shape.
USES:	Fall color, four-season interest, winter interest, easy care, shade tolerant, architecture
PROBLEMS:	Needs another clone for fruit set
INSIDER'S TIPS:	To ensure fruiting, plant two or more species in close proximity for cross-pollination. This has many similar traits to 'Winterthur' viburnum: glossy foliage, fall color, and pink to blue-black fruit. How it differs is its horizontal branching pattern, larger size, and a greater tolerance for shade. It is very resistant to powdery mildew. Native to Connecticut to Wisconsin, south to Florida and Texas.
COMBINES WITH:	In sun: *Sesleria autumnalis, Miscanthus sinensis* 'Adagio'; in shade: *Hosta* 'Gingko Craig' or 'Brim Cup'

Viburnum sieboldii 'Wave Crest'

'WAVE CREST' SIEBOLD VIBURNUM

PLANT TYPE:	Deciduous shrub
ZONE:	4–7
FLOWER/FRUIT:	Profuse creamy white, flat-top clusters; fruits beginning in August are rosy-red to black
HABIT/FOLIAGE:	Robust, upright form; large, dark green foliage turns red-purple in fall; leaves have nasty smell if crushed
HEIGHT:	15–20 feet
WIDTH/SPREAD:	10–12 feet
LIGHT:	Sun to part shade
SOIL:	Rich, moist, well-drained
CARE:	I found this plant growing at The Morton Arboretum in Lisle, Illinois, in a large parking lot bed. It had shoots to 8 feet and was only 6 feet wide. It could be pruned to manage the ultimate size, but I believe in choosing plants that meet the site's space requirements—remember: There is a viburnum to fit every space.
USES:	Fall color, profuse flowers, screen, bold accent
PROBLEMS:	Becomes very large—needs lots of space
INSIDER'S TIPS:	Roy Klehm has selected a newer one called 'Ironclad'. The name says it all! Although I did not find 'Wave Crest' on any deer-resistant lists, after smelling the leaves I suspect that the deer would leave it alone. Choose "bold and bodacious" perennials as companions.
COMBINES WITH:	*Eupatorium maculatum* 'Gateway', *Miscanthus sinensis* 'Gracillimus', *Vitex agnus-castus*

Viburnum trilobum 'Hah's'

'HAH'S' CRANBERRY VIBURNUM

PLANT TYPE:	Deciduous shrub
ZONE:	2–7
FLOWER/FRUIT:	Fragrant white lacecaps become clusters of glossy red "cranberries" that persists into spring
HABIT/FOLIAGE:	Rounded, not-too-tall form, more open than the denser 'Wentworth'; glossy, medium-green, three-lobed leaves turn red-purple in fall
HEIGHT:	5–7 feet
WIDTH/SPREAD:	5–7 feet
LIGHT:	Sun, part shade, shade
SOIL:	Rich, moist, well-drained
CARE:	This is a smaller cranberry viburnum than most. There is a viburnum to fit any space in the garden! I've included 14 in this book.
USES:	Fall color, persistent fruit, small space, winter interest
PROBLEMS:	Less problems with borers than other cultivars
INSIDER'S TIPS:	The best fall color is achieved with more sun. May only turn yellow with considerable shade. However, the amount of flower and fruiting does not seem to be affected in shadier sites.
COMBINES WITH:	*Ajuga reptans* 'Bronze Beauty' ('Gaiety'), *Aster divaricatus, Aconitum fischeri*

Stems

FOR WINTER COLOR AND STRUCTURE

Acer griseum

PAPERBARK MAPLE

PLANT TYPE:	Deciduous tree
ZONE:	5–7
FLOWER/FRUIT:	Few green pendent flowers, followed by green samaras
HABIT/FOLIAGE:	Oval-rounded form, showy peeling bark is red-brown to cinnamon colored; dark green leaves turn russet red in late fall (color is also dependent on colder temperatures)
HEIGHT:	Slowly to 20 feet
WIDTH/SPREAD:	10 feet
LIGHT:	Sun to part shade
SOIL:	Average to rich, moist, well-drained
CARE:	Although the growth rate on this maple is said to be 6–12 inches per year, judicious pruning at a young age will help to keep this one in bounds.
USES:	Winter interest/color, specimen, woodland edge, fall color
PROBLEMS:	Best fall color comes from colder temperatures
INSIDER'S TIPS:	I consider this a collector's plant—one for a collector who takes time to appreciate the subtlety of the interesting, colorful bark and can wait for the fall foliage color.
COMBINES WITH:	*Brunnera macrophylla, Lamium maculatum* 'White Nancy', *Kirengeshoma palmata, Hydrangea arborescens* 'Annabelle'

Betula nigra 'Little King', 'Fox Valley'

'LITTLE KING' DWARF RIVER BIRCH

PLANT TYPE:	Deciduous tree
ZONE:	4–9
FLOWER/FRUIT:	Slender brown catkins; fruits are small nutlets
HABIT/FOLIAGE:	Rounded to pyramidal form with branching to the ground; attractive exfoliating cinnamon-red bark; medium-green foliage turning yellow in fall
HEIGHT:	8–10 feet
WIDTH/SPREAD:	8–10 feet
LIGHT:	Full sun
SOIL:	Average to rich, evenly moist, not drought tolerant
CARE:	Birches should be pruned in summer, when sap is not flowing.
USES:	Winter interest, screen, disease resistant
PROBLEMS:	None
INSIDER'S TIPS:	Extremely wide with branching right to the ground, it takes up a lot of space! For an easy-care bed, you might consider using a wide-spreading evergreen such as *Juniperus sabina* 'Calgary Carpet' or 'Buffalo'. Any companion planting will do best in front of the ultimate drip line of 'Little King'.
COMBINES WITH:	*Astilbe* x *arendsii* 'Glow', *Buddleia davidii* 'Ellen's Blue', *Sorghastrum nutans* 'Sioux Blue'

Cercidiphyllum japonicum 'Pendula'

WEEPING KATSURA TREE

PLANT TYPE:	Deciduous tree
ZONE:	4–8
FLOWER/FRUIT:	Inconspicuous
HABIT/FOLIAGE:	Strong weeping form with branches arching to the ground, grafted to species; blue-green, heart-shaped leaves emerge red-purple, turning golden yellow in fall
HEIGHT:	15–25 feet
WIDTH/SPREAD:	10–15 feet
LIGHT:	Full sun
SOIL:	Rich, moist, well-drained
CARE:	Says John Beaudry of the Chicago Botanic Garden, "To keep tree in proportion to the garden, prune long branches all the way back to the point where they originate (drop-crotch pruning), sometimes taking more than one long shoot at a time by cutting back deeper into the plant. To keep it from dragging on the ground basically do the same as above but less drastically. I *never* cut a branch back halfway, as it would regrow from that point."
USES:	Showy form, specimen, winter architecture
PROBLEMS:	Top (crown) can easily sun scald
INSIDER'S TIPS:	A trained horticulturist may be needed to maintain your weeping katsura tree because proper pruning is so important. This specimen showing emergence from winter can be found in the English Walled Garden at Chicago Botanic Garden.
COMBINES WITH:	*Buxus* x 'Chicagoland Green', *Tulipa* 'Toronto', *Scilla sibirica*

Cornus alba 'Alleman's Compact'

'ALLEMAN'S COMPACT' RED-STEMMED DOGWOOD

PLANT TYPE:	Deciduous shrub
ZONE:	3–7
FLOWER/FRUIT:	Yellowish-white, flat-topped clusters in May–June are followed by white fruits
HABIT/FOLIAGE:	Compact rounded form with many red stems in winter; clean, rich green leaves turn reddish purple in fall
HEIGHT:	5–6 feet
WIDTH/SPREAD:	4–5 feet
LIGHT:	Sun to part shade
SOIL:	Rich, moist, well-drained
CARE:	Renovation prune a third of oldest stems each year to maintain stem color. As with all dogwoods, pay attention to good soil fertility and moisture.
USES:	Hedge, winter stems, background
PROBLEMS:	Possible canker if soil requirements are not met, but foliage has little to no leaf spot
INSIDER'S TIPS:	This is the best and most trouble-free red-stemmed dogwood for winter interest.
COMBINES WITH:	*Vinca minor, Narcissus* 'King Alfred', *Hemerocallis* 'Ice Carnival' or 'Baja'

Cornus sanguinea 'Midwinter Fire' ('Winter Flame')

'WINTER FLAME' OR 'MIDWINTER FIRE' DOGWOOD

PLANT TYPE:	Deciduous shrub
ZONE:	4–7
FLOWER/FRUIT:	Dull, white, flat clusters in late May; black fruit hidden by foliage
HABIT/FOLIAGE:	Rounded, twiggy form; showy stems start yellow and orange in fall then turn coral and back to green in spring; dark green leaves suffused with yellow, gold, and orange in fall
HEIGHT:	8–10 feet
TH/SPREAD:	8 feet
LIGHT:	Sun to part shade
SOIL:	Rich, moist
CARE:	For best coloration, cut back in late winter to encourage new growth. This also keeps the plant from getting too leggy. Most plants I have seen in landscapes are under 5 feet high.
USES:	Winter interest, flower arrangements, fall color, background
PROBLEMS:	So far rated as having no "serious" disease or insect problems and limited suckering
INSIDER'S TIPS:	This is advertised as a "bonfire" in your winter landscape. Not particularly exciting during the growing season until fall, when the leaves start coloring up.
COMBINES WITH:	*Sporobolus heterolepis*, *Veronica prostrata* 'Aztec Gold', *Tradescantia* 'Sweet Kate'

Cornus sericea 'Flaviramea'

YELLOW-STEMMED DOGWOOD

PLANT TYPE:	Deciduous shrub
ZONE:	3–8
FLOWER/FRUIT:	Flat-topped white clusters become bluish-white berries in fall; neither are showy
HABIT/FOLIAGE:	Vase-shaped form with yellow-green stems throughout winter and early spring; medium-green leaves turn purple or purple-tinged in fall
HEIGHT:	6–8 feet
WIDTH/SPREAD:	6–8 feet
LIGHT:	Tolerates both sun and shade, best in part shade
SOIL:	Rich, moist
CARE:	Easily pruned to desired height and width and to maintain stem color. Mulch annually with organic matter.
USES:	Winter stems, accent, background
PROBLEMS:	A little suckering is possible; tip die-back signals canker due to lack of sufficient water
INSIDER'S TIPS:	Maintaining soil moisture and good fertility will decrease the incidence of canker. For this reason, a mulch of composted organic material should be applied on an annual basis. This plant is a very much a plain Jane until the leaves drop in fall. Stems are still incredibly showy in spring when the daffodils are blooming. Give it an evergreen backdrop to highlight the yellow stems.
COMBINES WITH:	*Narcissus* 'King Alfred', *Taxus* x *media* 'Tauntonii', *Picea pungens* 'Montgomery'

225

Cotoneaster x 'Hessei'

HESSE ROCKSPRAY COTONEASTER

PLANT TYPE:	Semi-evergreen shrub
ZONE:	4–7
FLOWER/FRUIT:	Inconspicuous, pink flowers, then profuse red fruit persists into winter
HABIT/FOLIAGE:	Cascading rounded form of arching stems; stems showy red and dark brown even in winter; small, glossy, dark green leaves turn scarlet in fall
HEIGHT:	18 inches
WIDTH/SPREAD:	5 feet
LIGHT:	Full sun
SOIL:	Rich, moist, well-drained
CARE:	Cut back stems as needed to control the width.
USES:	Rock garden, cascade over walls, groundcover
PROBLEMS:	The fall foliage color may overpower the fruit
INSIDER'S TIPS:	This tolerates salt and many growing conditions such as clay, sandy soil, and high pH, but not soggy soil. Don't try to plant companions in front of this, but do your plantings behind so they will not be overgrown by the arching stems.
COMBINES WITH:	*Sedum* x 'Autumn Joy', *Caryopteris* x *clandonensis* 'First Choice', *Narcissus* 'Ice Follies'

226

Fagus sylvatica 'Tortuosa'
TWISTED EUROPEAN BEECH

PLANT TYPE:	Deciduous shrub
ZONE:	4–7 (8)
FLOWER/FRUIT:	Not showy
HABIT/FOLIAGE:	Dome shaped with twisted and curving gray branches; leaves are green, turning bronze in fall and finally tan
HEIGHT:	8–10 feet
WIDTH/SPREAD:	8–10 feet
LIGHT:	Sun to light shade
SOIL:	Average to rich, moist but not wet
CARE:	Usually pruned in winter when you can see the branching pattern
USES:	Winter interest, specimen, foundation
PROBLEMS:	Holds leaves into winter
INSIDER'S TIPS:	The twisted beech in this picture is the green-leafed form— rigorously prune to create a shape interesting for a Japanese-style garden. A similar branching pattern can be found on the cultivar 'Tortuosa Purpurea', with the added bonus of purple-burgundy foliage.
COMBINES WITH:	*Hemerocallis* 'Starlight Serenade', *Geranium pratense* 'Mrs. Kendall Clark', *Campanula lactiflora* 'Pouffe'

Kerria japonica

JAPANESE ROSE SHRUB

PLANT TYPE:	Deciduous shrub
ZONE:	4b–9
FLOWER/FRUIT:	Golden-yellow, single roselike blooms
HABIT/FOLIAGE:	Rounded habit with arching stems; bright green stems showy in winter; sharply pointed, bright green leaves with only occasional yellow fall color
HEIGHT:	3–6 feet
WIDTH/SPREAD:	5–8 feet
LIGHT:	Part shade, shade
SOIL:	Average, well-drained
CARE:	It blooms on old wood, so pruning should be done right after bloom. Prune at least a third of older stems to improve appearance. Stems may be cut back to a few inches from the ground.
USES:	Winter color, light texture, profuse bloom
PROBLEMS:	Spreads by runners; soil that is too rich promotes rampant growth
INSIDER'S TIPS:	Yellow-green stems are showiest in winter against an evergreen background or in spring with newly emerged foliage of bulbs.
COMBINES WITH:	Evergreen groundcovers will highlight the stems: *Vinca minor*, *Pachysandra terminalis* and sometimes evergreen *Lamium maculatum* 'White Nancy'

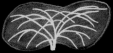

Malus 'Mary Potter'

'MARY POTTER' CRABAPPLE

PLANT TYPE:	Deciduous tree
ZONE:	4–8
FLOWER/FRUIT:	Pink buds open to white flowers, red fruit is persistent
HABIT/FOLIAGE:	Small, broadly spreading—but not quite weeping—on a central trunk; newer branches are reddish in winter; dark green leaves are yellow and gold in fall
HEIGHT:	6–8 feet
WIDTH/SPREAD:	12–15 feet
LIGHT:	Full sun
SOIL:	Rich, moist, well-drained
CARE:	The wider spreading habit is easily controlled with pruning.
USES:	Small stature, persistent fruit, winter interest
PROBLEMS:	Blooms are heaviest in alternate years
INSIDER'S TIPS:	This is my favorite small crabapple! Besides its small size, it has a great winter outline—looks like a standard decorated with tiny red balls. Friend Lee Randhava uses pink-flowered hydrangeas like a skirt around 'Mary Potter'. Use shade-tolerant plants underneath and sun lovers on the outskirts.
COMBINES WITH:	*Hydrangea serrata* 'Preziosa', *Hosta* 'Patriot', *Geranium* 'Rozanne'

Malus 'Red Jade'

'RED JADE' CRABAPPLE

PLANT TYPE:	Deciduous tree
ZONE:	4–8
FLOWER/FRUIT:	Rosy buds open to white flowers; glossy red fruit loved by birds
HABIT/FOLIAGE:	Broadly spreading weeper; bark is nearly black, with previous year's new stems showing red-black; medium-green leaves have little fall color
HEIGHT:	10–15 feet
WIDTH/SPREAD:	10–20 feet
LIGHT:	Full sun
SOIL:	Rich, moist, well-drained
CARE:	'Red Jade' is easily pruned to enhance the branching structure, and for this reason it's often seen in Japanese-style gardens, such as Anderson Gardens in Rockford, Illinois.
USES:	Weeping form, winter interest, attracts birds, Japanese garden
PROBLEMS:	Although moderately susceptible to apple scab, it does not defoliate; possible powdery mildew
INSIDER'S TIPS:	The beauty of *Malus* 'Red Jade' is the branching pattern in winter. I would prune this in late winter for the best opportunity to "see" how to prune artistically.
COMBINES WITH:	I am not one to do much underplanting with the low, wide-spreading crabs. Consider only using a low groundcover, or use your imagination on the outside edges.

Malus sargentii
SARGENT'S CRABAPPLE

PLANT TYPE:	Deciduous shrub
ZONE:	4–8
FLOWER/FRUIT:	Rosy buds open to white flowers; dark red persistent fruit
HABIT/FOLIAGE:	Low branched, wide spreading; branches are red-black in winter; dark green leaves with good disease resistance; some yellow fall color
HEIGHT:	6–8 feet
WIDTH/SPREAD:	8–15 feet
LIGHT:	Full sun
SOIL:	Rich, moist, well-drained
CARE:	Pruning for opening-up or thinning works best; tip-pruning or "heading back" is less successful. As with *Malus* 'Red Jade', prune it in late winter, even though you will lose some bloom.
USES:	Disease resistant, persistent fruit, winter interest, background
PROBLEMS:	Flowers profusely in alternate years
INSIDER'S TIPS:	This crabapple is a very wide spreader! This must be taken into account when planning a garden. Not many plants will be able to do well underneath the low-branching habit. But if you have space (up to 15 feet) to fill in with a great multi-season short tree, Sargent's crab would be a good choice. I have effectively used it as a softening screen on a very public corner.
COMBINES WITH:	This is another wide-spreading crab for which I rarely do a combination planting.

Salix alba 'Britzensis'

CORAL BARK WILLOW

PLANT TYPE:	Deciduous shrub
ZONE:	2–8
FLOWER/FRUIT:	Spring catkins
HABIT/FOLIAGE:	Rounded upright shrub with orange-red stems in winter; gray-green willowy leaves become golden-yellow in fall
HEIGHT:	6–10 feet (in only one year)
WIDTH/SPREAD:	5–7 feet (if cutting back each year)
LIGHT:	Full sun
SOIL:	Average to rich, evenly moist
CARE:	Must be coppiced (cut stems back to the ground) each early spring to ensure shrublike proportions as well as to maintain young stem color. Mike Dirr mentions seeing 10 feet of growth in one year in the South!
USES:	Winter color, specimen, easy, wet tolerant
PROBLEMS:	If left to grow on its own, it could reach a height of 80 feet!
INSIDER'S TIPS:	As more and more gardeners are looking beyond the summer blooming season, bright and colorful stems become an important to the winter landscape.
COMBINES WITH:	*Sporobolus heterolepis, Anemone* x *hybrida* 'Honorine Jobert', *Aster novae-angliae* 'Alma Potschke'

232

Salix elaeagnos

ROSEMARY WILLOW

PLANT TYPE:	Deciduous shrub
ZONE:	4–7
FLOWER/FRUIT:	Yellow catkins before the plant leafs out
HABIT/FOLIAGE:	Upright, somewhat vase-shaped with a nicely rounded top; stems are thin black-purple; green willowy leaves with white undersides look a fine-textured blue all summer, turning yellow in fall
HEIGHT:	15–20 feet
WIDTH/SPREAD:	15 feet
LIGHT:	Full sun
SOIL:	Average to rich, evenly moist
CARE:	Prune to the ground in late winter to promote new shoot growth, which has the best stem color.
USES:	Wet garden, textured foliage, winter stems, background
PROBLEMS:	Needs renewal pruning to avoid legginess
INSIDER'S TIPS:	I have never seen plants in the 15–20-foot range. When seen in the mixed border, they have been cut back hard, usually on an annual basis. This will help them develop the purple stems that provide winter color.
COMBINES WITH:	*Calamagrostis* x *acutiflora* 'Karl Foerster', *Helictotrichon sempervirens*, *Eupatorium maculatum* 'Gateway', *Solidago rugosa* 'Fireworks'

Salix 'Flame'

'FLAME' WILLOW

PLANT TYPE:	Deciduous shrub
ZONE:	2–8
FLOWER/FRUIT:	Yellow catkins in early spring before the plant leafs out
HABIT/FOLIAGE:	Upright rounded form with brilliant red-orange stems; silvery-green thin willow leaves become yellow in fall
HEIGHT:	10–12 feet
WIDTH/SPREAD:	10–12 feet
LIGHT:	Sun to light shade
SOIL:	Average to rich, evenly moist
CARE:	Cutting stems back in spring before new growth will improve the amount of new colored stems, as well as control the size of this shrub. 'Flame' willow is not as dependent on this stem cut back as is 'Britzensis'.
USES:	Winter color, background, wet tolerant
PROBLEMS:	No pests
INSIDER'S TIPS:	The 'Flame' willow in this picture was about 7 feet tall—I encourage you to manage the size of this plant to fit your garden. The reward will be one of the best displays of winter color from the flamelike stems.
COMBINES WITH:	*Lobelia cardinalis, Panicum virgatum* 'Northwind', *Hibiscus* 'Lord Baltimore', *Picea pungens* 'Montgomery'

Spiraea nipponica 'Halward's Silver'

'HALWARD'S SILVER' NIPPON SPIREA

PLANT TYPE:	Deciduous shrub
ZONE:	(3) 4–7 (8)
FLOWER/FRUIT:	Bright white-domed pom-poms in May
HABIT/FOLIAGE:	Densely mounded form with red-brown stems; narrow, dark blue-green leaves may turn yellow in fall
HEIGHT:	3 feet
WIDTH/SPREAD:	3 feet
LIGHT:	Sun to light shade
SOIL:	Average to rich, moist but not wet
CARE:	Easy—an occasional thinning of branches may be needed in spring.
USES:	Winter interest, small space, foundation, short hedge
PROBLEMS:	Hard to find—with so many choices now in spireas, it is hard for nurseries to carry all the cultivars
INSIDER'S TIPS:	Even smaller than 'Snowmound' spirea, which is described as a neater, denser form of 'Vanhoutte' spirea (bridalwreath). Most spireas have noticeably red-brown stems during winter.
COMBINES WITH:	*Iris sibirica* 'Caesar's Brother', *Paeonia lactiflora* 'Flame', *Hemerocallis* 'Happy Returns', *Rosa* 'Carefree Sunshine'

Stewartia pseudocamellia

JAPANESE STEWARTIA, CAMELLIA TREE

© Kris Bachtell

PLANT TYPE:	Deciduous tree
ZONE:	(4) 5–7
FLOWER/FRUIT:	Very white, cupped, camellia-like flowers in June and July
HABIT/FOLIAGE:	Pyramidal oval with bark in patches of red-brown, gray, and chalky white; clean, dark green leaves can be anywhere from orange to reddish purple in fall
HEIGHT:	At least to 20 feet
WIDTH/SPREAD:	12–15 feet
LIGHT:	Part shade to sun—protect from afternoon sun
SOIL:	Rich, moist, acidic
CARE:	Soil should be well supplemented with compost, and a layer of mulched leaves should be maintained over the root zone.
USES:	Accent, winter architecture, unusual bark and flowers
PROBLEMS:	Gets *big;* other than that, it is trouble-free
INSIDER'S TIPS:	If you have the space or would like to try to "manage" the size by consistent pruning, stewartia would be an interesting, fun tree. I have seen in catalogs some that stay under 15 feet (*Stewartia* 'Scarlet Sentinel' and *Stewartia pseudocamellia* 'Ballet'), but I have not yet seen them in the landscape.
COMBINES WITH:	I'm inclined to put this in a bed by itself with green groundcover to accent its four-season interest.

Viburnum plicatum var. *tomentosum* 'Mariesii'

'MARIESII' DOUBLEFILE VIBURNUM

PLANT TYPE:	Deciduous tree
ZONE:	5–8
FLOWER/FRUIT:	In May into June the flowers look like white pinwheels; red then black fruit if there has been cross-pollination from a nearby clone
HABIT/FOLIAGE:	Rounded form with horizontally branched tiered habit; light green leaves turn red-purple in fall
HEIGHT:	8–10 feet
WIDTH/SPREAD:	9–12 feet
LIGHT:	Sun to part shade—needs more shade in southern regions
SOIL:	Rich, moist, well-drained, does not tolerate heavy clay soils
CARE:	Careful pruning maintains the horizontal branching pattern.
USES:	Tiered winter branches, architectural accent, specimen, background, fall color
PROBLEMS:	For Zone 5 gardens, needs protection in winter
INSIDER'S TIPS:	This doublefile viburnum is growing in the garden of Barbara Miller, Evanston, Illinois. Protection from this 5-foot high fence is helpful surrounding a southwest corner.
COMBINES WITH:	In winter I like to see 'Mariesii' standing alone! The combination plantings were all perennial and were cut back to the ground in late fall (see this plant in chapter 3, May, page 58).

CHAPTER 12

EVERGREENS FOR YEAR-ROUND COLOR— AND NOT JUST CONIFERS!

Who says there is *no color* in winter? On April 7 and 8, 2003, while I was trying to finish writing this book, we had a 6-inch snowfall in northeastern Illinois. Driving around and observing the way shrubs and trees looked in my neighborhood reminded me that that there is a lot of color in the winter landscape that we just don't think about.

Check the previous year's new growth of crabapples and cherry trees. Then look at the barberries and spireas with their red-black and red-brown stems, respectively. And of course, willows, kerrias, and colored-stemmed dogwoods are easily recognized. Evergreens may be taken for granted, but they, too, add colors such as blue, silver, yellow, bronzed, and, naturally, green!

Take some time to recognize those winter shapes and colors that keep the landscape marching along in a progression of change.

Abies koreana 'Silberlocke'

SILVER CURLS KOREAN FIR

PLANT TYPE:	Evergreen
ZONE:	4–7
FLOWER/FRUIT:	Blue-purple, upright cones are produced on plants after 10 years
HABIT/FOLIAGE:	Narrow, irregular pyramid; medium-green needles curve upward, showing silvery undersides and giving a frosted appearance
HEIGHT:	6–15 feet in 10 years (ACS classification: Intermediate)
WIDTH/SPREAD:	4–5 feet
LIGHT:	Sun to light shade, likes some afternoon shade
SOIL:	Rich, moist
CARE:	Do not let plant become water stressed in dry periods. Mulch to retain soil moisture.
USES:	Accent, specimen, foundation
PROBLEMS:	May have deer or rabbit browse
INSIDER'S TIPS:	The showy coloring of this fir stands out in any garden, and it seems to fit in anywhere because of its slow-growing narrow shape. Shown in Brent Markus's garden with Japanese maples in autumn.
COMBINES WITH:	*Delphinium elatum, Aconitum napellus, Rosa* 'Knockout' or 'Betty Prior', *Acer shirasawanum* 'Aureum'

Buxus 'Green Mountain'

'GREEN MOUNTAIN' BOXWOOD

PLANT TYPE:	Broadleaf evergreen
ZONE:	4–8
FLOWER/FRUIT:	Small yellow flowers in March
HABIT/FOLIAGE:	Densely pyramidal shape; small, dark green, oval leaves that hold color well throughout winter
HEIGHT:	2–3 feet
WIDTH/SPREAD:	18–24 inches
LIGHT:	Part shade to sun
SOIL:	Average, well-drained
CARE:	May be sheared into shapes. Take care to not cultivate soils around surface roots.
USES:	Pyramidal accent, evergreen, topiary
PROBLEMS:	Protect from drying winds; may "bronze" in winter
INSIDER'S TIPS:	'Green Mountain' looks particularly good in a formal garden with a lot of structure. Here it is used in a private garden in Scotland (the Frasers' garden at Shepherd House) as accents for a parterre.
COMBINES WITH:	*Sidalcea* 'Party Girl', *Origanum vulgare* 'Aureum', *Nepeta mussinii* 'Blue Wonder', *Knautia macedonica* 'Mars Midget'

Buxus 'Green Velvet'

'GREET VELVET' BOXWOOD

PLANT TYPE:	Broadleaf evergreen
ZONE:	4–8
FLOWER/FRUIT:	Small yellow flowers in March or April
HABIT/FOLIAGE:	Densely, rounded mound, even ball shaped; dark, glossy evergreen ovals
HEIGHT:	2–4 feet
WIDTH/SPREAD:	2–4 feet
LIGHT:	Part shade to sun
SOIL:	Average, well-drained
CARE:	Although this boxwood can be sheared, I prefer to allow it to achieve a softer, more natural rounded form.
USES:	Formal edging, hedge, evergreen
PROBLEMS:	Does not winter-burn
INSIDER'S TIPS:	'Green Velvet' is a cross between Korean and English boxwoods that maintains its dark green foliage throughout winter—it doesn't look "peaked" at the beginning of spring.
COMBINES WITH:	*Iris ensata* 'Variegata', *Hosta tokudama* 'Aureo-nebulosa', *Begonia coccinea* (angel wing begonia)

Buxus sempervirens 'Graham Blandy'

'GRAHAM BLANDY' BOXWOOD

PLANT TYPE:	Broadleaf evergreen
ZONE:	5–8
FLOWER/FRUIT:	None
HABIT/FOLIAGE:	Upright, narrow column with straight sides; small, glossy, dark green ovals
HEIGHT:	9–15 feet in 20–35 years, respectively
WIDTH/SPREAD:	12–18 inches
LIGHT:	Part shade
SOIL:	Average, well-drained
CARE:	May prune to maintain straighter sides
USES:	Architectural accent, screen, evergreen, topiary
PROBLEMS:	Difficult to find in the Midwest, maybe due to a winterburn issue
INSIDER'S TIPS:	Shown here at Rosemary Verey's garden at Barnsley House in England. They look like exclamation marks or sentinels for the vegetable and cutting garden. Think of all the contrasting plant shapes this could go with!
COMBINES WITH:	*Caryopteris* or *Berberis* (ball), *Miscanthus sinensis* 'Morning Light' or *Lespedeza thunbergii* 'Pink Fountain' (fountain)

Buxus sempervirens 'Vardar Valley'

'VARDAR VALLEY' BOXWOOD

PLANT TYPE:	Broadleaf evergreen
ZONE:	4–8
FLOWER/FRUIT:	Yellow-green apetalous clusters in April and May
HABIT/FOLIAGE:	Low-growing, flat-topped mound; dark green ovals retain color through winter; new growth may appear bluish
HEIGHT:	2–3 feet
WIDTH/SPREAD:	3–4 feet
LIGHT:	Part shade to sun
SOIL:	Average, well-drained
CARE:	Easy care, but may be shaped. The hedge shown in this picture shows what it might look like without drastic shearing.
USES:	Evergreen, parterre hedge, edger
PROBLEMS:	Not so hardy (shows winter injury) in Zone 5
INSIDER'S TIPS:	I have seen this growing beautifully in areas of the country not affected by extremes of heat or cold. It is not readily available in my Chicagoland area, which tells me that it might be a risky plant to grow in Zones 4 and 5.
COMBINES WITH:	*Hemerocallis* 'Scarlet Tanager', *Geranium* 'Brookside', *Solidago rugosa* 'Fireworks', *Thalictrum aquilegiifolium*

Cephalotaxus harringtonia 'Prostrata'

PROSTRATE JAPANESE PLUM YEW

PLANT TYPE:	Evergreen
ZONE:	(5) 6–9
FLOWER/FRUIT:	Only on very mature plants
HABIT/FOLIAGE:	Horizontal, spreading oval shape with open, somewhat upswept branches; glossy, dark green needles are similar to yews, only larger and thicker
HEIGHT:	2–3 feet
WIDTH/SPREAD:	3–5 feet
LIGHT:	Part shade, shade, tolerates some sun
SOIL:	Rich, moist, well-drained
CARE:	Allow space for wide spreading habit, or prune when needed.
USES:	Shade tolerant, groundcover, deer resistant
PROBLEMS:	Availability in northeastern Illinois is by mail order only
INSIDER'S TIPS:	Tropical looking evergreen not often grown in Zone 5. It has survived at the Chicago Botanic Garden Conifer Collection for over five years. It's very resistant to deer browse.
COMBINES WITH:	*Hosta* 'Piedmont Gold', *Brunnera macrophylla* 'Dawson's White', *Lamium maculatum* 'Beedham's White'

Chamaecyparis nootkatensis 'Pendula'

PENDULOUS NOOTKA FALSE CYPRESS

PLANT TYPE:	Evergreen
ZONE:	4–7
FLOWER/FRUIT:	Small, glaucous cones
HABIT/FOLIAGE:	Very narrow with occasional ascending pendulous arms; dark green, flat sprays (with a hint of blue) along stems
HEIGHT:	7–15 feet in 10 years (ACS classification: Large)
WIDTH/SPREAD:	3–5 feet
LIGHT:	Sun to light shade
SOIL:	Average to rich, evenly moist
CARE:	Any pruning of browned branches should be done before spring growth. Don't crowd the lower branches with other plants.
USES:	Accent, evergreen, showy form, small space
PROBLEMS:	Site where protected from winter winds
INSIDER'S TIPS:	This is one of the best for hardiness in cold winters. I love this evergreen because it stays so narrow and does not take up too much valuable garden space. Also, it's unusual shape draws the eye into the landscape. One student likened it to a witch with pointed hat and arms held outstretched and draping downward, as if cloaked!
COMBINES WITH:	*Narcissus* 'King Alfred', *Leucanthemum* x *superbum* 'Ryan's White', *Hemerocallis* 'Mary Todd', *Echinacea purpurea* 'Springbrook's Crimson Star', *Hydrangea paniculata* 'Limelight'

Chamaecyparis obtusa 'Nana Gracilis'

DWARF HINOKI FALSE CYPRESS

PLANT TYPE:	Evergreen shrub
ZONE:	4–8
FLOWER/FRUIT:	Small brown cone
HABIT/FOLIAGE:	Upright oval shape is somewhat irregular; dark green, compact cupped fans; holds color where not exposed to winter winds
HEIGHT:	3–6 feet in 10 years (ACS classification: Dwarf)
WIDTH/SPREAD:	3–4 feet
LIGHT:	Sun to part shade
SOIL:	Rich, moist, well-drained
CARE:	This is a slow grower, so only pruning of winter-burned needles is necessary.
USES:	Evergreen accent, hedge, small space
PROBLEMS:	Needs protection from drying winds
INSIDER'S TIPS:	Said to be the most popular of the Hinoki cypresses, it is readily available. But there are many other selections to be tried, such as 'Blue Feathers' and 'Split Rock', which are blue, or 'Crippsii' and 'Golden Sprite', which have bright yellow foliage.
COMBINES WITH:	*Rosa* 'Knockout' or 'Carefree Wonder', *Platycodon grandiflorus* 'Mariesii', *Aster oblongifolius* 'Raydon's Favorite'

Chamaecyparis pisifera 'Filifera Aurea'

GOLDEN THREADLEAF SAWARA FALSE CYPRESS

PLANT TYPE:	Evergreen
ZONE:	4–8
FLOWER/FRUIT:	Tiny cone, not showy
HABIT/FOLIAGE:	Low, spreading form grafted onto a single trunk; threadlike needles will be yellow to yellow-green
HEIGHT:	3–4 feet (not including the standard)
WIDTH/SPREAD:	3–4 feet
LIGHT:	Sun to part shade
SOIL:	Rich, moist, well-drained, neutral to acidic
CARE:	Does best in moist atmosphere and protected from drying wind. The standard form takes a lot of pruning management to maintain the shape. Also prune out any leaders.
USES:	Architecture, color accent, specimen, winter interest
PROBLEMS:	Only to be found at a specialty nursery and will probably be very costly!
INSIDER'S TIPS:	I couldn't resist showing this incredible specimen from a garden in Toronto, Canada. I would practice pruning and care with other unusual conifers before making the investment. And who knows, you might find the same look with another less expensive plant.
COMBINES WITH:	*Pulmonaria longifolia* 'Bertram Anderson', *Hosta* 'Blue Arrow', *Corydalis lutea, Hemerocallis* 'Pink Embers'

Chamaecyparis pisifera 'Golden Mop' ('Gold Mops')

'GOLDEN MOP' SAWARA FALSE CYPRESS

PLANT TYPE:	Evergreen
ZONE:	3–7
FLOWER/FRUIT:	Inconspicuous flowers become yellowish brown cones
HABIT/FOLIAGE:	Densely mounded; threadlike bright golden-yellow leaves; showy texture
HEIGHT:	3–6 feet in 10–15 years (ACS classification: Dwarf)
WIDTH/SPREAD:	3–6 feet
LIGHT:	Sun to light shade
SOIL:	Rich, moist, well-drained
CARE:	Prune out any leaders
USES:	Edger, color accent, rock garden
PROBLEMS:	Too many in a single site gets tiresome
INSIDER'S TIPS:	This is one of the most popular and widely available dwarf conifers because of its texture and color. Use it to "face down" leggy plants, such as some *Aronia*.
COMBINES WITH:	Annual hot pink *Geranium*, black mondo grass used as an annual, *Helictotrichon sempervirens*, *Phlox paniculata* 'Little Princess'

Chamaecyparis pisifera 'Vintage Gold'

'VINTAGE GOLD' JAPANESE FALSE CYPRESS

PLANT TYPE:	Evergreen
ZONE:	(4) 5–8
FLOWER/FRUIT:	None
HABIT/FOLIAGE:	Compact, roundy-moundy; described as a fern-leaf form of 'Gold Mops'! Foliage is golden yellow in summer, softening to a more yellow color in cooler fall temperatures.
HEIGHT:	18–30 inches (no ACS classification as yet)
WIDTH/SPREAD:	18–30 inches
LIGHT:	Part shade to sun
SOIL:	Rich, moist, well-drained, neutral to acidic
CARE:	All *Chamaecyparis* do not do well in hot, drying winds!
USES:	Bright accent, soft texture, winter color
PROBLEMS:	Not readily available
INSIDER'S TIPS:	'Vintage Gold' is so new that I haven't been able to try it—yet. When I do, I will make sure I prepare the soil as I would for rhododendrons.
COMBINES WITH:	*Hemerocallis* 'Siloam Tiny Tim', *Veronica spicata* 'Blue Fox', *Tradescantia* x *andersoniana* 'Bilberry Ice'

Choisya ternata 'Sundance'

MEXICAN ORANGE BUSH

PLANT TYPE:	Evergreen
ZONE:	(6) 7–9
FLOWER/FRUIT:	Fragrant, white, flat-topped clusters resembling orange blossoms
HABIT/FOLIAGE:	Dense, rounded, fast grower; shiny yellow leaves that are evergreen
HEIGHT:	6–8 feet
WIDTH/SPREAD:	6–8 feet
LIGHT:	All-sun, part shade, shade
SOIL:	Acid, well-drained
CARE:	I tried it in a container in 2002. Because the container had a saucer and I did not pay attention or see that the saucer was holding water, my plant died. I usually need three chances to grow and/or kill a plant before I stop replacing it!
USES:	Evergreen, fragrant, color accent, container
PROBLEMS:	Root and crown rot in poorly drained sites; sucking insects
INSIDER'S TIPS:	If I could grow this shrub in Zone 5, it would be one of my first choices. In northern gardens where temperatures dip below 15°F, try growing in containers brought indoors over winter. But make sure that containers are well-drained.
COMBINES WITH:	*Campanula carpatica* 'Samantha', *Geranium wallichianum* 'Buxton's Blue', *Iris tectorum, Hemerocallis* 'Joan Senior', *Kirengeshoma palmata*

Ilex crenata 'Sky Pencil'

'SKY PENCIL' JAPANESE HOLLY

PLANT TYPE:	Evergreen
ZONE:	5–7 (8)
FLOWER/FRUIT:	None
HABIT/FOLIAGE:	Narrowly fastigiate resembling a telephone pole, with interesting contours; very slow-growing; forest green, glossy evergreen leaves are almost needlelike
HEIGHT:	6–8 feet
WIDTH/SPREAD:	18 inches feet
LIGHT:	Sun to part shade
SOIL:	Average to rich, evenly moist, slightly acidic
CARE:	This is low maintenance because it is so slow growing. Pay attention to soil preparation.
USES:	Bold architectural form, small space, entryway, container
PROBLEMS:	Hard to find in the Midwest
INSIDER'S TIPS:	Introduced by the National Arboretum in 1985.
COMBINES WITH:	*Rosa* 'All That Jazz', *Sedum* 'Frosty Morn', *Hibiscus* 'Kopper King'

Ilex glabra 'Compacta'

COMPACT INKBERRY HOLLY

PLANT TYPE:	Broadleaf evergreen
ZONE:	(3) 4–9
FLOWER/FRUIT:	Inconspicuous white flowers; blue-black inkberries
HABIT/FOLIAGE:	Compact, roundy-moundy; dark, glossy evergreen leaves are long ovals
HEIGHT:	3–4 feet
WIDTH/SPREAD:	3–4 feet
LIGHT:	Sun, part shade
SOIL:	Average to rich, evenly moist
CARE:	Because the species typically spreads by underground stems, gardeners should watch for this possibility in the cultivars.
USES:	Foundation, easy care, evergreen
PROBLEMS:	None
INSIDER'S TIPS:	This was a selection of 'Compacta' from F & F Nursery that Spring Meadow Nursery is selling to the trade. It has consistently held its lower leaves.
COMBINES WITH:	*Salix* 'Flame', *Rosa* 'Knockout', *Astilbe* x *arendsii* 'Snowdrift', *Myosotis sylvatica* 'Victoria Dark Blue'

Ilex glabra 'Shamrock'

SHAMROCK INKBERRY

PLANT TYPE:	Broadleaf evergreen
ZONE:	(4) 5–9
FLOWER/FRUIT:	Inconspicuous white flowers become blue-black inkberries in the following year
HABIT/FOLIAGE:	Nicely branched, mounded form; lustrous bright green foliage becomes dark green to bronzed in winter
HEIGHT:	3–5 feet
WIDTH/SPREAD:	3–5 feet
LIGHT:	Sun to part shade, somewhat shade tolerant
SOIL:	Average to rich, tolerates both wet or dry soil and not fussy about pH
CARE:	Because the species typically spreads by underground stems, gardeners should watch for this possibility in the cultivars.
USES:	Evergreen, wet tolerant, foundation, hedge, small space
PROBLEMS:	Not often seen in Midwestern landscapes and not readily available
INSIDER'S TIPS:	Is said to be slower growing than *Ilex glabra* 'Nordic', but both tend to drop their lower leaves with age. Use this small broadleaf evergreen as you would boxwood.
COMBINES WITH:	*Phlox maculata* 'Natascha', *Pulmonaria longifolia* 'Bertram Anderson', *Hosta* 'Diamond Tiara'

Juniperus chinensis 'Fairview'

'FAIRVIEW' CHINESE JUNIPER

PLANT TYPE:	Evergreen
ZONE:	4–9
FLOWER/FRUIT:	Silvery blue ball-like cones (juniper berries)
HABIT/FOLIAGE:	Narrow, loosely pyramidal shape with light brown, upward-arching stems; rich green, feathery fans are held on upright stems
HEIGHT:	10–15 feet in 10 years (ACS classification: Intermediate)
WIDTH/SPREAD:	3–5 feet
LIGHT:	Sun to light shade
SOIL:	Average to rich, evenly moist, tolerates drier soils at maturity
CARE:	May need tip pruning for browned foliage in the year after planting.
USES:	Screen, background, naturalistic form, narrow space
PROBLEMS:	Relatively trouble free
INSIDER'S TIPS:	This is my favorite background juniper because of color, showy fruit, and naturalistic shape.
COMBINES WITH:	*Rosa* 'Henry Kelsey' or *Rosa* 'Golden Showers', *Helianthus* 'Lemon Queen', *Eupatorium maculatum* 'Gateway'

Juniperus chinensis 'Plumosa Aurea'

'PLUMOSA AUREA' JUNIPER

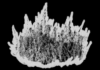

PLANT TYPE:	Evergreen
ZONE:	(4) 5–8
FLOWER/FRUIT:	Fruit not highly noticeable
HABIT/FOLIAGE:	Irregular, wide-spreading vase shape with plumy branches and nodding tips; yellow-green prickly needles become golden-bronze in winter
HEIGHT:	6–15 feet in 10–15 years (ACS classification: Intermediate)
WIDTH/SPREAD:	6–15 feet
LIGHT:	Sun to light shade
SOIL:	Average to rich, moist but not wet
CARE:	Pruning of no more than 20% will help slow the growth. Shearing will ruin the "natural" form!
USES:	Background brightener, accent, four-season color
PROBLEMS:	May be faster growing when well-established
INSIDER'S TIPS:	Give this juniper space to develop over time into its miniature golden mountain ridges. This would include removing other companion plantings, as they begin to shade out the branches of 'Plumosa Aurea', or using perennials and small shrubs as groundcovers.
COMBINES WITH:	*Miscanthus sinensis* 'Cosmopolitan' (not hardy in Zone 5), *Caryopteris* x *clandonensis* 'First Choice', *Phlox paniculata* 'Bright Eyes'

Juniperus communis 'Gold Cone'

'GOLD CONE' JUNIPER

© Ed Hasselkus

PLANT TYPE:	Evergreen
ZONE:	2–6 (7)
FLOWER/FRUIT:	Inconspicuous flower; only female flowers develop small, oval berry-like fruit
HABIT/FOLIAGE:	Compact, narrowly upright column with pointed top; bright yellow-tipped spiny needles in spring and early summer becoming gray-blue for remainder of the year
HEIGHT:	3–6 feet in 10–15 years (ACS classification: Dwarf)
WIDTH/SPREAD:	2–3 feet
LIGHT:	Full sun
SOIL:	Average, well-drained, very adaptable to any soil except for wet
CARE:	Because this is so slow-growing, only light pruning is needed. As with all junipers, this is best done in spring, while the plant is actively growing. Drastic shearing will result in leafless twigs and stems! Take care to not plant companions that will shade out any part of the plant.
USES:	Accent, narrow space, mixed border, evergreen
PROBLEMS:	None
INSIDER'S TIPS:	While the form is very noticeable in the mixed border, I was disappointed that it lost its yellow coloration in the heat of summer.
COMBINES WITH:	*Digitalis purpurea, Delphinium grandiflorum* 'Blue Butterfly', *Hemerocallis* 'Rosy Returns'

257

Juniperus communis 'Pencil Point'

'PENCIL POINT' COMMON JUNIPER

PLANT TYPE:	Evergreen
ZONE:	3–7
FLOWER/FRUIT:	Green to bluish Juniper berry cones—I have not seen these in the landscape
HABIT/FOLIAGE:	Narrow, columnar form; sharp, spiky green needles with silver bands
HEIGHT:	4–6 feet
WIDTH/SPREAD:	10–18 inches
LIGHT:	Full sun
SOIL:	Average, well-drained
CARE:	If branches are shaded by other surrounding plants, they will not grow back and green up.
USES:	Architectural accent, narrow space, low maintenance
PROBLEMS:	Does not do well in the Deep South
INSIDER'S TIPS:	This picture was taken at the National Arboretum—the huge golden evergreen is *Chamaecyparis obtusa* 'Crippsii'. 'Pencil Point' may also be sold under the cultivar name 'Sentinel'. This juniper looks good with other architectural plants.
COMBINES WITH:	*Helictotrichon sempervirens* 'Sapphire', *Weigela florida* 'Midnight Wine', *Berberis thunbergii* 'Bonanza Gold'

Juniperus sabina 'Calgary Carpet', 'Monna'

'CALGARY CARPET' SAVIN JUNIPER

PLANT TYPE:	Evergreen
ZONE:	4–7
FLOWER/FRUIT:	Not very showy, green, berry-like cones
HABIT/FOLIAGE:	Low-growing, wide spreader; stems curve outward and slightly upward; soft-feeling fans are light to bright green
HEIGHT:	9–12 inches
WIDTH/SPREAD:	May eventually grow to 10 feet wide
LIGHT:	Full sun
SOIL:	Average to poor, well-drained
CARE:	Some shearing on an annual basis (no more than 20%) will slow the spread, but see the Insider's Tip below.
USES:	Groundcover, edger, rock garden
PROBLEMS:	May be too wide-growing for the mixed border
INSIDER'S TIPS:	Ed Hasselkus suggests, "Pruning of creeping-type junipers to restrict their spread never seems to work very well. Probably they are best replaced when they outgrow their bounds."
COMBINES WITH:	*Rosa* 'Flower Carpet', *Panicum virgatum* 'Shenandoah', *Hibiscus* x 'Tosca'

Juniperus squamata 'Blue Star'

'BLUE STAR' JUNIPER

PLANT TYPE:	Evergreen
ZONE:	4–7 (8)
FLOWER/FRUIT:	Tiny, blue "berries," or cones
HABIT/FOLIAGE:	Irregularly mounded dwarf, star-shaped; prickly needles are silvery-blue
HEIGHT:	12–18 inches
WIDTH/SPREAD:	1–2 feet
LIGHT:	Full sun
SOIL:	Average to rich, moist but not wet, adaptable to even dry soils
CARE:	Easy—very slow growing. Does not like shading by other plant material.
USES:	Small space, blue accent, winter interest, easy care
PROBLEMS:	Not tolerant of humidity and high heat; very prickly to handle
INSIDER'S TIPS:	One of the most popular evergreens because of its color and small size.
COMBINES WITH:	*Coreopsis verticillata* 'Moonbeam', *Campanula carpatica* 'White Clips', *Heuchera* 'Plum Pudding'

Picea abies 'Pendula'

WEEPING NORWAY SPRUCE

PLANT TYPE:	Evergreen
ZONE:	3–7
FLOWER/FRUIT:	None
HABIT/FOLIAGE:	Prostrate or pendulous branches are often trained onto a post to make a slender upright form with weeping branches; very dark green needles are short and stiff
HEIGHT:	More than 15 feet in 10 years (ACS classification: Large)
WIDTH/SPREAD:	3–8 feet, dependent on training
LIGHT:	Full sun
SOIL:	Sandy, acidic, well-drained loam
CARE:	The natural tendency of this plant is to be a wide-spreading, undulating groundcover. With shaping and training, you will get a more upright specimen or possibly even an usual form resembling a dinosaur.
USES:	Specimen, architecture, four-season interest
PROBLEMS:	*Cytospora* canker
INSIDER'S TIPS:	Although best in sandy, acidic soils, it can be planted in average soil with adequate moisture while becoming established. Norway spruce does best in colder climates. The weeping Norway spruce will take time and attention to manage the shape that fits your garden.
COMBINES WITH:	Spring bulbs, *Leucanthemum* x *superba* 'Aglaya', *Agastache foeniculum* 'Blue Fortune', *Miscanthus sinensis* 'Huron Sunrise'

Picea glauca 'Conica'

DWARF ALBERTA SPRUCE

PLANT TYPE:	Evergreen
ZONE:	2–6
FLOWER/FRUIT:	Green, purple-tinged cones turn light brown with age
HABIT/FOLIAGE:	Densely pyramidal form; bright green needles are short and densely packed along the stems
HEIGHT:	3–6 feet in 10 years, 10–12 feet in 25 years (ACS classification: Dwarf)
WIDTH/SPREAD:	3–6 feet
LIGHT:	Sun to light shade
SOIL:	Rich, moist, well-drained
CARE:	Shield from winter winds to prevent burning
USES:	Rich color, foundation, screening
PROBLEMS:	Susceptible to red spiders during warm, dry periods
INSIDER'S TIPS:	The most popular dwarf conifer, but over time will be much bigger than the plant bought in a container. Plan ahead and don't try to squeeze the Alberta spruce into a space only 1 or 2 feet wide.
COMBINES WITH:	*Tulipa* 'Burgundy Lace', *Syringa meyeri* 'Paliban', *Platycodon grandiflorus* 'Mariesii', *Iris ensata* 'Variegata'

Picea omorika 'Nana'

DWARF SERBIAN SPRUCE

PLANT TYPE:	Evergreen
ZONE:	4–7
FLOWER/FRUIT:	Pendant cones are purple, turning cinnamon brown as they ripen
HABIT/FOLIAGE:	Short, densely-branched, conical shape; needles have a bicolored appearance, dark green on top with white stomata underneath
HEIGHT:	3–6 feet in 10–15 years (ACS classification: Dwarf)
WIDTH/SPREAD:	3–6 feet
LIGHT:	Full sun
SOIL:	Rich, moist, well-drained
CARE:	Very adaptable
USES:	Color accent, small space, four-season interest
PROBLEMS:	None
INSIDER'S TIPS:	This dwarf Serbian spruce (dense cone in the center) is in a garden done by Brent Markus. The plant is about 12 years old and only 3 feet tall.
COMBINES WITH:	*Rosa* 'Knockout', *Heuchera* 'Midnight Claret', *Coreopsis* x 'Limerock Ruby', *Hemerocallis* 'Rosy Returns'

Picea orientalis 'Skylands' ('Aurea Compacta')

'SKYLANDS' ORIENTAL SPRUCE

PLANT TYPE:	Evergreen
ZONE:	4–7
FLOWER/FRUIT:	Crimson male flowers; fruit is a pendulous purple-brown cone
HABIT/FOLIAGE:	Extremely slow-growing, narrow pyramid; lower branches make a "skirt" along the ground; short, golden yellow needles hold color all season
HEIGHT:	5–6 feet in 10 years (ACS classification: Intermediate)
WIDTH/SPREAD:	3–4 feet in 10 years, 6 feet in 20 years (plant in photo)
LIGHT:	Filtered shade in the afternoon
SOIL:	Average to rich, moist but not wet
CARE:	"Good drainage and good air circulation around this tree is essential in the Midwest!" says Ed Lyon, education director at Olbrich Botanical Gardens.
USES:	Color accent, architecture, specimen
PROBLEMS:	Needles will burn in winter on any side exposed to wind
INSIDER'S TIPS:	'Skylands' spruce was "found" at Skylands Farm, now Ringwood State Park, New Jersey. Allow it to stand alone without planting companions too closely. I know, someone will have to sit on me to make me obey my own advice!
COMBINES WITH:	*Hosta* 'Golden Tiara', *Heucherella* x 'Viking Ship', *Carex siderostricha* 'Island Brocade' (Zone 6), *Carex conica* 'Gold Fountains' (Zone 5)

Picea pungens 'Glauca Globosa'
Dwarf globe Colorado blue spruce

PLANT TYPE:	Evergreen
ZONE:	2–8
FLOWER/FRUIT:	Cones
HABIT/FOLIAGE:	Globe shaped, flat-topped; densely branched; bright silver-blue needles
HEIGHT:	3–5 feet
WIDTH/SPREAD:	5–6 feet
LIGHT:	Full sun
SOIL:	Rich, moist
CARE:	Must have good air circulation. Take care to not plant perennials too close to evergreens, or you will shade out the lower branches, causing the foliage to die and not grow back.
USES:	Blue highlight, specimen, slow growing, rounded form
PROBLEMS:	Susceptible to *Cytospora* canker
INSIDER'S TIPS:	*Picea pungens* is more drought tolerant than other spruces.
COMBINES WITH:	*Lavandula angustifolia* 'Hidcote', *Geranium sanguineum* var. *striatum*, *Coreopsis verticillata* 'Moonbeam', *Hemerocallis* 'Siloam Tiny Tim'

Picea pungens 'St. Mary's Broom'

'ST. MARY'S BROOM' BLUE SPRUCE

PLANT TYPE:	Evergreen
ZONE:	2–8
FLOWER/FRUIT:	None
HABIT/FOLIAGE:	Low-spreading, becoming more mounded with age; silvery blue, relatively longer needles grow at a wide angle
HEIGHT:	2–3 feet in 10 years (ACS classification: Miniature)
WIDTH/SPREAD:	3–5 feet in 10 years
LIGHT:	Full sun
SOIL:	Rich, moist
CARE:	Easy—just an occasional snip with the pruners.
USES:	Rock garden, groundcover, color highlight, winter interest
PROBLEMS:	Don't let other plants shade this out
INSIDER'S TIPS:	'St. Mary's Broom' seems to creep along the ground very slowly, providing that nice blue spruce color.
COMBINES WITH:	*Campanula poscharskyana, Coreopsis rosea* 'Sweet Dreams', *Echinacea purpurea* 'Cygnet', *Spiraea japonica* 'Lemon Princess'

Pieris x 'Forest Flame'

'FOREST FLAME' PIERIS

PLANT TYPE:	Broadleaf evergreen
ZONE:	6–9
FLOWER/FRUIT:	Lavender-scented flowers hang in white drooping clusters
HABIT/FOLIAGE:	Upright, rounded, similar to rhododendrons; spring foliage is red turning cream and green for the remainder of the year
HEIGHT:	6–8 feet
WIDTH/SPREAD:	4–6 feet
LIGHT:	Sun, part shade, shade
SOIL:	Rich, moist, well-drained, acidic
CARE:	Prune after blooming as needed, and prepare soils as you would for rhododendrons. A dose of Epsom salts in spring works like a "mineral tonic."
USES:	Evergreen, changing foliage color, fragrant, deer resistant
PROBLEMS:	Not hardy for Zone 5
INSIDER'S TIPS:	The red "new growth" of the cultivars is showiest early in the season when rhododendrons are in bloom. Take care to avoid color clashes with rosy-purple blooms. For Zone 5 gardeners, hardier *Pieris japonica* 'Mountain Fire' and 'Scarlet O'Hara' have similar foliage coloration.
COMBINES WITH:	*Coreopsis* x 'Limerock Ruby', *Cimicifuga simplex* 'Black Negligee', *Campanula carpatica* 'Samantha'

Pinus cembra 'Chalet'

'CHALET' SWISS STONE PINE

PLANT TYPE:	Evergreen
ZONE:	3–7
FLOWER/FRUIT:	Blue to purplish cones do not open and are held on the tree for 2–3 years
HABIT/FOLIAGE:	Narrowly conical form; soft blue-green needles in clusters of five; needles are held for 5 years on branches
HEIGHT:	6–15 feet in 10–15 years (ACS classification: Intermediate)
WIDTH/SPREAD:	5–6 feet
LIGHT:	Full sun
SOIL:	Average to rich, evenly moist, slightly acidic
CARE:	Annual candling keeps this plant more densely compact—removing half of the new candle growth will cause the formation of lateral buds below the cut.
USES:	Foundation, color accent, hedge
PROBLEMS:	None
INSIDER'S TIPS:	*Pinus cembra* 'Glauca' tends to have bluer needles than 'Chalet'.
COMBINES WITH:	*Calamagrostis* x *acutiflora*, *Iris sibirica* 'Caesar's Brother', *Rosa* 'All That Jazz'

Pinus x 'Jane Kluis' (*densi-thunbergii*)

'JANE KLUIS' JAPANESE RED PINE

PLANT TYPE:	Evergreen
ZONE:	4–8
FLOWER/FRUIT:	Starts with nice red buds but no cones
HABIT/FOLIAGE:	Dwarf, flat-topped globe; bright green two-needled pine
HEIGHT:	2–3 feet (ACS classification: Dwarf)
WIDTH/SPREAD:	3–4 feet
LIGHT:	Full sun
SOIL:	Average to rich, evenly moist, slightly acidic
CARE:	Easy—needs only occasional pinching of new growth in spring.
USES:	Foundation, specimen, mixed border, small space, formal ball shape
PROBLEMS:	None
INSIDER'S TIPS:	The rich green color stands out on this pine, and needles are softer and not so prickly. This could be a good substitute for globe forms of *Pinus strobus* (white pine), which can decline.
COMBINES WITH:	*Phlox paniculata* 'Fairest One' or 'Katherine', *Iris pallida* 'Variegata', *Euphorbia dulcis* 'Chameleon', *Heuchera* 'Midnight Claret'

Pinus leucodermis 'Green Bun'

'GREEN BUN' BOSNIAN PINE

PLANT TYPE:	Evergreen
ZONE:	4–7
FLOWER/FRUIT:	Although reported to have blue-purple cones, I have been unable to observe any on this plant over the past three years.
HABIT/FOLIAGE:	Slow-growing, roundy-moundy shape; rich green needles hold color well all season but are very stiff and sharp
HEIGHT:	3–4 feet in 10 years (ACS classification: Dwarf)
WIDTH/SPREAD:	3–4 feet
LIGHT:	Full sun
SOIL:	Rich, moist, well-drained
CARE:	'Green Bun' is so slow-growing that pruning is usually not necessary. The candles (new growth tips) could be pinched in half in spring.
USES:	Low hedge, evergreen accent, small space, foundation
PROBLEMS:	Beware of getting pricked by the sharp needles
INSIDER'S TIPS:	This Bosnian pine looks fresh in every season. You may also want to plant this to deter animals from your garden beds.
COMBINES WITH:	*Miscanthus sinensis* 'Kaskade', *Malva alcea* 'Fastigiata', *Perovskia atriplicifolia* 'Little Spire', *Hydrangea paniculata* 'Little Lamb'

Pinus mugo 'Aurea'

GOLDEN MUGO PINE

PLANT TYPE:	Evergreen
ZONE:	2–7
FLOWER/FRUIT:	Prominent yellow buds in winter
HABIT/FOLIAGE:	Densely globular form; stiff, medium-green needles become yellow-gold in late fall through winter; a two-needle pine
HEIGHT:	3–6 feet in 10–15 years (ACS classification: Dwarf)
WIDTH/SPREAD:	3–6 feet
LIGHT:	Sun to light shade
SOIL:	Rich, moist, well-drained
CARE:	Annual candling keeps this plant more densely compact—removing half of the new candle growth will cause the formation of lateral buds below the cut.
USES:	Winter interest, small space, textural contrast
PROBLEMS:	Susceptible to tip blight
INSIDER'S TIPS:	May be found grafted to a small tree to become a standard form. This will also give more planting space in the garden. The smallest mugo I have seen is *Pinus mugo* 'Mops', with densely compacted dark green needles on shortened stems.
COMBINES WITH:	*Scilla sibirica, Aster novae-angliae* 'Purple Dome' or 'Alert', *Campanula carpatica* 'Samantha', *Rosa* 'White Carpet'

Pinus parviflora 'Ibo-can'

'IBO-CAN' JAPANESE WHITE PINE

PLANT TYPE:	Evergreen
ZONE:	4–7
FLOWER/FRUIT:	Reportedly red-brown cones born on the ends of branches
HABIT/FOLIAGE:	Narrowly pyramidal with upswept branches and a loose-looking, open pattern; the twisted blue needles show white undersides and are in groups of five
HEIGHT:	4–5 feet in 10 years (ACS classification: Dwarf)
WIDTH/SPREAD:	4–5 feet
LIGHT:	Full sun
SOIL:	Rich, moist, well-drained
CARE:	When first planted, attention must be paid to consistent soil moisture.
USES:	Specimen, color accent, clay and salt tolerant.
PROBLEMS:	None
INSIDER'S TIPS:	This is a good "see-through" plant. It also compliments all plants around it. Used here with *Acer shirasawanum* 'Aureum' in the fall garden of Brent Markus. There are many other cultivars worth trying—choose them by form and needle color. Dirr mentions that the species shows salt tolerance in testing.
COMBINES WITH:	*Tulipa* 'Peachblossum', *Leucanthemum* x *superbum* 'Becky', *Salvia* x *superba* 'May Night', *Rosa* 'Carefree Wonder'

Pinus strobus 'Pendula'

WEEPING WHITE PINE

PLANT TYPE:	Evergreen
ZONE:	3–7
FLOWER/FRUIT:	Typical long, narrow, light brown cones on the ends of branches
HABIT/FOLIAGE:	Form can vary from low and broad to a conical, slender cascade; branches are pendulous and twisting; soft bluish-green needles in clusters of five
HEIGHT:	More than 15 feet in 10–15 years (ACS classification: Large)
WIDTH/SPREAD:	Highly dependent on training
LIGHT:	Sun to light shade
SOIL:	Rich, moist, well-drained
CARE:	Knowing that this becomes a large plant with growth of up to 12 inches per year, be prepared to prune and shape this pine to fit your garden space. The pendulous, twisting branches respond well to training.
USES:	Specimen, backdrop, unusual shape
PROBLEMS:	May be chlorotic in very alkaline soils (high pH); not tolerant of air pollution or salt
INSIDER'S TIPS:	Every plant seems to develop its own individual shape (Dirr calls this "personality"). But too many unusual shapes in a garden can be disconcerting! Shown here with *Chamaecyparis obtusa* 'Kosteri'.
COMBINES WITH:	*Rosa* 'Golden Wings', *Miscanthus sinensis* 'Variegatus', *Rhododendron* 'Olga Mezitt'

Pinus sylvestris 'Spaan's Fastigiate'
SPAAN'S COLUMNAR SCOTCH PINE

PLANT TYPE:	Evergreen
ZONE:	3–7
FLOWER/FRUIT:	Small cones only present on older plants; they begin red, turn green, and finally age to brown in the second summer
HABIT/FOLIAGE:	Slow-growing compact, columnar form with orange, peeling bark; stiff, twisted, blue-green needles in pairs
HEIGHT:	6–10 feet in 10–15 years (ACS classification: Intermediate)
WIDTH/SPREAD:	6–8 feet in 10 years
LIGHT:	Full sun
SOIL:	Most soils as long as they are well drained
CARE:	Candling will assure a more dense, compact habit over time. According to www.conifersociety.org, "When pruning pines, be aware that pines lack buds along the stem. Buds are only present at the tip of the current season's growth, so the time to prune pines is in the spring."
USES:	Small space, foundation, hedge, color accent
PROBLEMS:	None
INSIDER'S TIPS:	Choose your conifers to fit your garden. There will be a color and size to fit every space. And once you get started, you will soon be addicted. This pine is said to be more resilient to the weight of snow and ice than others are.
COMBINES WITH:	*Phlox paniculata* 'Laura', *Calamagrostis* x *acutiflora* 'Karl Foerster', *Lychnis chalcedonica*

Prunus laurocerasus 'Otto Luyken'

'OTTO LUYKEN' ENGLISH LAUREL

PLANT TYPE:	Broadleaf evergreen
ZONE:	6–9
FLOWER/FRUIT:	Fragrant white flower spikes in May; purple/black fruit
HABIT/FOLIAGE:	Compact globe; glossy, dark green ovals are evergreen, resembling bay leaves
HEIGHT:	3–4 feet
WIDTH/SPREAD:	3–4 feet
LIGHT:	Sun to part shade
SOIL:	Average, well-drained
CARE:	Responds well to regular pruning. Shearing will ruin the look of the leaves.
USES:	Foundation, hedge, background, evergreen
PROBLEMS:	None
INSIDER'S TIPS:	OK, this is one of those plants I have been wanting to try! Soon, I hope. I like to find out for myself that a plant is not truly hardy in my Zone 5 garden.
COMBINES WITH:	*Aster divaricatus*, *Iris pallida* 'Variegata', *Astilbe simplicifolia* 'Darwin's Snow Sprite', *Carex conica* 'Gold Fountains'

Taxus cuspidata 'Bright Gold'

'BRIGHT GOLD' JAPANESE YEW

PLANT TYPE:	Evergreen
ZONE:	4–7
FLOWER/FRUIT:	Red berry-like fruit (arils) on mature plants
HABIT/FOLIAGE:	Upright oval shape; flat needles have vertical green and yellow stripes
HEIGHT:	6–9 feet in 10–15 years (ACS classification: Intermediate)
WIDTH/SPREAD:	Width is somewhat less than the height
LIGHT:	Shade, part shade
SOIL:	Average, well-drained
CARE:	Prune as necessary to maintain size. Prune out any winter damage.
USES:	Woodland highlight, color accent, specimen, all-season interest
PROBLEMS:	May burn in too much sun
INSIDER'S TIPS:	From what I have seen of this plant, it seems to be a smaller intermediate size, at about 4–5 feet tall. And being a shade-tolerant evergreen, it has an all-season appeal and shows up in shade because of its yellow variegation.
COMBINES WITH:	*Chelone lyonii* 'Hot Lips', *Hosta fluctuans* 'Variegata' ('Sagae'), *Heucherella* x 'Viking Ship', *Astilbe* x *arendsii* 'Bridal Veil'

Taxus cuspidata 'Nana Aurescens'

DWARF GOLD JAPANESE YEW

© Ed Lyon

PLANT TYPE:	Evergreen
ZONE:	4–7
FLOWER/FRUIT:	Red berry-like fruit called arils only on mature plants
HABIT/FOLIAGE:	Low, spreading form; yellow, flat needles in spring on new growth become medium-green later in summer in shaded sites
HEIGHT:	3–6 feet in 10–15 years (ACS classification: Dwarf)
WIDTH/SPREAD:	Wider spreading than it is high
LIGHT:	Sun, part shade, shade
SOIL:	Average, well-drained
CARE:	Very easy care!
USES:	Woodland highlight, color accent, edger, all-season interest
PROBLEMS:	Variable color in full shade
INSIDER'S TIPS:	I have yet to see this plant get to more than 18–24 inches tall! I wonder if it doesn't classify as miniature. New young plants appear to be more globe-shaped than spreading, so give this a little time to mature.
COMBINES WITH:	*Tulipa* 'Angelique', *Aquilegia longissima* 'Maxistar', *Hosta fortunei* 'Aureomarginata', *Astilbe japonica* 'Bremen'

Taxus x *media* 'Flushing'

'FLUSHING' ANGLO-JAPANESE YEW

PLANT TYPE:	Evergreen
ZONE:	4–7
FLOWER/FRUIT:	Bright red berries (arils) when mature
HABIT/FOLIAGE:	Tight, very narrow, upright column—tends to be narrower than 'Beanpole' or 'Sentinalis'; dark green, glossy needles are very flat
HEIGHT:	6–15 feet in 10–15 years (ACS classification: Intermediate)
WIDTH/SPREAD:	18 inches
LIGHT:	Sun, part shade, shade
SOIL:	Rich, moist, well-drained
CARE:	Its very narrow width will not need pruning.
USES:	Shade tolerant, exclamation point, narrow hedge, small spaces
PROBLEMS:	May need tying in the winter
INSIDER'S TIPS:	The shape gives the feeling of an exclamation point in the garden and acts as an evergreen focal point, especially in the woodland garden.
COMBINES WITH:	*Miscanthus sinensis* 'Morning Light', *Hemerocallis* 'Pink Lavender Appeal', *Filipendula ulmaria* 'Aurea'

Taxus × *media* 'Margarita', 'Geers'

'MARGARITA' ANGLO-JAPANESE YEW

PLANT TYPE:	Evergreen
ZONE:	4–7
FLOWER/FRUIT:	This yew has the possibility of red fruit, but I have not observed it
HABIT/FOLIAGE:	Low, mounding form; lime-green, flat needles hold color all year long
HEIGHT:	4–5 feet in 10 years
WIDTH/SPREAD:	4–5 feet
LIGHT:	Sun, part shade, shade
SOIL:	Average, well-drained
CARE:	Easy—this is a slow-grower. Avoid soggy soils.
USES:	Short hedge (parterre), four-season interest, edger, shade tolerant
PROBLEMS:	None
INSIDER'S TIPS:	This is so new that it hasn't gotten an American Conifer Society classification; I'm guessing it may be considered a miniature. In this picture, 'Margarita' is under 2 feet tall.
COMBINES WITH:	*Hemerocallis* 'Siloam Tiny Tim', *Platycodon grandiflorus* 'Sentimental Blue', *Geranium endressii* 'Wargrave Pink'

Taxus × *media* 'Sentinalis' ('Sentinel')

'SENTINEL' ANGLO-JAPANESE YEW

PLANT TYPE:	Evergreen
ZONE:	4–7
FLOWER/FRUIT:	Red cuplike berries (arils)—of the columnar yews, this has the most fruit
HABIT/FOLIAGE:	Narrow, upright column; flat, dark green needles are glossy
HEIGHT:	8 feet in 10 years (ACS classification: Intermediate)
WIDTH/SPREAD:	2 feet
LIGHT:	Sun, part shade, shade
SOIL:	Rich, evenly moist, well-drained
CARE:	Prune any winterkill.
USES:	Shade tolerant, exclamation point, narrow hedge
PROBLEMS:	May need tying at top to prevent damage from heavy winter snows
INSIDER'S TIPS:	It is interesting to see this young 'Sentinel' yew next to the dwarf Alberta spruce in its maturity. Remember: Size is relative! Even more narrow is *Taxus* × *media* 'Flushing', maturing at 18 inches wide.
COMBINES WITH:	*Aruncus dioicus, Hakonechloa macra* 'Aureola', *Astilbe simplicifolia* 'Praecox Alba', *Rosa* 'Golden Showers'

Taxus × *media* 'Tauntonii'

TAUNTON YEW

PLANT TYPE:	Evergreen
ZONE:	4–8
FLOWER/FRUIT:	Often has red berries (arils)
HABIT/FOLIAGE:	Densely mounded medium-sized shape; glossy, dark green needles that hold their color throughout the winter
HEIGHT:	3–4 feet
WIDTH/SPREAD:	3–5 feet
LIGHT:	Sun, part shade, shade
SOIL:	Rich, moist, well-drained
CARE:	It's easily pruned to shape, but it develops a very regular ball shape if left alone.
USES:	Reliable, shade tolerant, foundation
PROBLEMS:	Deer love to browse all yews
INSIDER'S TIPS:	This is my favorite all-purpose yew! I know, yews are as common as can be, but 'Tauntonii' has very good winter color and is widely adaptable.
COMBINES WITH:	*Dryopteris goldiana, Hosta* 'Brim Cup', *Digitalis ambigua, Corydalis lutea, Astilbe* × *arendsii* 'Ellie'

Thuja occidentalis 'DeGroot's Spire'

'DeGroot's Spire' ARBORVITAE

PLANT TYPE:	Evergreen
ZONE:	3–7
FLOWER/FRUIT:	Little noticed
HABIT/FOLIAGE:	Extremely narrow column is very dense and slow growing; rich green twisted fans become bronze in winter
HEIGHT:	6–8 feet in 10–15 years (ACS classification: Dwarf)
WIDTH/SPREAD:	1–2 feet, possibly 4 feet in 20 years
LIGHT:	Sun to light shade
SOIL:	Rich, moist, well-drained
CARE:	Easy—you will only need to trim out any winterkill.
USES:	Small space, architecture accent, winter interest
PROBLEMS:	None
INSIDER'S TIPS:	Dwarf-conifer nurseryman Ed Lyon states, "Conifers do not perform well with other plants touching or shading them. The lack of sun and trapped humidity will cause the foliage affected to die, and it will *not* grow back next season." The 'DeGroot's Spires' shown here are in Brent Markus's garden as "tuck ins" with Japanese maples.
COMBINES WITH:	*Lysimachia nummularia* 'Aurea', *Callirhoë involucrata*, *Veronica* 'Minuet', *Viola* 'Dancing Geisha'

Thuja occidentalis 'Emerald', 'Smaragd'

'EMERALD' EASTERN OR AMERICAN ARBORVITAE

PLANT TYPE:	Evergreen
ZONE:	3–7
FLOWER/FRUIT:	Little noticed
HABIT/FOLIAGE:	Dense, narrow conical (almost columnar) form; bright, emerald green fans hold color through winter
HEIGHT:	10–15 feet
WIDTH/SPREAD:	3–4 feet
LIGHT:	Sun to light shade
SOIL:	Average to rich, moist but not wet, adapts to both sand and clay
CARE:	Easy—no need to prune, as the girth is not huge. According to www.conifer society.org, all arborvitaes "form a thin shell of green growth surrounding a zone of leafless twigs and limbs. Take care not to open this shell during pruning, since the unsightly scar may not be covered for many years."
USES:	Tight spaces, hedge, screening, architectural accent
PROBLEMS:	Could burn and brown when exposed to drying wind
INSIDER'S TIPS:	This is a favorite hedge or screen for me in a narrow space (as in a side yard with a path). After years of trying to maintain the width of 'Techny' arborvitae, I finally replaced mine. Just remember that arborvitaes are difficult to maintain their size with pruning. Another I would consider for its columnar form and rich, green color is *Thuja* 'Brandon'.
COMBINES WITH:	*Narcissus* 'Carlton', *Tulipa* 'Ollioules', *Myosotis sylvatica*, *Alchemilla mollis*, *Veronica spicata* 'Lilac Karina'

Thuja occidentalis 'Filiformis'

THREADLEAFED EASTERN ARBORVITAE

PLANT TYPE:	Evergreen
ZONE:	3–7
FLOWER/FRUIT:	I have not observed cones on this plant
HABIT/FOLIAGE:	Pyramidal shape with drooping branches—an unusual, overall weeping pyramid; green needles clasp tightly to tan stems, become bronzed in winter
HEIGHT:	6–10 feet in 10–15 years (ACS classification: Intermediate)
WIDTH/SPREAD:	6–8 feet in 10–15 years
LIGHT:	Full sun
SOIL:	Rich, moist, well-drained
CARE:	Please plan for the ultimate size of this plant and be mindful that arborvitaes are not readily pruned. Arborvitaes, junipers, and false cypress (*Chamaecyparis*) are the most difficult to maintain at a particular size. This group's buds are present only where there are green leaves; a branch cut back to a non-leafy region will not produce new foliage.
USES:	Architectural accent, winter interest, background
PROBLEMS:	Hard to find—a collector's plant
INSIDER'S TIPS:	If you need something really unusual, this could be the plant for your garden. Plant it among other plants with some stature.
COMBINES WITH:	*Gaura lindheimeri, Iris sibirica* 'Orville Fay', *Phlox* x 'Chattahoochie', *Solidago rugosa* 'Fireworks'

Thuja occidentalis 'Golden Globe'

'GOLDEN GLOBE' ARBORVITAE

PLANT TYPE:	Evergreen
ZONE:	3–7
FLOWER/FRUIT:	Little noticed
HABIT/FOLIAGE:	Globular to upright oval form; non-burning, golden yellow lacy foliage
HEIGHT:	3–6 feet in 10–15 years [ACS classification: Dwarf]
WIDTH/SPREAD:	3–6 feet in 10–15 years
LIGHT:	Sun to light shade
SOIL:	Rich, moist, well-drained
CARE:	Easy—only prune out any winterkill. Do not plant close to others, as other plants are likely to shade the lower branches of 'Golden Globe'.
USES:	Color accent, evergreen, small garden, formal garden
PROBLEMS:	Not as orange-tipped as 'Rheingold'
INSIDER'S TIPS:	Using the dwarf evergreens as color accents is fun, but don't get carried away with combinations of perennials that might shade out and kill the evergreen foliage. Also, using too many plants with yellow foliage can be overwhelming to the viewer. A little dab will do ya'!
COMBINES WITH:	*Alchemilla mollis, Physostegia virginiana* 'Miss Manners', *Geranium clarkei* 'Kashmir White', *Hemerocallis* 'Janice Brown'

Thuja (*Platycladus*) *orientalis* 'Beverlyensis'

BEVERLY HILLS GOLDEN ARBORVITAE

PLANT TYPE:	Evergreen
ZONE:	(5) 6–8
FLOWER/FRUIT:	I have not observed cones
HABIT/FOLIAGE:	Narrow pyramidal form; soft, bright yellow, fernlike fans are displayed on a vertical plane, becoming yellow-green in winter
HEIGHT:	8–10 feet in 10 years (ACS classification: Intermediate)
WIDTH/SPREAD:	6–8 feet in 10 years
LIGHT:	Sun to light shade
SOIL:	Average to rich, evenly moist
CARE:	Arborvitaes, junipers, and false cypress (*Chamaecyparis*) are the most difficult to maintain at a particular size. A branch cut back to a non-leafy region will not produce new foliage.
USES:	Color accent, winter color, specimen, background
PROBLEMS:	Will need protection to grow this one in Zone 5
INSIDER'S TIPS:	I fell in love with this beautifully colored arborvitae because of the unusual arrangement (texture) of its fernlike fans. As yet, I have been unable to buy my own. It will definitely need "the right-place treatment" because of its ultimate size and its need for protection in Zone 5. I will only buy it if I can afford to lose it—see the Introduction.
COMBINES WITH:	*Digitalis grandiflora, Iris sibirica* 'Pink Haze', *Phlox paniculata* 'Bright Eyes'

Tsuga canadensis

CANADIAN OR EASTERN HEMLOCK

PLANT TYPE:	Native evergreen
ZONE:	4–7 (8)
FLOWER/FRUIT:	Tiny, light brown cones
HABIT/FOLIAGE:	Slow-growing, slightly open, pyramidal form; drooping branches; medium-green, glossy needles are only $1/2$ inch long
HEIGHT:	6–15 feet in 10 years (ACS classification: Intermediate)
WIDTH/SPREAD:	5–6 feet, wider after 10 years
LIGHT:	Part shade
SOIL:	Sandy, well-drained loam
CARE:	This is a shade-tolerant species that can be sheared for denseness or used as a hedge. Pruning just before spring growth will assure that cuts will be covered by new growth. Rich Eyre of Rich's Foxwillow Pines warns, "Hemlocks do not tolerate wind, heavy clay soil, drought, or hot afternoon sun."
USES:	Hedge, shade tolerant, evergreen, architecture
PROBLEMS:	Easily drowns in heavy clay
INSIDER'S TIPS:	Growth rates seem to vary throughout the United States—very old hemlocks can be 100 feet tall! Despite this, hemlocks are very popular because of the soft, graceful habit and their shade tolerance. If sited in too much shade, they become very open and misshapen. A white-tipped cultivar with a smaller pyramidal habit is *Tsuga canadensis* 'Gentsch White'.
COMBINES WITH:	Shown in photo with *Hydrangea arborescens, Pachysandra terminalis*; others to combine with are *Hosta* 'Fair Maiden', *Brunnera macrophylla* 'Dawson's White', *Iris pallida* 'Variegata'

Tsuga canadensis 'Jeddeloh'

'JEDDELOH' DWARF HEMLOCK

PLANT TYPE:	Evergreen
ZONE:	4–7 (8)
FLOWER/FRUIT:	Small, light brown cones
HABIT/FOLIAGE:	Dwarf, rounded bird's nest (indented top) form; bright green needles are glossy and not sharp
HEIGHT:	12–30 inches in 10 years (ACS classification: Dwarf)
WIDTH/SPREAD:	2–3 feet
LIGHT:	Part shade
SOIL:	Average to rich, moist but not wet
CARE:	From www.conifersociety.org: "Yews and hemlocks are the easiest to prune. Both have abundant buds on old and new wood; these develop into twigs when the wood above is cut. Pruning in the spring just before the new growth begins allows the pruning cuts to be covered with new growth very rapidly, preventing the 'just sheared' look."
USES:	Shade garden, slow growing, definitive form
PROBLEMS:	Will not tolerate very wet soils
INSIDER'S TIPS:	There is an evergreen conifer for every garden. It's every gardener's opportunity to collect ones that work as the "right plant for the right place."
COMBINES WITH:	*Tiarella* 'Iron Butterfly', *Hosta* 'Hi Ho Silver', *Heucherella* x 'Viking Ship', *Chelone lyoni* 'Hot Lips'

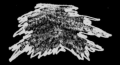

Tsuga canadensis 'Pendula'

WEEPING HEMLOCK

PLANT TYPE:	Evergreen
ZONE:	3b–7
FLOWER/FRUIT:	Small, light brown cones
HABIT/FOLIAGE:	Weeping form staked to maintain a narrow, pendulous character
HEIGHT:	More than 15 feet in 10–15 years (ACS classification: Large)
WIDTH/SPREAD:	Dependent on training
LIGHT:	Part shade
SOIL:	Rich, moist, well-drained, somewhat acidic
CARE:	Weeping hemlock requires training onto a stake, as well as on-going pruning. Pruning should be done in early spring before new growth.
USES:	Focal point, unusual accent, winter interest
PROBLEMS:	Get your soil and light requirements right, or this plant dies
INSIDER'S TIPS:	A collector's evergreen that is easier to manage than weeping forms of pine or spruce. Shown here in the Chicago Botanic Garden rock garden; notice it is in the background, where it will be shaded in late afternoon. It is sited where it has good soil drainage.
COMBINES WITH:	*Veronica incana, Sedum sexangulare, Achillea* x 'Appleblossom', *Brunnera machrophylla*

CHAPTER 13

Let's GET STARTED

© Ed Lyon

Now that you've read all about the shrubs and small trees available, it's time to choose the plants that best fit your garden. And the most important gardening tip I can share is: Begin by selecting shrubs and small trees to fit the space available.

Size is relative! Know what you are planting. This is a different lilac standard than appeared on page 57. The same plant allowed to grow to mature size is huge!

Shrubs and small trees can be expensive and difficult to move or remove if they outgrow their location, and they may require time-consuming pruning to maintain a desired size. Save yourself time, energy, and money by selecting plants by their mature height and width. Choose a plant that grows naturally into the shape you need for that space—columnar, pyramidal, round, upright vase, weeping.

Other limiting factors to plan for now are overhangs and proximity to walks, driveways, patios, buildings, or surrounding plantings. And, finally, consider the maintenance factors for fruits, nuts, and seedpods, as they are likely to be messy near patios, walkways, entrances, and driveways.

Poor pruning results in misshapen plants. This juniper was planted too close to the foundation and a roof overhang.

A classic example of what not to do is the Colorado spruce planted too close to the house. When purchased and installed, it might have been 4–5' tall and about 3' wide. But in 10 or 15 years, this spruce will have a spread of 15' and be over 30' tall. If planted only 6' from the house, it will soon need pruning away from the house and become a misshapen giant.

Not enough space or light. The Norway maple outgrew the blue spruces, and the lack of light produced a spruce without branches on one side.

Other pruning issues are most obvious in winter for deciduous shrubs and trees. Without leaves to hide the dense, new tip growth, the effects of shearing are particularly noticeable. Hedges have a top-heavy look; bushes with colored stems have color only at the top; and sheared, spreading trees such as crabapples, redbuds, dogwoods, and serviceberries look more like giant toadstools than graceful trees!

Sheared, not pruned—all the new tip growth is the unsightly end product. Observe branching patterns in the winter and see the pruning mistakes.

So think before you buy and/or plant. Don't just look at the light and soil conditions for the site—consider the size and shape of the plant needed.

The Scoop on Soils

Everyone wishes for that perfect soil—rich, crumbly loam that is moist but well drained! It almost seems like an oxymoron. How do you get both moist and well drained? It's in the gardener's best interest to work to provide the best soil environment for plant survival.

Most plant loss can be attributed to improper or poor drainage. HEAVY CLAY SOIL can act like a water saucer, causing plant roots to drown from lack of oxygen. Since both water and oxygen are needed to sustain plant life, add coarse composted material to open up the finely compacted clay particles. This will allow oxygen and water to percolate through the soil and allow plant roots to grow downward. Each time a new planting hole is dug (and even if only planting bulbs), mix one-third coarse, decomposed compost into the existing heavy clay. My personal recommendation to improve drainage under the roots is to add clay soil conditioner (one to three handfuls dependent on the size of the hole). Soil conditioner is a crushed ceramic with a consistency similar to kitty litter and is readily available at garden centers. Both the composted materials and the soil conditioner help open up pore space in heavy clay soil and greatly improve its drainage.

SANDY SOIL has the opposite problem; it drains away too quickly, leaving the roots searching for water. The second cause of plant loss is not enough water. Sandy soil also does not hold nutrients well. These problems will both be improved with the addition of compost as well as topsoil, about a third of each.

In the fall, continue to "make dirt" by layering ground-up fallen leaves back onto all garden beds. Let the worms, snow, and frost break down this SHEET COMPOST over winter, and in spring you will have an already-decomposing mulch in place that will not need to be worked into the soil. By letting nature do the work, in spring about 50% of the sheet compost will have broken down to increase soil friability while the rest will serve as a moisture-conserving mulch.

No discussion of soil is complete without a little understanding of the pH, or ALKALINE VS. ACID SOILS. Bill Cullina, in *Native Trees, Shrubs, and Vines,* has the best discussion of soil pH: "Acid-loving plants do not really love acids; rather, they have evolved on a diet rich in iron but low in most other nutrients, so they are 'lazy' about scavenging iron." For those plants that need only slightly acidic soil, I have found that they will do quite nicely in soil that has been improved over time with compost and in which drainage is good. Where soil is not waterlogged and "squeezing" out oxygen, dogwoods, fothergillas, iteas, magnolias, and Japanese maples are thriving.

If you plan to grow plants such as azaleas, rhododendrons, mountain laurels, and pieris and have alkaline clay soil, some changes in the soil will need to be made. See the following discussion on planting.

Planting New Plants

Make sure you have the planting location decided first. Place your newly acquired plant in the garden and move it around until you know that the light is correct, that it will fit the space at maturity, and that it works well with the surrounding plants in terms of color and texture. Even if it takes a few weeks to make a decision, save time and the plant's energy by not having to dig and move at a later date.

My general system for planting is as follows:

1. Dig a "good" hole, one that is about 2" deeper and wider than the root ball.
2. Mix excavated soil with one-third coarse composted material.
   - For clay: also add clay soil conditioner or very coarse sand
   - For sand: add one-third topsoil
3. Remove container or burlap and "tease" the root ends out and downward. It's OK to lose some roots in the process.
4. Put soil mix into bottom of hole and set root ball so that it is even with the soil level.

Take the burlap off before planting. The center yew did not have the burlap removed, and the roots never had a chance to move out into the soil to get established. Result: plant death.

5. Fill outer edge of hole and water in the plant. Then add the remaining soil as watered soil sinks in around roots.
6. A mulch of 1–2" of compost will help conserve soil moisture.

And, of course, there are the exceptions. Rhododendrons and azaleas planted in clay soil require you to:

1. Dig a shallower hole three-times the width of the root ball. The idea in heavy clay soil is to plant high.
2. Mix excavated soil with a very coarse compost such as "pine fines," which improves both pH and drainage.
3. After removing the container or burlap, vigorously cut away the bottom half of the root ball.
   • Trust me — this works!
   • This drastic treatment will encourage/force the roots to move out into the soil.
   • Rhododendrons are shallowly rooted, and roots only occupy the top 8" of the soil.
4. Add soil mix to bottom of the hole along with a generous handful of Ironite (urea, ferrous oxide, ferric sulfate).
5. Place the plant so that it is higher than the existing soil line.
6. Fill with soil mix, water in, and add remaining soil so that roots make contact with new soil.
7. A coarse mulch to 3" of pine bark will allow air circulation and help maintain soil moisture.

• Mound mulch at the edge of the planting hole so that water drains into the plant.
• Do not mulch around base of the plant.

With all newly planted specimens, make sure they receive adequate moisture throughout the first growing season and remove weeds, which will compete for this moisture. Hand weeding is particularly important around shallow-rooted plants such as rhododendrons—take care to not damage the root systems. Mulch will also help to suppress weeds.

Even at maturity, all plants need water to thrive and grow! And in years with low rainfall, the gardener needs to provide supplemental water.

Pruning

I can't help repeating this important gardening rule: *Choose shrubs and trees to fit the site!* If you have chosen your plant material properly, only minimal pruning will be necessary. Learn by observing well-pruned examples at a botanic garden, take pruning classes, or have a pruning expert teach you.

Pruning at the Chicago Botanic Garden, by the professionals.

The key to good pruning is to WORK WITH THE NATURAL HABIT of the plant being pruned. Some people call proper pruning an art. And this art must be learned if you do not choose to hire a professional. Take time when pruning.

Step back from the plant often and consider each cut to only improve the natural habit.

Prune to shape! Observe good pruning techniques at a local botanic garden.

PRUNING OUT DEAD WOOD is an obvious task. These cuts are best done as needed and will help maintain the health of the entire plant. Pruning in late winter or early spring is easiest for seeing where to prune deciduous trees and shrubs. This dormant-season pruning will also result in better spring growth.

Managed pruning the Japanese way. Annual tight pruning and branch thinning produce a rigorously trained tree.

THINNING smaller trees, such as crabapples, may be easier in the dormant season, when the branching pattern can be seen clearly. But spring is still a good time to prune out water sprouts or suckers and to open the branching pattern for increased light and air.

Which stems need renewal? When colored-stemmed dogwoods are only sheared at the top, the older stems lose their color, becoming brown. The brown stems should be renewal pruned.

Renewal pruning of a yellow-stemmed dogwood.

RENEWAL PRUNING is the selective removal of older plant stems. For the colored-stemmed dogwoods, willows, kerrias, spireas, and barberries, cut one-third of the oldest stems close to the ground each year. Selectively prune the old, less colorful branches from different sections of the entire plant so that all cuts are not made from one side. These colored-stemmed shrubs might also be stooled. STOOLING is a term used to describe another method of renewal pruning. All stems are cut back close to the ground in early spring. The resultant dense new growth produces more stems and somewhat larger leaves with more intense coloration, as in the purple-leaf smoke shrub.

Plants that BLOOM ON OLD WOOD should be pruned right after blooming because they form buds for the following year's blossoms about a month after their bloom time. These shrubs are generally spring bloomers, such as azaleas, rhododendrons, forsythias, lilacs, and viburnums.

A close-up look at a stooled *Heptacodium miconioides*.

PRUNING FOR CONIFERS should be done during the active growing season to avoid tip burn since evergreens are never fully dormant in the winter. If pruned in spring, the new growth will cover pruning cuts. Yews and hemlocks are the easiest to prune and can even be sheared into hedges, as long as some air and light get into the interior. Firs, spruce, and cedars can tolerate pruning when the new growth is soft, but selection of the more slow-growing cultivars (dwarf conifers) are better suited to the garden setting.

Pines need more careful pruning and/or selection. The only buds are at the tips of branches and become soft new growth in spring, called candles. CANDLING (pinching or cutting this new growth) will result in a more compact plant.

Junipers, arborvitaes, and false cypresses are the most difficult to manage by pruning. Buds only develop where there are green leaves/needles. Branches cut back to leafless twigs will not produce new growth. New growth will also not develop on branches shaded by other plant material growing too closely.

Other special pruning needs are noted under "Care" with each plant portrait. For further information on pruning, I have often used *Easy, Practical Pruning* by Barbara Ellis (Peter Smith, 1999) and the Web site for the American Conifer Society, www.conifersociety.org.

CHAPTER 14

EASY "YOU CAN PLAN" GARDEN CHARTS

While deciding which shrubs and small trees to choose for my very normal-sized, suburban garden, I created a system of looking at these plants by their seasonal characteristics. And because of limited space, I wanted to pick plants that had more than just one season of interest.

I started by simply making a chart of the flowers, foliage color, fall fruit, fall color, and winter interest/ color. Then I filled in the information for each plant I was interested in, and I could readily see which plants had features covering the most seasons.

The first chart, "Choosing Plants for Continuous Color," is where to start. The following charts on crabapples, viburnums, and conifers provide a way to differentiate the various cultivars and species and give you quick answers for which shrub or small tree can best fit into your garden. I have also left a section of this "Choosing Plants" chart blank, so you can photocopy the chart and fill in your own favorites.

Choosing Plants for Continuous Color

	BLOOMS	COLORED FOLIAGE	FALL COLOR	FRUIT	WINTER INTEREST	STRUCTURE & FORM	USE
Acer shirasawanum 'Aureum'	Red-purple in April	Yellow to chartreuse	Bright red	Red samara	Layered branching	Columnar	Highlight
Acer palmatum 'Crimson Queen'	Small red-purple in May	Crimson	Scarlet	Red samara	Newer branches wine red	Cascading	Highlight
Chamaecyparis nootkatensis 'Pendula'	N/A	Dark green	Evergreen	N/A	Evergreen	Narrow, weeping	Winter evergreen
Cornus sericea 'Silver and Gold'	Small cream clusters	Variegated	Insignificant	Few bluish white berries	Yellow stems	Upright vase shape	4-season color
Fagus sylvatica 'Purple Fountain'	N/A	Purple all season	Purple	N/A	Branch outline	Narrow weeper	Form
Forsythia x *intermedia* 'Gold Leaf'	Yellow, very early	Yellow	Bronzed yellow	N/A	Light tan stems	Weeping vase shape	Glows in shade
Hydrangea paniculata 'Kyushu'	July–Oct.	Glossy green	Yellow-gold	N/A	Dried flowers	Upright vase shape	Long blooming
Hydrangea quercifolia	June–July	Green oak leaves	Red/ burgundy	Red	Dried flowers	Large roundy-moundy	3-season interest
Itea virginica 'Henry's Garnet'	June, fragrant	Light green	Scarlet	N/A	Holds fall color into January	Arching stems	Shade tolerant
Juniperus communis 'Gold Cone'	N/A	Yellow over blue	Blue-green	Tiny green berries	Evergreen	Narrow cone	Winter evergreen
Physocarpus opulifolius 'Diabolo'	Cream-pink clusters	Burgundy or deep wine	Burgundy	Wine red	Peeling bark with age	Vase shape	4-season background
Picea pungens 'Glauca Globosa'	N/A	Chalky blue	Chalky blue	N/A	Evergreen	Globe	Blue highlight

	BLOOMS	COLORED FOLIAGE	FALL COLOR	FRUIT	WINTER INTEREST	STRUCTURE & FORM	USE
Rhododendron catawbiense 'Nova Zembla'	Showy crimson trusses	Broadleaf evergreen	Unchanging dark green	N/A	Evergreen	Roundy-moundy	Broadleaf evergreen
Rosa 'Knockout'	Repeating crimson	New growth burgundy	Crimson blooms	Rose hips	Rose hips	Short, upright vase	2-season color
Sambucus nigra 'Madonna'	White in spring	Yellow and green	Cream and green	Possible	Light tan stems	Arching habit to 8'	Color backdrop
Spiraea japonica 'Lemon Princess'	Pink repeats	Yellow	Orange/ bronze	Brown capsule	Red-brown stems	Roundy-moundy	4-season color
Taxus x *media* 'Tauntonii'	N/A	Evergreen	Evergreen	Red	Evergreen	Roundy-moundy	Shade tolerant
Viburnum trilobum 'Redwing'	Scented cream lacecaps for 4 weeks	Green	Purple-red	Red	Fruit persistent	Arching vase shape	Screening
Weigela florida 'Midnight Wine'	Rosy red for 4 weeks	Burgundy	Burgundy	N/A	Dense, tan stems	Roundy-moundy	Small highlight

Let's add to the list! Remember to choose plants that have at least two seasons of interest.

	BLOOMS	COLORED FOLIAGE	FALL COLOR	FRUIT	WINTER INTEREST	STRUCTURE & FORM	USE

Foliage Color

COLOR	BOTANIC NAME	COMMON NAME
Burgundy-red	*Acer palmatum* (many cultivars)	Japanese maple
	Berberis thunbergii 'Crimson Pygmy'	'Crimson Pygmy' barberry
	Berberis thunbergii 'Helmond's Pillar'	Pillar barberry
	Cercis canadensis 'Forest Pansy' (new growth)	'Forest Pansy' redbud
	Malus 'Prairifire' (new growth)	'Prairifire' crabapple
	Nandina domestica (new growth)	Heavenly bamboo
	Spiraea bumalda (new growth on most cultivars)	Bumald spirea
	Spiraea japonica 'Neon Flash' (new growth)	'Neon Flash' spirea
Pink to red	*Berberis thunbergii* 'Rosy Glow'	'Rosy Glow' barberry
	Pieris x 'Forest Flame'	Red-tinged pieris
Purple	*Berberis thunbergii* 'Concorde'	Purple globe barberry
	Berberis thunbergii 'Royal Cloak'	Purple barberry
	Cotinus coggygria 'Royal Purple'	Purple smoke bush
	Fagus sylvatica 'Purple Fountain'	Weeping purple beech
	Fagus sylvatica 'Purpurea Nana'	Dwarf purple beech
	Physocarpus opulifolius 'Diabolo'	Purple ninebark
	Prunus x *cerasifera* 'Thundercloud'	Purpleleaf plum
	Prunus x *cistena*	Purpleleaf sand cherry
	Sambucus nigra 'Black Beauty'	'Black Beauty' elderberry
	Weigela florida 'Wine & Roses'	Purpleleaf weigela
	Weigela florida 'Midnight Wine'	Dwarf purpleleaf weigela

COLOR	BOTANIC NAME	COMMON NAME
Blue	*Picea pungens* 'Glauca Globosa'	Globe blue spruce
	Picea pungens 'St. Mary's Broom'	Dwarf blue spruce
	Pinus parviflora 'Ibo-can'	Japanese white pine
Blue-green	*Chamaecyparis nootkatensis* 'Pendula'	Pendulous nootka false cypress
	Cercidiphyllum japonicum 'Pendula'	Weeping Japanese katsura tree
	Enkianthus campanulatus	Redvein enkianthus
	Fothergilla spp.	Fothergilla
	Hypericum spp.	St. John's wort
	Pinus sylvestris 'Glauca Nana'	Dwarf Scotch pine
	Salix purpurea 'Nana'	Dwarf Arctic willow
	Spiraea x *cinerea* 'Grefsheim'	Thinleaf spirea
	Spiraea betulifolia 'Tor'	Birchleaf spirea
Silver-green	*Caryopteris* x *clandonensis* 'Dark Knight'	Blue mist shrub
	Potentilla fruticosa 'Primrose Beauty'	'Primrose Beauty' bush cinquefoil
	Picea omorika 'Nana'	Dwarf Serbian spruce
	Salix alba 'Britzensis'	Red-stemmed willow
	Salix eleagnos	Rosemary willow
	Salix repens var. *argentea*	Creeping willow
	Salix x 'Flame'	Red-stemmed willow
Silver	Abies koreana 'Silberlocke'	Silver curls Korean fir
	Pyrus salicifolia 'Silver Frost'	Willowleaf pear

COLOR	BOTANIC NAME	COMMON NAME
White variegated	*Aralia elata* 'Variegata'	Japanese angelica
	Cornus alba 'Ivory Halo'	Red-stemmed dogwood
	Cornus controversa 'Variegata'	Variegated giant dogwood
	Cornus kousa 'Snow Boy'	Kousa dogwood
	Cornus sericea 'Silver and Gold'	Dogwood
	Daphne x *burkwoodii* 'Carol Mackie'	'Carol Mackie' daphne
	Deutzia gracilis 'Variegatus'	Slender deutzia
	Eleutherococcus sieboldianus 'Variegata'	Variegated fiveleaf aralia
	Kerria japonica 'Picta'	Variegated Japanese kerria
	Philadelphus coronarius 'Vareigatus'	Variegated mock orange
	Salix integra 'Hakuro Nishiki'	Dappled willow
	Sambucus nigra 'Pulverulenta'	Elderberry
	Weigela florida 'Variegata'	Weigela
Chartreuse	*Forsythia* x 'Gold Leaf'	Forsythia
	Philadelphus coronarius 'Aureus'	Mock orange
	Physocarpus opulifolius 'Dart's Golden'	Golden ninebark
	Spiraea x *bumalda* 'Golden Carpet'	Spirea
Yellow	*Acer shirasawanum* 'Aureum'	Full moon Japanese maple
	Berberis thunbergii 'Aurea'	Yellow barberry
	Berberis thunbergii 'Bonanza Gold'	Yellow barberry
	Chamaecyparis pisifera 'Golden Mop'	Threadleaf false cypress

COLOR	BOTANIC NAME	COMMON NAME
Yellow	*Choisya ternata* 'Sundance'	Mexican orange
	Ligustrum x *vicaryi*	Golden privet
	Sambucus racemosa 'Sutherland's Gold'	Elderberry
	Spiraea japonica 'Goldmound', 'Lemon Princess'	Japanese spirea
	Spirea thunbergii 'Ogon'	Thunberg spirea
	Thuja 'Golden Globe', 'Teddy'	Arborvitae
	Thuja orientalis 'Beverly Hills'	Arborvitae
	Weigela florida 'Briant's Rubidor'	Weigela
Yellow/red/bronze	*Spiraea japonica* 'Magic Carpet'	Spirea
	Spiraea japonica 'Dakota Goldcharm'	Spirea
Yellow variegated	*Cornus alternifolia* 'Golden Shadows'	Pagoda dogwood
	Cornus stolonifera 'Hedgerow's Gold'	Redosier dogwood
	Euonymus fortunei 'Emerald 'n Gold', 'Gold Splash'	'Emerald 'n Gold' winter creeper
	Sambucus nigra 'Madonna'	Elderberry

Fall Foliage Color

FALL COLOR	BOTANIC NAME	COMMON NAME
Burgundy-red	*Acer griseum*	Paperbark maple
	Aronia melanocarpa 'Grandiflora'	Black chokeberry
	Berberis thunbergii var. *atropurpurea*	Purpleleaf Japanese barberry
	Cornus alternifolia 'Golden Shadows'	'Golden Shadows' pagoda dogwood
	Cornus kousa 'Snowboy'	'Snowboy' kousa dogwood
	Crataegus crus-galli var. *inermis*	Cockspur hawthorn (thornless)
	Hydrangea quercifolia cultivars	Oakleaf hydrangea
	Hydrangea serrata 'Preziosa'	Sawtooth hydrangea
	Itea virginica cultivars	Virginia sweetspire
	Mahonia aquifolium	Oregon grape holly
	Malus 'Prairifire'	'Prairifire' crabapple
	Rhododendron 'Aglo'	'Aglo' rhododendron
	Rhododendron yedoense poukhanense 'Compacta'	Compact Korean azalea
	Spirea x *bumalda* 'Everblooming'	'Everblooming' spirea
	Viburnum plicatum var. *tomentosum* 'Mariesii', 'Watanabei'	Doublefile viburnum
	Viburnum prunifolium	Blackhaw viburnum
	Viburnum sieboldii ' Wave Crest'	Siebold viburnum
	Viburnum x 'Juddii'	Judd's viburnum
Dark maroon	*Rhododendron* 'Ginny Gee'	'Ginny Gee' rhododendron
Burgundy-purple	*Berberis thunbergii* 'Concorde'	'Concorde' barberry

FALL COLOR	BOTANIC NAME	COMMON NAME
Burgundy-purple	*Berberis thunbergii* 'Royal Cloak'	'Royal Cloak' Japanese barberry
	Cornus kousa chinensis	Kousa dogwood
	Cotoneaster apiculatus 'Nana'	Dwarf cranberry cotoneaster
	Cotinus coggygria 'Royal Purple'	'Royal Purple' smoke bush
	Deutzia gracilis 'Nikko'	'Nikko' slender deutzia
	Hydrangea quercifolia (most cultivars)	Oakleaf hydrangea
	Mahonia aquifolium	Oregon grape holly
	Physocarpus opulifolius 'Diabolo'	'Diabolo' ninebark
	Spiraea japonica 'Neon Flash'	'Neon Flash' spirea
	Viburnum carlesii 'Compactum'	Compact Korean spice viburnum
	Weigela 'Midnight Wine'	'Midnight Wine' weigela
Purple and red-purple	*Abelia* x *grandiflora*	Glossy abelia
	Acer palmatum 'Bloodgood'	'Bloodgood' Japanese maple
	Acer palmatum 'Emperor I'	'Emperor I' Japanese maple
	Cornus alba 'Alleman's Compact'	'Alleman's Compact' red-stemmed dogwood
	Cornus mas	Cornelian cherry dogwood
	Cornus mas 'Golden Glory'	'Golden Glory' Cornelian cherry dogwood
	Cornus sericea 'Flaviramea'	Yellow stemmed dogwood
	Forsythia x 'Courtasol' 'Gold Tide'	'Gold Tide' forsythia
	Hamamelis vernalis 'Autumn Embers'	'Autumn Embers' vernal witch hazel

FALL COLOR	BOTANIC NAME	COMMON NAME
Purple and red-purple	*Hydrangea serrata* 'Preziosa'	'Preziosa' sawtooth hydrangea
	Leucothoë spp.	Drooping leucothoë
	Rhododendron 'PJM'	PJM Hybrid rhododendron
	Rhododendron (Azalea) 'Northern Lights'	'Northern Lights' azalea
	Viburnum nudum 'Winterthur'	'Winterthur' possum-haw
	Viburnum prunifolium	Blackhaw viburnum
Light plum	*Spiraea betulifolia* 'Tor'	'Tor' birchleaf spirea
Red	*Acer palmatum* 'Crimson Queen'	'Crimson Queen' Japanese maple
	Acer palmatum dissectum 'Ever Red'	'Ever Red' cutleaf Japanese maple
	Acer shirasawanum 'Aureum'	Full moon maple
	Aronia arbutifolia 'Brilliantissima'	Very brilliant red chokeberry
	Berberis thunbergii 'Helmond's Pillar'	'Helmond's Pillar' barberry
	Berberis thunbergii 'Rosey Glow'	'Rosey Glow' barberry
	Cotoneaster 'Hessei'	Hesse cotoneaster
	Malus 'Satin Clouds'	'Satin Clouds' crabapple
	Rhododendron 'Aglo'	'Aglo' rhododendron
	Rhododendron 'Staccato'	'Staccato' rhododendron
	Rhododendron (Azalea) vaseyi	Pinkshell azalea
	Rhododendron viscosum	Swamp azalea
	Viburnum sieboldii 'Wave Crest'	'Wave Crest' siebold viburnum
	Viburnum trilobum 'Hah's'	'Hah's' cranberry viburnum

FALL COLOR	BOTANIC NAME	COMMON NAME
Red	*Viburnum trilobum* 'J.N. Select', 'Redwing'	'Redwing' cranberry viburnum
	Viburnum trilobum 'Wentworth'	'Wentworth' cranberry viburnum
Pink-red	*Cornus controversa* 'Variegata'	Variegated giant dogwood
	Cornus stolonifera 'Hedgerow's Gold'	'Hedgerow's Gold' dogwood
Red-orange	*Amelanchier alnifolia* 'Regent'	'Regent' serviceberry
	Aralia elata 'Aureovariegata' or 'Variegata'	Variegated Japanese angelica
	Aronia melanocarpa 'Morton' ('Iroquois Beauty')	'Morton' black chokeberry
	Aronia melanocarpa 'Viking'	Viking black chokeberry
	Berberis thunbergii 'Crimson Pygmy'	'Crimson Pygmy' barberry
	Cotinus coggygria 'Young Lady'	'Young Lady' smoke bush
	Pyrus calleryana 'Autumn Blaze'	'Autumn Blaze' callery pear
	Rhododendron yedoense poukhanense 'Compacta'	Compact Korean azalea
	Rhus aromatica 'Gro-Low'	'Gro-Low' fragrant sumac
	Rhus copallina var. *latifolia* 'Morton'	Prairie Flame shining sumac
	Spiraea japonica 'Dakota Goldcharm'	'Dakota Goldcharm' spirea
	Stewartia pseudocamellia	Japanese stewartia, camellia tree
	Viburnum dilatatum 'Cardinal Candy', 'Michael Dodge'	'Cardinal Candy' and 'Michael Dodge' linden viburnum
Yellow to red-orange	*Acer truncatum*	Purpleblow maple
	Amelanchier canadensis 'Spring Glory'	'Spring Glory' shadblow serviceberry
	Amelanchier x *grandiflora* cultivars	Apple serviceberry

FALL COLOR	BOTANIC NAME	COMMON NAME
Yellow to red-orange	*Cornus sericea* 'Midwinter Fire' (syn. 'Winter Flame')	'Midwinter Fire' dogwood
	Enkianthus campanulatus	Redvein enkianthus
	Fothergilla spp.	Fothergilla
	Hamamelis x *intermedia* 'Diana'	'Diana' witch hazel
	Prunus x 'Snofozam', 'Snow Fountains'	'Snow Fountains' weeping cherry
	Rhododendron calendulaceum	Flame azalea
	Rhus typhina 'Laciniata'	Cutleaf sumac
	Viburnum dentatum 'Blue Muffin'	'Blue Muffin' arrowwood
Orange	*Acer palmatum dissectum* 'Atropurpureum'	Red cutleaf Japanese maple
	Cotoneaster lucidus	Hedge cotoneaster
	Spirea fritschiana 'Pink Parasols'	'Pink Parasols' spirea
	Spiraea x *bumalda* 'Magic Carpet'	'Magic Carpet' spirea
	Spiraea japonica 'Neon Flash'	'Neon Flash' spirea
	Spiraea japonica 'Goldmound'	'Goldmound' Japanese spirea
	Spiraea thunbergii 'Ogon'	'Ogon' golden spirea
Gold	*Cercidiphyllum japonicum* 'Pendula'	Weeping katsura tree
	Prunus x 'Snow Fountains' 'Snofozam'	'Snow Fountains' Yoshino cherry
	Pseudolarix amabilis	Golden larch
	Spiraea thunbergii 'Mt. Fuji'	Thunberg spirea
	Viburnum trilobum 'Alfredo'	Cranberry viburnum

FALL COLOR	BOTANIC NAME	COMMON NAME
Yellow	*Aesculus parviflora*	Bottlebrush buckeye
	Berberis thunbergii 'Aurea'	Yellow Japanese barberry
	Betula nigra 'Little King'	'Little King' river birch
	Calycanthus floridus 'Athens'	Carolina allspice
	Cephalanthus occidentalis	Buttonbush
	Cercis canadensis	Redbud
	Cercis canadensis 'Lavender Twist' 'Covey'	'Covey' weeping redbud
	Chionanthus virginicus	Fringetree
	Clethra alnifolia (most cultivars)	Summersweet
	Daphne genkwa	Lilac daphne
	Deutzia x *lemoinei* 'Magician'	'Magician' deutzia
	Dirca palustris	Leatherwood
	Hamamelis virginiana	Common witch hazel
	Hypericum erectum 'Gemo'	'Gemo' St. John's wort
	Ilex verticillata 'Afterglow'	'Afterglow' winterberry
	Lindera benzoin	Spicebush
	Magnolia stellata 'Royal Star'	'Royal Star' magnolia
	Malus (many cultivars)	Crabapple
	Prunus tomentosa	Nanking cherry
	Rhamnus frangula 'Fine Line', 'Ron Williams'	'Fine Line' alder buckthorn
	Rhododendron dauricum 'Madison Snow'	'Madison Snow' Dahurian rhododendron

FALL COLOR	BOTANIC NAME	COMMON NAME
Yellow	*Salix elaeagnos*	Rosemary willow
	Salix 'Flame'	'Flame' willow
	Salix alba 'Britzensis'	'Britzensis' red-stemmed willow
	Spiraea x *bumalda* 'Golden Carpet'	'Golden Carpet' spirea
	Spiraea x *cinerea* 'Grefsheim'	'Grefsheim' spirea
Bronze	*Fagus* spp.	Beech
	Forsythia x 'Gold Tide'	'Gold Tide' forsythia
	Forsythia x 'Northern Gold'	'Northern Gold' forsythia
	Myrica pensylvanica 'Silver Sprite'	'Silver Sprite' northern bayberry
	Rhododendron (Azalea) *viscosum*	Swamp azalea
	Syringa patula 'Miss Kim'	'Miss Kim' Manchurian lilac
Golden brown	*Hypericum* x 'Hidcote'	'Hidcote' St. John's wort
	Magnolia x 'Betty'	Little girl hybrid magnolia
	Magnolia x 'Elizabeth'	'Elizabeth' magnolia
Chartreuse (stays the same spring through fall)	*Callicarpa dichotoma*	Purple beautyberry
	Corylopsis glabrescens	Fragrant winter hazel
	Corylus avellana 'Contorta'	Harry Lauder's walking stick or contorted European filbert
	Kerria japonica	Japanese kerria
	Hydrangea arborescens	Smooth hydrangea

FALL COLOR	BOTANIC NAME	COMMON NAME
Chartreuse (stays the same spring through fall)	*Hydrangea paniculata* 'Kyushu'	'Kyushu' panicled hydrangea

Conifer Forms

BOTANIC NAME	HEIGHT IN 10 YEARS	WIDTH IN 10 YEARS	FORM
Abies koreana 'Silberlocke'	6–9'	4–5'	Pyramid
Cephalotaxus harringtonia 'Prostrata'	2–3'	3–5'	Oval
Chamaecyparis nootkatensis 'Pendula'	7–15'	3–5'	Pyramid
Chamaecyparis obtusa 'Nana Gracilis'	3–6'	3–4'	Oval
Chamaecyparis pisifera 'Filifera Aurea'	3–4'	3–4'	Grown on standard
Chamaecyparis pisifera 'Golden Mop'	3–6'	3–6'	Mound
Chamaecyparis pisifera 'Vintage Gold'	18–30"	18–30"	Mound
Juniperus chinensis 'Fairview'	10–15'	3–5'	Pyramid
Juniperus communis 'Gold Cone'	3–6'	2–3'	Column
Juniperus communis 'Pencil Point'	4–6'	10–18"	Column
Juniperus sabina 'Calgary Carpet'	9–12"	Over 10'	Spreader
Juniperus squamata 'Blue Star'	12–18"	1–2'	Mound
Larix decidua 'Pendula'	6', dependent on staking	3–6'	Staked weeper
Picea abies 'Pendula'	Over 15'	3–8'	Staked weeper
Picea glauca 'Conica'	3–6'	3–6'	Pyramid
Picea omorika 'Nana'	3–6'	3–6'	Conical
Picea orientalis 'Skylands'	5–6'	3–4'	Narrow pyramid
Picea pungens 'Glauca Globosa'	3–5'	5–6'	Globe
Picea pungens 'St. Mary's Broom'	2–3'	3–5'	Spreader
Pinus cembra 'Chalet'	6–10'	5–6'	Conical
Pinus leucodermis 'Green Bun'	3–4'	3–4'	Globe

BOTANIC NAME	HEIGHT IN 10 YEARS	WIDTH IN 10 YEARS	FORM
Pinus mugo 'Aurea'	3–6'	3–6'	Globe
Pinus parviflora 'Ibo-can'	4–5'	3–4'	Pyramid
Pinus strobus 'Pendula'	Over 15'	Depends on training	Staked weeper
Pinus sylvestris 'Spaan's Fastigiate'	6–10'	6–8'	Column
Pinus x 'Jane Kluis'	2–3'	3–4'	Globe
Taxus cuspidata 'Bright Gold'	6–10'	5–8'	Oval-upright
Taxus cuspidata 'Nana Aurescens'	3–6'	4–8'	Oval-horizontal
Taxus x *media* 'Flushing'	5–10'	18"	Column
Taxus x *media* 'Margarita'	4–5'	4–5'	Mound
Taxus x *media* 'Sentinalis'	6–8'	2'	Column
Taxus x *media* 'Tauntonii'	3–4'	3–5'	Mound
Thuja occidentalis 'DeGroot's Spire'	6–8'	1–2'	Column
Thuja occidentalis 'Emerald', 'Smaragd'	10–15'	3–4'	Conical
Thuja occidentalis 'Filiformis'	6–10'	6–8'	Pyramid
Thuja occidentalis 'Golden Globe'	3–6'	3–6'	Globe
Thuja (*Platycladus*) *orientalis* 'Beverlyensis'	8–10'	6–8'	Pyramid
Tsuga canadensis	10–15'	5–6'	Pyramid
Tsuga canadensis 'Jeddeloh'	12–30"	2–3'	Bird's nest
Tsuga canadensis 'Pendula'	Over 15'	Depends on training	Staked weeper

Crabapple (Malus) Varieties

	RESISTS APPLE SCAB	SHAPE	HEIGHT	WIDTH	FLOWER	FOLIAGE	FALL COLOR	FRUIT	PERSISTS	ATTRACTS BIRDS
'Adams'	Yes	Rounded	20'	20'	Pink	Light green	Apricot-yellow	Red	Yes	Yes
'Adirondack'	Yes	Columnar	18'	10'	White	Dark green		Orange-red	No	Yes
'Christmas Holly'	Slight	Rounded	15'	15'	White	Dark green	Yellow-tinged	Red	Yes	Yes
'David'	Yes	Compact round	12'	12'	White	Dark green		Bright red	Yes	?
'Donald Wyman'	Slight	Rounded	20'	20'	White	Glossy, mid-green	Yellow to gold	Bright red	Yes	Yes
floribunda	Yes	Horizontal spreader	12'	18'	Pink	Green		Yellow-red	Dec.	Yes
'Harvest Gold'	Yes	Upright, oval	20'	15'	White	Dark green	Some yellow	Yellow-gold	Dec.	Yes
'Lancelot'	Yes	Upright, oval	10'	8'	White	Dark green	Gold	Gold	Yes	?
'Lollipop'	Yes	Dwarf, rounded	10'	10'	White	Green	Some gold	Golden amber	Jan.	?
'Louisa'	Yes	Weeping	15'	15'	Pink	Glossy, dark green	Yellow-tinged	Yellow	Dec.	Yes
'Mary Potter'	Yes	Horizontal weeper	6–8'	18'	White	Dark green	Yellow to gold	Red	Yes	Yes
'Molten Lava'	Yes	Broad weeper	15'	12–15'	White	Medium green		Red-orange	Yes	Yes
'Pink Princess'	Yes	Low, spreader	8'	12'	Rose-pink	Bronze-green	Bronze-green	Deep red	No	Yes

	RESISTS APPLE SCAB	SHAPE	HEIGHT	WIDTH	FLOWER	FOLIAGE	FALL COLOR	FRUIT	PERSISTS	ATTRACTS BIRDS
'Prairifire'	Yes	Upright spreader	20'	20'	Red-purple	Maroon to bronze green	More bronzed	Purple-red	Yes	Yes
'Profusion'	Yes	Upright spreader	20'	20'	Purple pink	Purple to bronze green	Some apricot-yellow	Maroon	Yes	Yes
'Purple Prince'	Yes	Rounded	15'	15'	Rose red	Purple green	More purple	Maroon	Yes	?
'Red Jade'	Yes	Weeping	12'	12'	White	Green	Yellow-tinged	Bright red	Dec.	Yes
sargentii	Yes	Horizontal spreader	6–8'	15'	White	Dark green	Some yellow	Dark red	Yes	Yes
sargentii 'Tina'	Yes	Dwarf, rounded	5'	6'	White	Small, medium-green	Little yellow	Bright red	Yes	Yes
'Satin Clouds'	Yes	Dwarf, rounded	6–8'	6–8'	White	Dark green	Bright red	Yellow	Dec.	Yes
'Snowdrift'	Moderate	Rounded	20'	20'	White	Glossy, bright green		Orange-red	Yes	Yes
'Sugar Tyme'	Yes	Upright, oval	18'	15'	White fragrant	Dark green		Red	Yes	Yes
x *zumi* 'Calocarpa'	Yes	Rounded	15'	15'	White fragrant	Dark green	Apricot-yellow	Bright red	Dec.	Yes

Viburnum Varieties

	HEIGHT	WIDTH	FLOWER	FRUIT	FALL COLOR	FORM	ATTRACTS	NOTES
Viburnum acerifolium	4–6'	3–4'	Yellow-white	Black	Pink to burgundy	Open, twiggy	Birds	Very shade tolerant; suckering
Viburnum x *burkwoodii*	8–10'	6–8'	Pink fragrant	Sparse	Almost evergreen	Upright, rounded	N/A	Holds leaves into winter
Viburnum carlesii	5'	5'	Fragrant	Red turns black	Wine-red	Rounded	Butterflies	Similar to *juddii*
Viburnum carlesii 'Compactum'	30–40"	3–5'	White	Red turns black	Burgundy	Compact round	Butterflies	More compact
Viburnum cassinoides	12–15'	12–15'	Creamy-white	Pink, red, blue	Red-purple	Upright, rounded	Birds	Looks like *V. nudum* but hardier
Viburnum dentatum 'Blue Muffin'	5–7'	5–7'	Cream	Blue	Red, orange, gold	Compact rounded	Birds	Sun, partial shade
Viburnum dentatum 'Northern Burgundy'	10–12'	6–10'	Flat-top cream	Red to purple	Burgundy	More upright	Birds	Leggy in too much shade
Viburnum dilatatum 'Cardinal Candy'	5–6'	5–6'	Cream	Bright red	Red orange	Upright, rounded	Butterflies, birds	Sun, partial shade
Viburnum dilatatum 'Michael Dodge'	4–5'	5–6'	Cream	Yellow	Orange-red	Rounded	Butterflies, birds	Sun, partial shade
Viburnum x *juddii*	6–8'	6–8'	White fragrant	Red turns black	Red	Rounded	Butterflies	Sun, partial shade; more heat tolerant than *carlesii*

Not included in this chart are varieties I would not recommend for the following reasons: *Viburnum lantana* has escaped to naturalize in the Midwest; *Viburnum lentago* (nannyberry) has a problem with mildew; and *Viburnum opulus* is a nuisance weed in the Midwest.

	HEIGHT	WIDTH	FLOWER	FRUIT	FALL COLOR	FORM	ATTRACTS	NOTES
Viburnum nudum 'Winterthur'	5–6'	4–5'	White	Pink, red, blue	Red-purple	Upright. Rounded	Birds	Sun, partial shade; slightly acid
Viburnum plicatum var. *tomentosum* 'Mariesii'	8–10'	9–12'	White	Red turns black	Red-purple	Hori-zontally tiered	Birds	Sun, partial shade; not tolerant of clay
Viburnum plic-atum var. *tomen-tosum* 'Summer Snowflake'	5–6'	5–6'	White	Red turns black	Red-purple	Hori-zontally tiered	Birds	Prune out water sprouts
Viburnum prunifolium	12–15'	8–12'	Cream	Pink-blue	Red-purple	Similar to Hawthorn	Birds	Sun, partial shade
Viburnum x *rhytidophylloides* 'Allegheny'	8–10'	10–12'	Yellow/white	Red turns black	Almost evergreen	Upright, rounded	Birds	Needs clone for cross-pollination
Viburnum rufidulum 'Emerald Charm'	10–12'	8–10'	Creamy-white	Dark blue	Burgundy	Rounded	Butterflies	Sun, partial shade
Viburnum sieboldii 'Wave Crest'	15–20'	10–12'	Creamy-white	Rose red to black	Red-purple	Upright	Birds	Sun, partial shade
Viburnum trilobum 'Hah's'	5–7'	5–7'	All 3	Red	Red-purple	Rounded	Birds	Shade tolerant; mildew resistant
Viburnum trilobum 'Redwing'	8–10'	6–8'	Fragrant	Red	Bright red	Upright, rounded	Birds	Sun, partial shade; mildew resistant
Viburnum trilobum 'Wentworth'	10–12'	10–12'	White	Red	Red-purple	Densely, rounded	Birds	Most dense; mildew resistant

Appendix A
USDA HARDINESS ZONE MAP

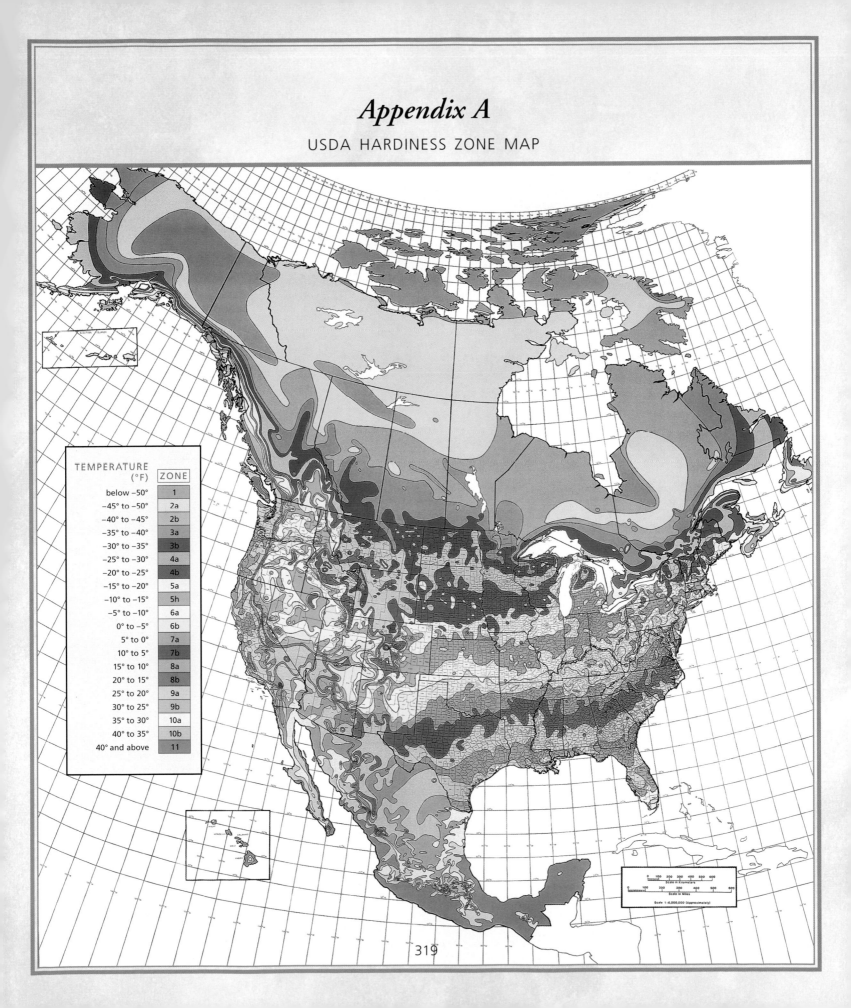

TEMPERATURE (°F)	ZONE
below –50°	1
–45° to –50°	2a
–40° to –45°	2b
–35° to –40°	3a
–30° to –35°	3b
–25° to –30°	4a
–20° to –25°	4b
–15° to –20°	5a
–10° to –15°	5h
–5° to –10°	6a
0° to –5°	6b
5° to 0°	7a
10° to 5°	7b
15° to 10°	8a
20° to 15°	8b
25° to 20°	9a
30° to 25°	9b
35° to 30°	10a
40° to 35°	10b
40° and above	11

Appendix B

Each region of the country has its own list of plants that are invading and taking over natural plant communities. To be "environmentally correct," gardeners should keep updated on those plants being evaluated but definitely should *not* plant invasive species if they garden near a natural site such as a woodland or prairie/meadow.

Further information can be found on the Web at: http://www.chicagobotanic.org/research/conservation/invasive_chicago.html. Check with local extension offices or botanic gardens for the status of plants in your region.

The following lists of plants refer to status in the Midwest, and these plants are not included in this book.

INVASIVE	
Acer ginnala (amur maple)	
Alnus glutinosa (black or European alder)	
Berberis thunbergii (barberry)	Species only; cultivars are being evaluated
Cotoneaster multiflorus (many-flowered cotoneaster)	
Elaeagnus angustifolia (Russian olive)	
Euonymus alatus (burning bush)	Cultivars are being evaluated, but any with numerous fall fruits should be avoided
Hippophaë rhamnoides (common sea buckthorn)	
Ligustrum obtusifolium, L. vulgare (common privet)	
Lonicera maackii, L. morrowii, L. tatarica (honeysuckle)	
Rhamnus catharticus (buckthorn)	
Robinia pseudoacacia (black locust)	
Viburnum opulus (European cranberry viburnum)	Cultivars are being evaluated
ON THE WATCH LIST!	
Spiraea japonica (Japanese spirea)	Species only; cultivars are being evaluated
Syringa reticulata (Japanese tree lilac)	Species only; cultivars may be evaluated in the future

Appendix C
PLANT SOCIETIES

**American Association of
Botanical Gardens and Arboreta**
100 West 10th Street, Suite 614
Wilmington, DE 19808
Phone: (302) 655-7100, ext. 10
www.aabga.org

American Botanical Council
6200 Manor Road
Austin, TX 78723
Phone: (512) 926-4900
www.herbalgram.org

The American Conifer Society
John Martin
P.O. Box 3422
Crofton, MD 21114-0422
Phone: (410) 721-6611
www.conifersociety.org

American Hibiscus Society
P.O. Box 321540W
Cocoa Beach, FL 32932-1540
Phone: (321) 783-2576
http://americanhibiscus.org

American Horticultural Society
7931 East Boulevard Drive
Alexandria VA 22308
Phone: (703) 768-5700; (800) 777-7931
www.ahs.org

The American Hydrangea Society
P.O. Box 11645
Atlanta, GA 30355
www.americanhydrangeasociety.org

American Rhododendron Society
11 Pinecrest Drive
Fortuna, CA 95540
Phone: (707) 725-3043
www.rhododendron.org

The American Rose Society
P.O. Box 30000
Shreveport, LA 71130
www.ars.org

Azalea Society of America
1000 Moody Bridge Road
Cleveland, SC 29635-9789
www.azaleas.org

The Herb Society of America
9019 Kirtland Chardon Road
Kirtland, OH 44094
Phone: (440) 256-0514
www.herbsociety.org

Holly Society of America
309 Buck Street, #803
Millville, NJ 08332-3819
Phone: (856) 825-4300
www.hollysocam.org

International Lilac Society
3 Paradise Court
Cohoes, NY 12047-14228
http://lilacs.freeservers.com

The International Ornamental Crabapple Society
C/O David Allen
The Holden Arboretum
9500 Sperry Road
Kirtland, OH 44094-5172
Phone: (440) 256-1110
www.malus.net

Lady Bird Johnson Wildflower Center
4801 La Crosse Avenue
Austin, TX 78739
Phone: (512) 292-4100
www.wildflower.org

The Magnolia Society, International
518 Parker Street
Gibson, TN 38338
Phone: (731) 787-6873
www.magnoliasociety.org

The Nature Conservancy
4245 N. Fairfax Drive, Suite 100
Arlington, VA 22203
Phone: (800) 628-6860
http://nature.org

New England Wildflower Society
180 Hemenway Road
Framingham, MA 01701-2699
Phone: (508) 877-7630
www.newfs.org

New Ornamentals Society
Membership Secretary
P.O Box 12011, Raleigh, NC 27605
http://members.tripod.com/~Hatch_L/nos.html#what

The North American Rock Garden Society
P.O. Box 67
Millwood, NY 10546
www.nargs.org

Perennial Plant Association
3383 Schirtzinger Road
Hilliard, OH 43026
Phone: (614) 771-8431
www.perennialplant.org

The Royal Horticultural Society
80 Vincent Square
London
SW1P 2PE
United Kingdom
Phone: (44) 020 7834 4333
www.rhs.org.uk

The United States National Arboretum
3501 New York Avenue, NE
Washington, DC 20002
Phone: (202) 245-4539
www.usna.usda.gov

Appendix D
A FEW MAIL-ORDER CATALOGS TO COLLECT

Bluestone Perennials
7211 Middle Ridge Road
Madison, OH 44057-3096
(800) 852-5243
www.bluestoneperennials.com

Brent and Becky's Bulbs
7900 Daffodil Lane
Gloucester, VA 23061
(804) 693-3966
http://store.brentandbeckysbulbs.com

Fairweather Gardens
P.O. Box 330
Greenwich, NJ 08323
(856) 451-6261
http://fairweathergardens.com/

Forest Farm
990 Tetherow Road
Williams, OR 97544-9599
(541) 846-7269
www.forestfarm.com

Gardens Alive
5100 Schenley Place
Lawrenceburg, IN 47025
(812) 537-8650
www.gardensalive.com
(Organic supplies)

Gardener's Supply
128 Intervale Road
Burlington, VT 05401
(888) 833-1412
http://gardeners.com
(Organic supplies and tools)

Heirloom Old Garden Roses
P.O. Box 9106
Halifax, Nova Scotia
B3K 5M7
Canada
(902) 471-3364
www.oldheirloomroses.com

Heronswood Nursery
7530 NE 288th Street
Kingston, WA 98346-9502
(360) 297-4172
www.heronswood.com

Hydrangeas Plus
P.O. Box 389
Aurora, OR 97022
(866) 433-7896
www.hydrangeasplus.com

Jackson & Perkins
P.O. Box 712
Medford, OR 97501
(877) 322-2300
www.jacksonperkins.com

Joy Creek Nursery
20300 NW Watson Road
Scappoose, OR 97056
(503) 543-7474
www.joycreek.com

Klehm's Songsparrow Nursery
13101 E. Rye Road
Avalon, WI 53505
(800) 553-3715
www.songsparrow.com

Mountain Maples
54561 Registered Guest Road
P.O. Box 1329
Laytonville, CA 95454-1326
(888) 707-6522
www.mountainmaples.com

Plant Delights Nursery
9241 Sauls Road
Raleigh, NC 27603
(919) 772-4790
www.plantdelights.com

Prairie Nursery
P.O. Box 306
Westfield, WI 53964
(800) 476-9456
www.prairienursery.com

Rich's Foxwillow Pines
11618 McConnell Road
Woodstock, IL 60098
(815) 338-7442
www.richsfoxwillowpines.com

Roslyn Nursery
211 Burrs Lane
Dix Hills, NY 11746
(631) 643-9347
http://roslynnursery.com

Thompson & Morgan
P.O. Box 1308
Jackson, NJ 08527-0308
(800) 274-7333
www.thompson-morgan.com

Wayside Gardens
1 Garden Lane
Hodges, SC 29695
(800) 213-0379
www.waysidegardens.com

White Flower Farm
P.O. Box 50
Litchfield, CT 06759-0050
(800) 503-9624
www.whiteflowerfarm.com

Woodlander's
1128 Colleton Ave.
Aiken, SC 29801
(803) 648-7522
http://www.woodlanders.net

Wholesale Only

Brotzman's Nursery, Inc.
6899 Chapel Road
East Madison, OH 44057
(440) 428-3361
brotzmannsry@ncweb.com

Lake County Nursery
Route 84
Box 122
Perry, OH 44081-0122
(800) 522-5253
www.lakecountynursery.com

Spring Meadow Nursery Inc.
12601 120th Avenue
Grand Haven, MI 49417-9621
(800) 633-8859
www.springmeadownursery.com
www.colorchoiceplants.com

Bibliography

Batdorf, Lynn R. 1995. *Boxwood Handbook: A Practical Guide to Knowing and Growing Boxwood.* Boyce, Va.: The American Boxwood Society.

Bloom, Adrian. 2002. *Gardening with Conifers.* Buffalo, N.Y.: Firefly Books.

Bridwell, Ferrell M. 1994. *Landscape Plants.* Albany, N.Y.: Delmar Publishers.

Brooklyn Botanic Garden Record. 1993. *Hollies: A Gardener's Guide.* Brooklyn, N.Y.: Brooklyn Botanic Garden.

Clark, Ethne. 1999. *Autumn Gardens.* San Francisco: Soma Books.

Clark, Ethne. 1997. *Gardening with Foliage Plants: Leaf, Bark and Berry.* New York: Abbeville Press.

Cox, Jeff and Marilyn. 1987. *Flowers for All Seasons.* Emmaus, Penn.: Rodale Press.

Cullina, William. 2002. *Native Trees, Shrubs, and Vines.* New York: Houghton Mifflin Company.

Cutler, Sandra McLean. 1997. *Dwarf and Unusual Conifers Coming of Age.* North Olmstead, Ohio: Barton-Bradley Crossroads Publishing Company.

Darke, Rick. 2002. *The American Woodland Garden.* Portland, Ore.: Timber Press.

Davis, Brian. 1987. *The Gardener's Illustrated Encyclopedia of Trees and Shrubs.* Emmaus, Penn.: Rodale Press.

Davis, Karan Cutler. 2003. *Pruning Trees, Shrubs & Vines.* Brooklyn, N.Y.: Brooklyn Botanic Garden.

Dirr, Michael A. 1997. *Dirr's Hardy Trees and Shrubs.* Portland, Ore.: Timber Press.

Dirr, Michael A. 1998. *Manual of Woody Landscape Plants.* 5th edition. Champaign, Ill.: Stipes Publishing.

Ellis, Barbara. 1997. *Easy, Practical Pruning.* New York: Houghton Mifflin Company.

Flint, Harrison. 1983. *Landscape Plants for Eastern North America.* New York: John Wiley & Sons.

Gates, Galen, Chris Graham, and Ethan Johnson. 1994. *The American Garden Guides: Shrubs and Vines.* New York: Pantheon Books.

Harper, Pamela J. 2000. *Time-Tested Plants: Thirty Years in a Four-Season Garden.* Portland, Ore.: Timber Press.

Hightshoe, Gary L. 1988. *Native Trees, Shrubs, and Vines for Urban and Rural America.* New York: Van Nostrand Reinhold.

Hyland, Bob, ed. 1994. *Shrubs: The New Glamour Plants.* Brooklyn, N.Y.: Brooklyn Botanic Garden.

Iles, Jeff. 1999. *Crabapples for Midwestern Landscapes.* Kirtland, Ohio: International Ornamental Crabapple Society.

Kourik, Robert. 2000. *The Tree and Shrub Finder.* Newtown, Conn.: Taunton Press.

Lawson, Andrew. 1992. *Plants for All Seasons.* London: Frances Lincoln.

The Morton Arboretum. 2002. *Tree and Shrub Handbook.* Lisle, Ill. Morton Arboretum.

Odenwald, Neil G., Charles F. Fryling Jr., and Thomas E. Pope. 1996. *Plants for American Landscapes.* Baton Rouge, La.: Louisiana State University Press.

Poor, Janet Meakin and Nancy Peterson Brewster. 1996. *Plants That Merit Attention, Volume II—Shrubs.* Portland, Ore.: Timber Press.

Randall, John M. and Janet Marinelli, eds. 1996. *Invasive Plants: Weeds of the Global Garden.* Brooklyn, N.Y.: Brooklyn Botanic Garden.

Reader's Digest. 1991. *A Garden for All Seasons.* London: The Reader's Digest Association Limited.

Reiley, H. Edward. 1992. *Success with Rhododendrons and Azaleas.* Portland, Ore.: Timber Press.

Rose, Nancy, Don Selinger, and John Whitman. 2001. *Growing Shrubs and Small Trees in Cold Climates.* Lincolnwood, Ill.: Contemporary Books.

Snyder, Dr. Leon C. 2000. *Trees and Shrubs for Northern Gardens.* Revised edition. Chanhassen, Minn.: Andersen Horticultural Library.

Thomas, R. William, ed. 1992. *Hearst Garden Guides: Trees and Shrubs.* New York: William Morrow and Company.

Thomas, R. William, Susan F. Martin, and Kim Tripp. 1997. *Growing Conifers.* Brooklyn, N.Y.: Brooklyn Botanic Garden.

Tripp, Kim and J. C. Raulston. 1997. *The Year in Trees: Superb Woody Plants for Four-Season Gardens.* Portland, Ore.: Timber Press.

Vertrees, J. D., revised by Peter Gregory. 2001. *Japanese Maples.* Portland, Ore.: Timber Press.

Index to Common Names

Index to Scientific Names